The Philadelphia Barrio

The Arts, Branding, and
Neighborhood Transformation

The Philadelphia Barrio

FREDERICK F. WHERRY

with photographs by Tony Rocco

The University of Chicago Press
Chicago and London

FREDERICK F. WHERRY is associate professor of sociology at the University of Michigan. He is the author of *Global Markets and Local Crafts: Thailand and Costa Rica Compared.*

The University of Chicago Press, Chicago 60637
The University of Chicago Press, Ltd., London
© 2011 by The University of Chicago
All rights reserved. Published 2011.
Printed in the United States of America

20 19 18 17 16 15 14 13 12 11   1 2 3 4 5

ISBN-13: 978-0-226-89431-7 (cloth)
ISBN-10: 0-226-89431-2 (cloth)
ISBN-13: 978-0-226-89432-4 (paper)
ISBN-10: 0-226-89432-0 (paper)

Library of Congress Cataloging-in-Publication Data

Wherry, Frederick F.
    The Philadelphia barrio: the arts, branding, and neighborhood transformation / Frederick F. Wherry ; with photographs by Tony Rocco.
        p. cm.
    Includes bibliographical references and index.
        ISBN-13: 978-0-226-89431-7 (cloth: alk. paper)
        ISBN-10: 0-226-89431-2 (cloth: alk. paper)
        ISBN-13: 978-0-226-89432-4 (pbk.: alk. paper)
        ISBN-10: 0-226-89432-0 (pbk.: alk. paper)
    1. Hispanic American neighborhoods—Pennsylvania—Philadelphia. 2. Community development—Pennsylvania—Philadelphia.
    3. Community arts projects—Pennsylvania—Philadelphia. I. Rocco, Tony. II. Title.
    HT177.P4W54 2011
    307.7609748′11—dc22
    2010049106

For *Charlie* and *Peggy*, my parents
And to the memory of *William Bryant Wellons III*

Behold, I will do a new thing; now it shall
spring forth; shall ye not know it? I will even
make a way in the wilderness, and rivers
in the desert.

ISAIAH 43:19

Contents

Preface

Now that the book is written, I can say that I know a little about how neighborhoods change and even more about the role of the arts in shaping and transforming their character. When I started doing the research for this book, I read the work of other social scientists whose analyses were at odds with what was happening in the Philadelphia barrio. Much of what I read was cynical: No good could come from capitalism, so attempts to use the arts and tourism to promote economic development could only result in the exploitation of the neighborhood, sowing the seeds of the community's demise. As some scholars tell it, the arts become an instrument for making the neighborhood more attractive so that richer people would inhabit it. Once the members of the community succeed in making their neighborhood a better place, they are forced to move elsewhere. The services already rendered, the servicers are sent packing.

The cynics hold this perspective on neighborhood change because they have witnessed it firsthand. When newspaper reporters, real estate agents, and city officials talk about neighborhoods "turning around," they are usually referring to a bounded territory rather than the people who live there. And they are almost never talking about the actual performances that initiate, maintain, and contest the type of transformation the neighborhood experiences. Even the demographic indicators of change are misleading. Poverty levels may drop considerably because most of the poor have moved. The crime rate may decline because the criminals (as well as anyone too near the scene of an alleged misdeed) have been incarcerated. New property owners (along with some old-timers who now have a fresh set of allies) find themselves needing to "teach" the longtime residents that cars in the midst of repair on public streets are unsightly and that trash on the sidewalks is unacceptable. Murals begin to replace graffiti as the public art of choice, with images of a conga drum braced between a man's thighs, a local poet singing as he plucks his guitar, a clump of dancers poised for performance with small red bows dotting their white dresses, and a tamed jungle sheltering a lion, a waterfall, a blue parrot.

With these murals forming the backdrop to locally owned stores selling items from Puerto Rico, Latin America, and the Caribbean, the whole area might easily be seen as a stage and its artists, business owners, and residents as merely players. But such a depiction belies what the performers do and why. Some of the graffiti artists write regardless of the presence of tourists. Many of the dancers perform to satisfy their own desires to participate in local festivals or to develop and show off their talents.

I witnessed how musical jam sessions provide opportunities for friends and acquaintances to shake off worry while stepping, twisting, and twirling in the streets. I came to understand how art events attract different people, institutions, and resources into the community, and how these resources and the resulting visibility can be used for other development purposes. I overheard parents talking with their children about feeling beautiful and proud. Business owners explained why they established their enterprises in this neighborhood and why some of them have stayed even though they had opportunities to move their businesses elsewhere. It dawned on me that the experience of business owners and residents in a neighborhood drenched with the arts probably differs from the experience of people in neighborhoods with similar poverty levels where the arts do not thrive. But their neighborhood does not look like other places that have "turned around." Progress and transformation mean revival and redemption—the return of life, the cleansing and nurturing of a new spirit.

This book focuses on how people within the Philadelphia barrio are defining and bringing about this transformation. Rather than presenting a caricature of individuals in stock roles that the reader can easily pin down, this book shows community leaders, artists, and business owners engaged in constant negotiations over what they should be doing and why. How should the community be represented in public parades, and how should the various Latino cultures be represented to different audiences? Which narratives are stigmatizing and which ones uplifting? How can local organizations sell the ethnic and cultural authenticity of their artists without selling out—distorting what's real for the sake of what consumers and funders seem willing to pay for? How do the neighborhood's history and prevailing urban myths influence the types of narratives told about the neighborhood's characteristics and the repertoire of symbols that marketers can use to promote those characteristics? These questions highlight how culture—symbols, myths, and ways of perceiving and talking about the world—and emotions are implicated in attempts to improve neighborhoods and the business districts anchoring them.

All over the country, community development corporations and city officials have touted tourism and the arts as pathways to urban revitalization. In San Francisco, for example, tourists have long flocked to the city's ethnic and gay neighborhoods, but the rough Tenderloin District was not high on the list of attractions. Now, even the Tenderloin is a candidate for transformation. Just as culture has become hot, so too has grittiness. The Tenderloin's single-room occupancy hotels house the nearly homeless, and the local police have asked for special powers to combat the illegal drug trade thriving there. These facts may contribute to rather than detract from the Tenderloin's allure. And when reality gets mixed with history and myth, the resulting combination sells, especially when the neighborhood can be safely experienced with only a hint of peril. Can this strategy lead to positive development outcomes for the people of the Tenderloin? How might the story of the Philadelphia barrio help us understand the promises and pitfalls of such strategies in different city and community contexts?

People in other urban locales such as Chicago's blues clubs and New York's Lower East Side have used grittiness and cultural authenticity to transform their businesses and their neighborhoods into viable tourist destinations. How local people engage in, and whether they benefit from, these efforts forms the core of this book, whose title is inspired by *The Philadelphia Negro*, by W. E. B. DuBois. *The Philadelphia Barrio* may remind readers of *Blue Chicago*, in which David Grazian talks about the performance of authenticity in Chicago's blues clubs; *Barrio Dreams*, in which Arlene Dávila documents how Puerto Ricans in Spanish Harlem have fared in the cultural economy; *City on the Edge*, in which Alejandro Portes and Alex Stepick examine ethnic entrepreneurship and the rise of Little Havana in Miami; and *Villa Victoria*, in which Mario Luis Small reminds us that the way people think about their neighborhood matters for what they do to and in it. This book differs from those in tying the arts and the performance of authenticity with ethnic entrepreneurship, community participation, and local economic development. Although *The Philadelphia Barrio* does build on existing studies, it does not dwell on them. The book allows the stories of the artists, the entrepreneurs, and the community leaders to take center stage, with discussions of the various books and journal articles relevant to the narrative appearing in the notes. And the book's use of photographs by Tony Rocco provides a visual rendering of the neighborhood's character from someone who knows it well.

I want the people and the events in this book to be recognizable to those I studied. I also want my readers to comprehend how culture is intermingled in local economies and the implications of those entanglements for economic development and neighborhood change. These lessons come from the experiences of people generous enough to share their stories and caring enough to correct my misunderstandings. Apathy would have allowed some of my initial hunches to stand unchallenged; thankfully, apathy did not prevail. The transformation of the Philadelphia barrio has many sides, and no one person can see it all clearly or right away. I pray that I have rendered this one side of the story and the characters populating it with reasonable fidelity.

ANN ARBOR, MICHIGAN
SEPTEMBER 2010

Acknowledgments

This book would not have been possible without the willingness of the barrio residents, business owners, community leaders, and others to open their offices, their businesses, and their homes to me. Johnny Irizarry, Jesse Bermudez, Yolanda Alcorta, Mike Esposito, Carmen Febo, Bill Salas, Nilda Ruiz, Marcus Delgado (now deceased), Rose Gray, Jennifer Rodriguez, Evelyn Aponte, Daniel de Jesus, Monica Rodrigo, Veronica Castillo-Pérez, and Gilberto González, along with the staff and board members at Raíces, Taller, HACE, and APM helped me gain access to people in the community. I began writing this book while on a Mellon Postdoctoral Fellowship in the Humanities and Social Sciences at the University of Pennsylvania, where Elijah Anderson and Randall Collins served informally as my mentors. Upon my arrival in Philadelphia, I remained in touch with Alejandro Portes and Viviana Zelizer, who mentored me during my years at Princeton and who kept showing up to guide me in those moments when I felt a little lost. Patricia Fernandez-Kelley introduced me to qualitative research methods and remained a source of encouragement. Jeffrey Alexander and Phil Smith along with others at Yale's Center for Cultural Sociology offered me intellectual resources to better my work, and Pat Egan pushed me to think more about redemption and revitalization in the story I am telling.

Doug Mitchell's good cheer, ability to keep the external reviewers on schedule, and incandescent e-mails helped me stay focused on the revisions. One of the reviewers, Mitch Duneier, arrived at Princeton after I left; after he revealed his identity as a reviewer, we began a series of e-mail and in-person exchanges that proved to be invaluable for the manuscript and for my development as an ethnographer. I also benefited richly from the other external reviewer, Bruce Haynes, who kindly revealed his identity to me. David Grazian saw early drafts of my chapters and my book prospectus and pushed me to make them better. And Eli Anderson talked me through my engagement with his work and urged me to develop the poverty and community development component of the arts chapters.

Leslie Keros copyedited the manuscript as I was responding to reviewer comments and lavished it with care. We talked about turns of phrase, how scenes were set, and musical memories some of the chapters evoked. She was heaven-sent. And Danielle Gwinn produced the maps for the book.

A Rackham Junior Faculty Grant at the University of Michigan and start-up funds provided by the Department of Sociology enabled me to travel frequently to Philadelphia to complete my fieldwork. The department's willingness to release me from some courses also gave me the time to travel, think, and write. The department's chair, Howard Kimmeldorf, and the chair's secretary, Linda Williams, as well as the department's financial specialist, Pat Preston, were skillful at making sure that I had the resources I needed to do my work. Provost Lester Monts and the director of the Center for Southeast Asian Studies, Linda Lim, also encouraged me mightily.

A number of my colleagues in the department offered advice, read drafts, and helped me keep my project on track: Mark Mizruchi, Michael Kennedy, Jason Owen-Smith, David Harding, Karyn Lacy, Rene Anspach, Peggy Somers, Barbara Anderson, and Al Young. I also benefited from the feedback I received from colloquium talks I gave at Yale, Stanford, Cornell, the University of Pennsylvania, and New York University. During these talks, I recall especially useful interventions from Janice Madden, Annette Laureau, Richard Swedberg, Mabel Berezin, Mark Granovetter, Harvey Molotch, Ann Morning, Pat Egan, and Gabi Abend. When I traveled to Philadelphia, I could count on Peter Barberie, Virgil Marti, David Grazian, Meredith Broussard, Rich Horrow, Nana Bogis, Boon Nguyen, Dustin Kidd, Keith Brown, and William Meredith "Bill" Wood III for food and shelter. And Will and Junko Meschievitz, Dario Gaggio, Anthony Mora, Tony Dupuis, Terry Thiesen, and Michael Woodford helped me out as I bounced between Ann Arbor and Philadelphia. During the writing stage, Paolo Asso, Wendy Cadge, James Furst, Rachel Havrelock, Cory Knobel, Patrick Peirce, and Claiborne Kenneth Hutchins Smith offered their insights and their encouragement. I also received some much-needed inspiration from my visits to Hotel Griffou in New York and the Morehead-Cain Foundation's Alumni Forum at the University of North Carolina at Chapel Hill. Larry Poston, Ross Advincula, Jeff Schulden, Shelley Senterfitt, James Wilson, Reuel Rogers, Bill Wood, and Clay Smith helped me stay on balance, while Jess Reynolds kept me going to the gym. Jan Boxill, Kenneth Janken, and Donna

LeFevre nudged me toward academia, and Ell Close and Katherine Marshall remained wonderful mentors before and after my "academic turn."

As I was wrapping up the manuscript, a family medical emergency drove me to despair, and Jeff Schulden and Erika Gantt Lumsden intervened in ways that remind me how durable friendships are over time. I dedicate this work to my parents, Charlie and Peggy, and to the memory of William Bryant Wellons III, my friend at Asheville School who introduced me to the stage and who passed away while we were in the Fifth Form (eleventh grade). My brothers (Bernard, Sam, Reggie, and Scott) and especially my twin sister, Frances, have been a constant source of joy.

We have never seen anything quite as bad as this section of north Philadelphia.... Almost everything about this part of town is cheap, sleazy, decaying, and sad. It is an overripe cliché, down to the name the residents have given their neighborhood: the Badlands. It is the worst of what happens when the drug trade takes over.... It's as invasive as crabgrass, as destructive as cancer.... One of the heroin addicts... suggested that what's missing these days is a sense of shame.

TED KOPPEL, "Badlands: The Death of an American Neighborhood," *Nightline*, 1995

In front of *Congreso de Latinos Unidos* last month, on American Street just above Lehigh, a Latin percussion band was jamming on a *plena* to celebrate the newest arts night out in town, *Noches de Arte*. A tow truck came easing by, the driver jamming along, both hands thundering out the beat on the steering wheel. Clearly, this is an event that the community can get behind. If Old City and First Friday seem a bit too precious, reserve second Fridays for a trip north to the business heart of the barrio.

MARY ARMSTRONG, "Artpicks: Noches de Arte en el Barrio," *City Paper*, 2003

1 » Culture at Work

*The Arts, Branding, and
Neighborhood Transformation*

THE QUESTION

In 2003, the Latino neighborhood in Philadelphia was featured in a local newspaper as a place teeming with arts and culture, attractive to urban explorers wanting to venture out of Philadelphia's Center City and ripe with possibilities. Yet barely a decade earlier, it had been regarded as a hopeless section of town, a district portrayed on national television as a devastated place whose "shameless" residents lacked dignity and self-respect. What happened?

To understand the neighborhood's transformation, I read dozens of newspaper articles depicting the character of the neighborhood and interviewed the individuals who were instrumental in changing outsiders' perception of it. In the Latino commercial district known as the Centro de Oro, or Golden District, I met the community's cultural entrepreneurs, whose mission is to "brand" their neighborhood in the service of social and economic development. They lead Philadelphia Neighborhood Tours through the barrio, host community-wide art openings, mount theatrical, musical, and dance performances, and prepare floats for the annual Puerto Rican Day Parade. Leaders of the Hispanic Association of Contractors and Enterprises (HACE) told me that they hire architects to develop streetscapes and storefront window displays that reflect the Latino character of the district. I learned that local business owners volunteer their time and money to ensure that the trash is privately collected and that a security guard is visibly patrolling the sidewalk outside their shops. Some business owners go so far as to rearrange their retail space to accommodate paintings or photography exhibitions by artists who might not otherwise be able to display their works. Other business owners provide food at deeply discounted prices for local arts organizations' receptions and donate prizes for fundraising events.

A banner for the Centro de Oro business and cultural district.

It may seem surprising that such a systematic approach to changing the community's image could come from a community reputed to be disorganized. It may also come as a surprise that so much energy would go into managing the image of the place rather than dealing with unemployment, joblessness, the drug trade, and the homicide rate, yet the one cannot be resolved without the other. When bad things are "supposed to happen" in a neighborhood, people have little incentive to turn their neighborhood around. To change what people do in a neighborhood, one first has to change what they think is typically done there.

The most common attitude toward neighborhood branding is a cynical one: Every city must have ethnic enclaves; if an ethnic community does not exist, savvy capitalists will create one. No cosmopolitan city in the United States is complete without at least a Chinatown, if not also a barrio. Add "Havana" to the neighborhood's moniker, open a dash of Mexican restaurants along the strip, string up a row of Spanish-language signs, assemble an outdoor festival or two, and witness the city's cultural credibility rise. After all, Miami, New York, Chicago, Los Angeles, and San Francisco have their barrios and stand out as representing the "real" multicultural cities of the country as opposed to those cities still stuck in the black–white divide. For Philadelphia to count herself as their multicultural peer, she too needs to claim ownership of a barrio, where the musical rhythms, the flavorful cuisine, and the style of life evident on the sidewalks complement the city's other cultural offerings. Yet when the cultural entrepreneurs succeed, they become the victims of their own success, as gentrification sends property taxes up and poor residents out.[1] Simply put, there is a growing demand for things ethnic; consequently, city elites along with local entrepreneurs exploit the raw cultural materials at hand to meet that demand without regard for the residents who populate the place of cultural production. According to this perspective, to brand the neighborhood is to commodify it.[2] Money becomes king.

To anyone who has witnessed the process of neighborhood branding firsthand, this supply-and-demand view is at best simplistic. Arts organizations in the Centro de Oro have turned down opportunities to apply for large grants from national foundations in order to preserve their autonomy. These same organizations struggle to meet payroll from time to time, so it is not as if they can afford to forgo foundation funding. Some Latino property owners have refused to sell their properties or to move to areas of the city where customers might be more plentiful. They are not staying in the barrio "for the money" alone, but also for their emotional attachment to the community that they have helped to build.[3] People's lives are drenched with meanings, and these meanings are not simply switched off when people interact in commercial markets.[4] People and the places they inhabit carry memories and meanings and invite emotional attachment.[5] The arts make these memories and meanings resonate.

OVERVIEW

In this book we explore the process of branding in two parts. In part 1, we look at what people do to brand their neighborhood, how visitors to the community respond to these efforts, and why some local business owners participate in the process but not others. In part 2, we go beyond the mechanics of branding to try to understand what makes some images resonate more than others.[6] There we look at the ways in which these symbols and understandings limit how the image of the neighborhood can be believably transformed.

The Branding Process

A brand has many components.[7] In the context of a neighborhood, the brand is apparent from what businesses sell, how their storefronts are designed, what kind of music emanates from open neighborhood windows and passing cars, and what kinds of themes are depicted on the neighborhood's plentiful murals.[8] Special events featuring the music and dance traditions of particular countries reinforce the brand. What people do intentionally and unintentionally to brand their neighborhood is the focus of the first three chapters of the book.

I observed direct and indirect branding activities in the barrio during the two years I spent living in Philadelphia and the other three traveling there frequently. I donned the costume of the *caballero* to march in the Puerto Rican Day Parade, swept the floors of the rehearsal space before and after major events, carried movable stages from the back of a minivan to outdoor performance sites, hauled trash bags down to the sidewalk, carefully mounted masks onto walls, shopped at Cousin's Supermarket for the refreshments used at dance rehearsals and for receptions, contributed narrative sections to grant proposals, and engaged in strategic planning as a board member of the pan-Latino performance arts organization Raíces Culturales Latinoamericanas (Latin American Cultural Roots). Through my volunteer work, I encountered visitors to the district (some for the first time) who talked about why they came to the area and how the reputation of the community kept some of them from visiting earlier. From community insiders, I heard a great deal about how outsiders insulted the good people of the community by focusing only on the people engaged in antisocial behavior, and about how this one-sided view affected neighborhood commerce by discouraging the "right" kinds of investments (chic clothing boutiques, higher-end restaurants, and cultural performance spaces) and encouraging the "wrong" kinds (check-cashing vendors and pawnshops).[9]

To attract the right kinds of investment, neighborhood leaders focused on changing the impressions that outsiders have of the neighborhood. Chapter 2 explores how the tours and cultural workshops organized by community leaders shape outsiders' understandings of the neighborhood's reputation. I contrast the experiences of the Philadelphia Neighborhood Tours

Tree on North Fifth Street carved by Robert Smith-Shabazz.

in this Latino neighborhood with those described in David Grazian's *Blue Chicago* to illustrate the nuances of marketing ethnic identities and places. (Chicago and Philadelphia have comparable populations of Puerto Ricans and rank as the second and third largest Puerto Rican populations in the United States, numbering 111,055 and 91,527, respectively, in the year 2000.) How individuals demonstrate their authenticity in the cultural economy of the ethnic neighborhood tour need not be seen as a confidence game. I agree with Grazian that there are situations in which "confidence men" dupe cultural tourists, luring them to a prefabricated setting where shills cheer them to spend their money on what these consumers believe to be an authentic experience, but those involved in the confidence game know that these consumers are purchasing a counterfeit good (a less-than-authentic performance).[10] Such situations of deception are not ubiquitous, however, for I did not observe them in this neighborhood. The members of the arts organization and of the community development corporation have a sense of integrity and self-respect, and there are some things they are not willing to do just to attract dollars to the district. What types of businesses establish themselves and what types of performances they enact speak not only to the financial bottom line but also to their identity and their place in society. I end the chapter with a discussion of what one Latino leader called the "American Cultural Stock Exchange" and the unspoken regulations that help maintain collective identity in the marketplace.

In the third chapter, I describe three arts organizations that are leading the branding efforts and how they, the artists, and other performers create an ethnic art scene.[11] The art world is not a unified entity, and it does not paint a coherent portrait of the neighborhood's cultural identity. Rather, arts organizations strive to balance what their leadership sees as authentic expressions of Latino cultural identity and what the foundations funding them consider worthwhile cultural productions. "We have a mission. When we are only trying to satisfy the funders to get the money, we've strayed from the mission. At that point, there's no use in doing this kind of work anymore," explains Mike Esposito, one of the cofounders of Raíces. From conversations with him, Yolanda Alcorta (the other cofounder), Carmen Febo (executive director of Taller Puertorriqueño), and Jesse Bermudez (AMLA), I discern a common theme: Art is a vocation, and artists and organizations are motivated to answer the call—even at a financial loss, if the integrity of the work requires it. The sense of calling can spark conflict among the collective artists when they do not agree on how or whether some public events should be staged. But such vocal disagreements indicate passion, not disorganization. The neutrality that marks professional behavior in other fields mars the cultural authenticity of players in the art world. Aglow with passion, this world attracts artists, funding organizations, city agencies, business owners, cultural consumers, and private citizens into its orbit.

Artistic activities also influence the image that insiders have of their neighborhood. In chapter 4, we see how local businesses participate in neighborhood branding efforts. The different ways that business owners envision the neighborhood influences the types of investments they make to improve the neighborhood in general and their own businesses in particular.[12] A business owner may describe the commercial section as the

Golden District, but it matters whether she believes "the gold" will shine again or is tainted. The business owners in the neighborhood are central to the branding efforts because their storefronts, the types of goods they sell, and their interactions with customers are the routine ways in which the neighborhood's identity manifests itself. Without these unscripted performances of authenticity, the scripted narratives about the neighborhood's character could not stand.

The Cultural and Social Constraints on Branding

The narratives that branders construct about the neighborhood rely on the accumulated narratives that have characterized the community and its inhabitants. These histories of representation make some depictions of the neighborhood seem so "true" that evidence indicating otherwise is more easily discounted. The most widely circulated stories about a stigmatized neighborhood perpetuate the stigma; therefore, it is instructive to see how community leaders, business owners, artists, residents, and others work to stage the positive character of a stigmatized place in the service of community development.[13]

In chapter 5 we look at the "environment of reception" for Puerto Ricans and other Latinos in Philadelphia—the degree of prejudice shown toward them by the majority of non-Latinos and how that gives rise to a widespread image of the barrio as a struggling, sometimes dangerous place. Our focus is not on how these prejudices affect assimilation but on how they shape the types of branding projects that will resonate as authentic.[14] The chapter draws on surveys from the 1950s about the perceptions of Philadelphians toward Puerto Ricans, testimony before the Human Relations Commission in the 1960s about racial tensions, mob violence, and prejudicial beliefs toward Latinos in Philadelphia, marketing surveys from the late 1970s about the Latino commercial district, and more recent national surveys about the contributions that different ethnic groups have made to the United States. The chapter also draws on letters and memoranda written between community leaders and their consultants about how to brand the Latino commercial district, my interviews with individuals who participated in those branding efforts, and newspaper reports about the Latino neighborhood and its ethnically themed (branding) events.

Newspaper reports provide a glimpse into the core beliefs about the neighborhood and the ethnic group populating it. I analyze these articles in chapter 6 to demonstrate how coverage of the Latino district has changed over time. The chapter presents both a quantitative content analysis and a qualitative discourse analysis to show how the neighborhood was depicted during three periods. In the 1970s, newspapers portrayed Puerto Ricans as "hard-working," and articles highlighted a mix of positive and negative community characteristics. During the 1980s and 1990s, positive images gave way to a discourse of Puerto Ricans as welfare recipients and trouble-makers. The most recent coverage focuses on how neighborhood residents and other Latinos have contributed to American society and worked to overcome their own social ills. Running through all these media accounts is a series of cultural codes or binaries that describe the barrio as "good," "bad," "constructive," "destructive," "safe," or "dangerous."[15] Such binaries represent the limits that constrain branding entrepreneurs.

These neighborhood codes also constrain how city government, community development corporations, local entrepreneurs, and the newspaper and television media can appeal to tourists and other cultural consumers to boost spending in the city. As leaders in postindustrial cities have worked to replace lost manufacturing jobs with employment in cultural tourism or related cultural industries, they have confronted the realities of managing visitors' impressions of the city's neighborhoods. The attitude of outsiders derives not simply from racism or ignorance but from an overarching cultural code of the city that defines which neighborhoods are "decent" and which ones "street."[16] These categories of evaluation affect the neighborhoods' attractiveness for investment.

Although situated places as well as historical events may be seen as having certain characteristics, the characteristics do not reflect the essential nature of these places.[17] Whether a community viewed as dangerous or disorganized can be transformed into a desirable, culturally distinct district depends partly on representation. Some representations may cast a neighborhood's characteristics as contingent and relative, the implication being that its dangers can be ameliorated by better parking facilities, neighborhood watch programs, greater police presence, improved police-community relations, and improved trash collection and community clean-up campaigns, along with public art and community gatherings that bring the neighborhood residents and business owners into contact with one another for a common purpose. Other representations may render the neighborhood's characteristics as inherent and fixed; people who are "culturally deficient" or "antagonistic" toward civil society are not going to benefit from external interventions, so they should be geographically contained and let alone. Community leaders intuitively understand how their neighborhood is recognizable because they appreciate how its characteristics can be contrasted with other neighborhoods. These leaders strategically address the negative as well as the positive perceptions of their community, for they know that ignoring the negative characteristics will only amplify them.

How local Latino leaders wish to represent their culture differs somewhat from how the news media choose to represent them representing it; therefore, I add my own observations as a participant in the parade (dancing and wearing a costume) and as an observer of the parade (walking along the sidelines). Some of the participants are fully aware that they are representing the Latino community; in their preparations for the parade, some of the adults remind children about how "they" (mainstream Americans) think about "us" (people of color) and why it is so important that "they" be proved wrong. Community members know that the media coverage of the parade makes references to Latino people, culture, and character as well as specific streets in the Latino neighborhoods and specific, newsworthy events that have nothing to do with what is happening in the parade. The parade serves as a yearly ritual in which the dominant characteristics that the members of mainstream society attribute to the Latino community are articulated in newsprint. These articulations partly reflect the background representations of the community, and these representations provide the raw materials for branding entrepreneurs to write scripts and construct narrative accounts of the barrio. Before saying much more about how the barrio has been talked about and how the experience of the barrio teaches us how neighborhoods change, I will first sketch how the barrio came to be.

WHEN AND WHY THEY CAME

After the Spanish-Cuban-American War of 1898, Puerto Rico became a protectorate of the United States under the Foraker Act of 1900. By 1917 Congress had promulgated the Jones-Shafroth Act, granting Puerto Ricans U.S. citizenship, and by 1952 Puerto Rico had established itself as a Commonwealth with close economic ties to the United States. Perhaps this explains why the Puerto Ricans have been an exceptional Latino group, because while some of them speak Spanish and may have come from Puerto Rico, they are not immigrants. Puerto Rican Latinos are labor migrants in the same way that African Americans traveling to the Northeast in search of opportunity are, but neither this distinction nor their racial classification by the government matched the general sentiment of white America. After World War II, historian Carmen Teresa Whalen writes, "U.S. policy makers officially classified Puerto Ricans as mostly 'white' and as 'citizens,' while many people in the States defined Puerto Ricans as 'colored' and as 'foreigners.'"[18]

Many Puerto Rican migrants came to the mainland with the official help and encouragement of the United States government and of large, labor-hungry agricultural and manufacturing companies. Whalen describes the role played by public-private partnerships for recruiting Puerto Rican labor:

In 1943, a member of the Gloucester County Board of Agriculture in New Jersey, Willard B. Kille, wrote to Puerto Rico's Governor Rexford G. Tugwell. Kille wanted New Jersey's labor camps "filled with Puerto Ricans instead of Jamaicans." He described the Jamaicans as "slow and exceedingly contentious" and claimed that on wages they had "bested practically every grower." He wanted to know why these "English subjects" were "here working and demanding [the] highest wages while our own Puerto Ricans were starving."[19]

Whereas the Jamaican workers could be denied continued residence in the United States as noncitizens and sent home when their labor was no longer required, the Puerto Ricans could remain on the mainland for as long as they liked. Consequently, roughly 39 percent of the Puerto Rican men in Philadelphia in 1953 had come from farms in New York, New Jersey, and Pennsylvania where their labor was once in high demand.[20]

Labor arrived in Philadelphia through informal and formal migration chains. Samuel Freedman, a Puerto Rican of German descent and one of the key nodes in the migration chain, convinced local farmers that employing Puerto Ricans as farmworkers would be beneficial both for the recruiters and for the farm owners. Freedman persuaded one friend to hire recruiters to travel to Puerto Rico and to pay the recruiters twenty-five dollars for each Puerto Rican contracted. Freedman also worked with Gospel Mission and First Spanish Baptist Church to extend social services to newly arrived Puerto Ricans to help them adjust to their new environment. Ironically, some of the new Puerto Rican farmworkers were housed in an old prisoner-of-war camp in New Jersey by a farmers' cooperative to facilitate their adjustment.[21]

Not only the farms but also the factories craved labor. The Campbell Soup Company, located in Camden just across the river from Philadelphia, served as a major labor recruiter in the 1940s. In her 1965 dissertation, anthropologist Joan Dee Koss describes how some of the founders of Philadelphia's Puerto Rican community arrived in the area by way of Campbell Soup:

The first few founders of the Puerto Rican community in Philadelphia came under contract to the Campbell Soup Company in Camden in 1943. (Of the original 1,000 workers, 65 were still with the company in 1961.) Initially, they were cared for and provided with housing by the company. The majority of those who decided to settle in the States after the war sent for their families and remained in

Camden, having prospered there. However, some viewed Philadelphia as a better place in which to get a good job.[22]

Another member of Philadelphia's Puerto Rican community recalls how
his father came to Camden in 1944 to work for Campbell Soup and later
sent for his wife, their kids, and their relatives after becoming established.
"I lived with cousins in an apartment house, with my cousins and my aunt.
They came from Puerto Rico because my father sent for them after we got
here and got established."[23]

The migrants arrived by air, because as U.S. citizens they had no need
for a clandestine arrival; however, the city of brotherly love did not welcome them with open arms. One migrant who participated in the community's Oral History Project in the 1970s recalls what life was like two decades
earlier:

In 1952 there were few Hispanics in the [Spring Garden] area, you could count
them in one hand. The Hispanics that lived there sat on the stairs in front of the
houses and the [white] people on the third and second floor would throw water
on our backs. We saw signs that read APARTMENT FOR RENT—WHITES
ONLY.... A lot of times I was in the street. I was 14 or 15 at the time. The police
would see us in the street and would take us to police headquarters. There they
would hit us with a rubber hose.[24]

The tension with police was palpable. Two musicians who grew up in the
area, Johnny and Aida Cruz, remember having to be aware of neighborhood boundaries for fear of violence from non–Puerto Ricans (see discussion in chapter 5). Johnny and Aida recall that rocks and bottles were hurled
at school buses filled with Puerto Rican children and that a Puerto Rican
family had to flee the Spring Garden neighborhood after their house was
firebombed. Puerto Ricans understood that they were not welcome in most
Philadelphia neighborhoods. In response to mob violence and then to gentrification, Puerto Ricans and other Latino groups found themselves concentrated in Kensington and Lower North Philadelphia.

THE NEIGHBORHOOD AND THE CITY

In 1980, just under 4 percent of the city's population was Latino. By 2000,
the most recent year for which census results are available, the number had
risen to nearly 9 percent (see table 1). At the same time, the city's white
population went from being a numerical majority in 1980 and 1990 to becoming smaller than the combined black and Latino populations in 2000.

TABLE 1. Philadelphia City Population by Race, 1980, 1990, and 2000

Year	White (%)	Black (%)	Latino (%)*	Asian (%)	Total Population
1980	58	38	4	1	1,688,210
1990	54	40	6	3	1,585,577
2000	45	43	9	5	1,517,550

Source: U.S. Bureau of the Census, as reported in *City Stats*, Philadelphia Planning Commission (January 2005), p. 7.

*Persons indicating Latino could be of any race.

Most of the Latino population lives in a few of the city's contiguous neighborhoods. The Philadelphia City Planning Commission has combined the smaller neighborhoods into Planning Analysis Sections and provided demographic statistics for these sections. Statistics from these areas help us see how racially segregated the different parts of the city are and how the Latino population, in particular, is geographically concentrated. Figures 1 and 2 show nine of these sections in 1980 and 2000. Center City was 90 percent white in 1980 and nearly 79 percent white in 2000. In 1980, the Lower North Philadelphia section had the largest proportion of Latino residents (11.5 percent), followed closely by Upper North Philadelphia (9.8 percent), where the Latino cultural and business district is anchored. In 2000 the proportion of Latinos in Lower North had remained basically the same, but in Upper North it had risen to 35 percent. Meanwhile, the Kensington/Richmond section, which had been 98.6 percent white and 1.1 percent Latino in 1980, was 70.3 percent white and 21.2 percent Latino in 2000.

When we break up the planning sections into census tracts, the racial concentration of the residents is even more apparent. In the 2000 census, the proportion of Latino residents ranged from 77 to 88 percent across the three contiguous census tracts in the Centro de Oro, averaging 81 percent.[25] When we map the population statistics for 2000 from the U.S. Census,[26] we find that the Latino population is spatially concentrated in Lower North Philadelphia, with its census block groups registering more than 60 percent Latinos and its buffering tracts registering between 40 and 59 percent (see figs. 3 and 4). As these data on the spatial distribution of the Latino population show, the neighborhood and commercial district studied in this book form the core of Latino settlement in Philadelphia.

To understand how people touring this neighborhood evaluate it, consider an April 2008 article in the *Philadelphia Inquirer* describing a five-hour tour of the Centro de Oro cultural and business district.[27] The district includes the Fairhill and St. Hugh neighborhoods, but the Latino community

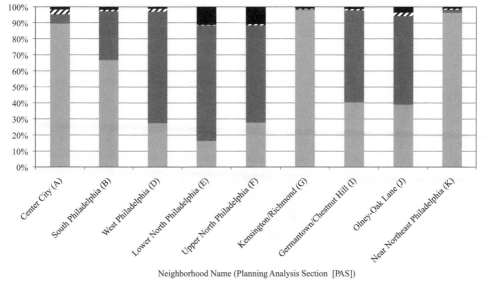

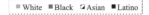

Neighborhood Name (Planning Analysis Section [PAS])

White   Black   Asian   Latino

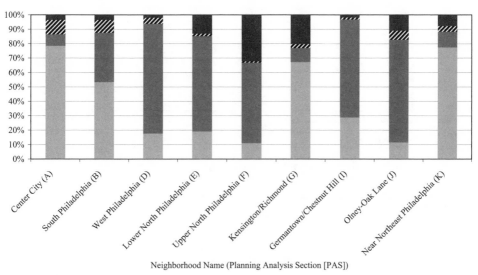

Neighborhood Name (Planning Analysis Section [PAS])

White   Black   Asian   Latino

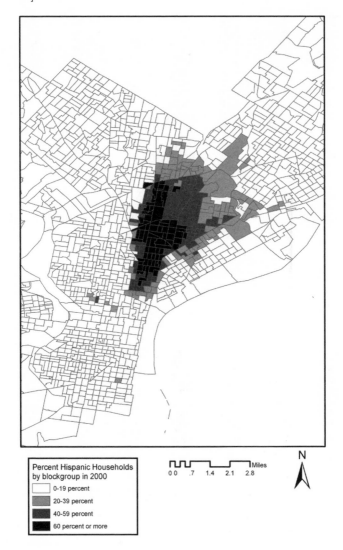

Percent Hispanic Households by blockgroup in 2000

☐ 0-19 percent

▨ 20-39 percent

▨ 40-59 percent

■ 60 percent or more

Miles

0 0 .7 1.4 2.1 2.8

N

in Philadelphia begins in what is known as Hartranft, at Fifth and Berks streets.[28] There are murals on both sides of Fifth Street, and the commercial shopping center, the Borinquen Plaza (where Cousin's Supermarket is located), is at the northwest corner, marking the unofficial beginning of neighborhood. At Fifth and Lehigh, the Golden District officially begins, with a larger proportion of commercial buildings than the area along Fifth just south of Lehigh Avenue. According to the Philadelphia City Planning Commission, stores in the district average 1,357 square feet, and in 2004 the

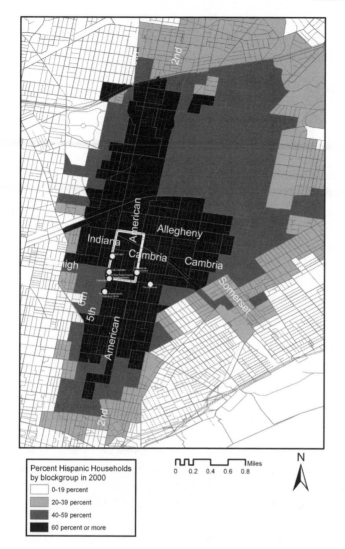

Percent Hispanic Households
by blockgroup in 2000

☐ 0-19 percent
▨ 20-39 percent
▨ 40-59 percent
■ 60 percent or more

0   0.2   0.4   0.6   0.8   Miles

N

district had 400,000 square feet of commercial space with a 16 percent vacancy rate. The *Philadelphia Inquirer*'s description of the Centro de Oro tour
suggests that outsiders have a mixed view of the barrio.

The tour of the district was connected to a conference discussing Main
Street development projects across the country. The National Trust for Historic Preservation funded the tour, and some participants said they were
especially interested in the Centro de Oro. Their own cities' Latino populations were rapidly growing, and they wanted to see how Latinos had assim-

ilated into Philadelphia and how they functioned as contributing members of civil society and as a new group of consumers and producers who helped spur economic growth.

Wearing a button on his lapel reading "*Yo Prometo Respetar a mi Barrio*"—"I promise to respect my neighborhood"—Cesar Santiago, HACE's Main Street manager, held the door while the tour group filed in to visit the well-established arts and cultural center Taller Puertorriqueño.... Having poured his heart and soul into the work, Santiago winced when he learned that a member of the tour group from Cleveland had just been overheard saying, "There are the same issues in every city, but this is worse in terms of filth. They ought to put some money together and clean up."

"We had extra crews cleaning this morning," Santiago said with a sigh.

[Tom] Tikkanen [a resident of Calumet, Michigan] and his family, however, were impressed. "We're both real estate brokers," said Tikkanen's wife 15 minutes into the tour. "See those for-sale signs on those buildings? They're not put there 'by owner,' but by commercial real estate companies. That's a sign of vibrancy."[29]

The question is not whether the neighborhood's transformation has enabled it to clone the characteristics of other established neighborhoods but rather how many of the public "bads" have been replaced with public "goods," and how some people manage to see "filth" even after a sidewalk has been cleaned while others manage to see signs of vibrancy. Although the street is not as clean as one of the visitors had expected, it is cleaner than it had been in a long while. Although the entire community is not free of illicit drugmongers, it has had much less visible drug activity than it did in years past. Indeed, I never witnessed such activity along the main thoroughfare of North Fifth Street during the five years I spent in the neighborhood.

Guillermo "Bill" Salas, the executive director of HACE, understands how critical it is to manage outsiders' impressions of the neighborhood and the commercial district anchoring it. He sees the emphasis on arts and culture for economic development as necessary yet not sufficient.

Author: With the '95 [strategic] plan, you mentioned that some people were talking about arts and culture as the main engine [of growth] and that there are lots of other things that have to happen. Did you have a conversation with people about the importance of those other components?

Bill Salas: Oh yeah. I think that's where the debate is today. Not only [at the level of] the neighborhoods, but when you look across the country, there are neighborhood arts organizations who are really trying to survive. And there is a general recognition finally ... that CDCs [community development corporations] are more involved and much more supportive of arts and culture, and [the] arts and culture [sector] recognizes that we're not the enemy; therefore, there needs to be a collaboration between [the arts and culture sector and] the CDCs who are doing the physical development of the community, and we need to think of it a little more holistically.

Bill went on to observe that other components of development—such as safety, trash collection, and mixed-use zones—were also necessary to create "communities of choice, where people want to raise their children. ... It's not just about the arts and culture."[30] Moreover, Bill suggested that thinking about arts and culture as occupying a *separate sphere* from that of economic development can have a deleterious effect on both. Without arts and culture, the community cannot attract good investments or the right kind of foot traffic for local businesses, and vice versa. Those branding the neighborhood need the raw cultural materials along with the appropriately appointed physical space to make the branding efforts work.

These branding efforts affect how attractive the barrio may become. Rose Gray—a consultant with the service agency Asociación de Puertorriqueños en Marcha, or APM (Association of Puerto Ricans on the Move), since 1989—views the success of the agency's mixed-income housing developments, in part, as a triumph of rebranding the neighborhood's image for investors. "We were designing some of these [housing] programs with the state," she recalls. "Let's be honest about it. People would say, 'Why the hell would you waste your money in these communities?' And you know [what they really meant was] 'minority communities.'"[31] The implication was that these people, by virtue of their poverty and minority status, would not care for their homes or their yards, and this impression of Latinos had to be managed in order to get the state to agree to APM's building plans.

APM also had to manage impressions to attract talent to the neighborhood. Marcus Delgado, a former gang member who rose to become a vice president at APM, told me that the neighborhood's image affected the types of employees he could attract and the types of grants his organization could bring to the community. According to Marcus, even with the offer of a competitive salary, applicants balked at the location: "'Oh, that's the Badlands. I don't want to go there. What about my car? My life?' ... We really had to work hard at doing a public relations campaign about the neighborhood and how it's changed."[32]

New housing by APM (foreground) amid old housing (background).

MY POSITIONS ON AND IN THE FIELD

Hearing people's dismay at how they were perceived by the outside world made me sympathetic to their cause. As a researcher, I am not without emotion, political instinct, or moral bearings, nor should I be lacking in these qualities as a human being. Whenever I came to a conclusion that portrayed the community in a positive light, I asked myself whether the evidence supported the portrayal or whether my sympathies were leading me to ignore contradictory evidence. I found myself being especially careful not to let my emotions get the better of me, and I felt more capable of guarding against my emotions and my personal politics by specifying how they might lead me to ignore some statements or observations in favor of others. Ironically, by being honest about my sympathies, I am better able to guard against rendering a biased examination of my subject matter, thereby exposing myself to more rigorous critiques about how my own personal sympathies might have "colored" my research report.[33]

It is my intention to convey the dignity and self-respect of the people I study. I do not hone in on the antisocial activities of a select few and thereby occlude the constructive activities of the many. Rather, I focus on those who try to change others' perceptions of their neighborhood and in so doing encourage fellow residents, local business owners, and empathetic outsiders to participate in the neighborhood's transformation. While I admire what this mobilized contingent is doing, I am aware that others in the community are not enthusiastic about branding efforts. A good example of the dichotomy can be found in chapter 3, where we meet Gilberto "Gil" González, an artist who has been a key player in the ethnic art world of the barrio. In his fictional memoir *Three Rings*, Gil opens with a vehement critique of some of the nonprofit organizations that he sees as benefiting financially from foundation and state grants at the expense of the community; Gil's work is critical of the neighborhood's branding projects, as we shall see in chapter 3. There are also published interviews in the newspapers with individuals who are trying to get out of the barrio and who say, "It's still the badlands." Although I do not interview people who are not somehow involved in the neighborhood's branding efforts, I do recognize that there are reasons why some neighborhood residents want to leave it. Some of them have lost family members or close friends to violence. In *Three Rings*, Gil recalls attending the funeral of a friend whose casket was closed because his face was blown off; however, I do not dwell on these episodes. To keep the focus of the book on how branding works, I have interviewed the people involved in constructing the neighborhood's identity. I leave to other ethnographers the task of describing the ethnic poor as competing violently for status and respect.

Because I am African American and I do not reside in the Latino community that I study, I wanted to have a second set of eyes to serve as a check on my assumptions and to provide alternative, concrete observations of the community. (I talk more about how my ethnicity, class position, and sexual orientation affected my research in the appendix.) I use photographs to document the lived experiences of the barrio's residents, community leaders, and business owners.[34] The photographer whose work I used, Tony Rocco, served as the primary photographer for the Historical Society of Pennsylvania's project on Latinos in Philadelphia and has himself served on the board of Taller and as a member of the Police-Community Relations Committee.

When I explained to Tony why I decided to write this book, it became clear to both of us how important the arts are for shaping how outsiders see the neighborhood. It was because of the arts that I visited the neighborhood for the first time. I had just moved to Philadelphia in the summer of 2004 when Boon Nguyen told me about the barrio. When we ran into each other at Thirteenth and Locust streets in Center City, we exchanged phone numbers and marveled how quickly time had flown since we had met at the University of Wisconsin's advanced Asian language program four years prior. Boon telephoned to invite me to the Latino community festival, the Feria del Barrio. I confessed that I didn't really know that there was a big Latino community in Philadelphia. "There is," he assured me, "but it's mostly Puerto Rican." Boon had been in the ethnic studies PhD program at the University of California at San Diego and had heard me talking about my own research interests while we were in Madison; he is now a documentary filmmaker at a community-based organization in Philadelphia, but at the time, he was thinking about doing some work in Philadelphia related to his ethnic studies program and wanted to give me a tour of the city's ethnic neighborhoods. (He also took me to a party of Cambodians and Laotians a few months later.)

I asked Boon what kind of festival he was taking me to see. "Trust me," he replied, "It's the kind of thing you'd like." He piqued my curiosity by talking about the arts. "There's this great bookstore at Taller Puertorriqueño and a really professional art gallery on its second floor. You'll see. It really is *your kind of thing*." With that, Boon had enrolled me in the ranks of others who may not know much about the Latino community in Philadelphia but who possess a cosmopolitan curiosity, a taste for the ethnic, and a willingness to undertake an urban adventure. It was significant that my initial foray into the community did not happen on a *random* day of the week, just to see what the barrio had to offer, but on a *specific* day, the Feria del Barrio. Indeed, it was the social activities of the festival that made the barrio relevant and accessible to me. The landscape, with its high concentration of Puerto Rican flags draped from people's windows and Latino-themed murals (starting at Fifth and Berks streets and continuing past the epicenter of the festival at Fifth and Lehigh), provided the physical evidence of the barrio's spatial boundaries and its character, but the social activities of the festival made these cultural symbols resonate as belonging to a distinct community with a valued heritage.

It struck me that urban neighborhoods carry reputations as places with distinct characteristics; whether a place's reputation resonates with outsiders depends on what types of social activities are organized in the community, what the news media report about the neighborhood, and how an outsider's usual circuit of friends and associates respond to an announcement that she has gone there for a festival or an art event. Would friends and associates take for granted that something artistic—not too lowbrow, but "real"—could happen in "a place like that," or would they be skeptical of the neighborhood's ability to change for the better? When I later spoke with colleagues at the University of Pennsylvania, I learned about the com-

Observers of performers outside of Raíces.

munity's infamous past. Could this be the same place that some of my colleagues described? If so, why was I seeing it differently now than they had five to ten years ago? At the festival, I added my name to the mailing list of La Colectiva, the organizer of Art Night in the barrio. David Mendez, one of the founders of La Colectiva (whom we will meet in chapter 3), was manning the table and invited me to meet with him to discuss the group's activities and to attend its events. I found myself going to Taller and Raíces, drawn to events featuring novelists, multicultural hip-hop artists, dancers, instrumentalists, photographers, and painters. As I attended one event after another, I became thoroughly convinced that the people of this community have a story that needs to be told. Theirs is the story of how arts and culture contribute to neighborhood change.

2 » Latin Soul, Latin Flavor

Performing the Authenticity of Place

THE CITY OF NEIGHBORHOODS AND THE AUTHENTICITY OF THE BARRIO

City boosters in Philadelphia may wish to portray ethnic neighborhoods as authentic sites ripe for exploration, but they may not do this in any way they please. The Latino neighborhood is not a Disneyland showplace, functioning solely for the pleasure of its paying customers. It is a community whose dignity and self-respect are tied into how it is represented. While community members want to get into the authenticity game, they want to do it in a way that is true to their cultural heritage.

This is not to say that money is not a motivating factor. Tourism is viewed as a panacea for northeastern cities that have lost manufacturing jobs, according to Patricia Washington, one of the initiators of the Philadelphia Neighborhood Tours and vice president of the Greater Philadelphia Tourism Marketing Corporation (GPTMC). The idea for the neighborhood tour to the Latino community came from within the community and happened, in part, because the tour's founder, Jesse Bermudez (president of Artistas y Músicos Latino Americanos, or AMLA), already knew Patricia from her years of working with nonprofits. She and Jesse wanted to learn from what Chicago had done without necessarily duplicating Chicago's program (developed by Juana Guzman). After applying for a planning grant from a local organization called the Independence Foundation, they traveled to Chicago, where they met with neighborhood groups and representatives of the Chicago Cultural Affairs Office and took several neighborhood tours.

We saw what Chicago had done, and coming from that experience, we realized that there are a lot of similarities between Philadelphia and Chicago. Both are cities of ethnic neighborhoods, . . . but we decided that we could actually create a program that went more in-depth [than the one in Chicago] . . . because we really wanted to give people a context for how to view the neighborhood and its evolution and why it is [in the condition] it is right now. We wanted to give a sense of the history, the culture, the people. At the same time, we wanted to humanize the neighborhoods and so we definitely didn't want it to be a voyeuristic experience where people were on the bus just pointing and looking.[1]

The focus on humanizing the neighborhood meant that its history and the experiences of its residents could not be ignored for the sake of the visitor's comfort. Jesse Bermudez recalls the tours' early days:

The trolley would arrive at AMLA's facility at 2726 North 6th Street. I would greet the tourists and bring them into our school of music. We had café tables set up with Spanish coffee and Spanish pastry for them to enjoy, while I spoke about AMLA, the school, and the artist. When they were done, we would show a two-minute film of dance and drumming.... Then our artists would create a performance with the tourists. So [within] 20 minutes they are dancing and drumming. They became different people... with the cultural experience that they were part of. They left [AMLA] ready to go into their next experience at Taller. Then I would take them to La Botanica and then to Centro Musical to get their Latin music.... The idea was to take control of their experience from the minute they get off that bus. After AMLA lost its facility, HACE created the current tours with Taller and Raíces.[2]

The collaborative nature of the effort also emphasized the autonomy of the local actors and the need during the tour to patronize "homegrown" businesses and cultural organizations that the tourists might return to in the future.[3]

The challenge lay in how to talk about the neighborhood's evolution and address urban blight in a way that would make the tour enjoyable and a return visit to the neighborhood by the tourists more likely. The probability that tourists would return to these neighborhoods is hard to estimate, but their proximity to the neighborhood is one indicator. Between 2002 and 2006 (the years for which data were available), most of the tourists came from within the state of Pennsylvania; only 14 percent came from another state and 13 percent from another country. Among the tourists from within the state, about 41 percent came from Philadelphia, 29 percent from the five-county outlying region (excluding Philadelphia), and 28 percent from the state of Pennsylvania (outside of the five-county region).[4] Eighty-one percent of tour participants said they wanted to visit the neighborhood again independent of the tour.[5] The neighborhood tours were piloted in 2001, although the tours of Center City began much earlier.

Between 1997 and 2006 the GPTMC awarded nearly $4 million in grants to support cultural tourism. This included a $15,000 grant to Taller Puertorriqueño for three events during Hispanic Heritage Month. The GPTMC also led workshops for neighborhood organizations on such topics as tourism readiness. The GPTMC arranged for a representative from the Four Seasons hotel to conduct a workshop with members of Philadelphia's Neighborhood Tourism Network on how to maintain a high level of hospitality for cultural tourists. Patricia describes the core content of these workshops as focusing on "the little things" that make a big difference: "Are the bathrooms clean [and easily accessible]; is someone there to greet them; you know, is it safe; are the sidewalks clean; you know, it's just those little things." When the neighborhood tours began, Patricia recalls an initial sense of bemusement on the part of the public that Philadelphia would be promoting its ethnic neighborhoods. We shared a chuckle as she explained that some people in the news media initially thought that the GPTMC was now promoting "the ghetto" because "they thought the neighborhoods were synonymous with 'the ghetto.'" The GPTMC, the Neighborhood Tourism Network, and the local community development corporations had to manage impressions carefully on the ground to transform discussions about "the ghetto" into discussions about the realness, the authenticity, and the cultural assets to be discovered in ethnic neighborhood life.

PACKAGING THE AUTHENTICITY OF NEIGHBORHOOD LIFE

The Philadelphia Neighborhood Tour invited tourists to "get to know the real Philadelphia" by venturing into the city's ethnic neighborhoods. The GPTMC, the Neighborhood Tourism Network, and the city of Philadelphia appealed both to locals and to visiting tourists to explore a small sample of neighborhoods representing the 158, "to be almost exact," neighborhoods that comprise the city.[6] The print and Internet advertisements for the neighborhood tours emphasized that no single locale constituted Philadelphia; therefore, the visitor would be embarking on a journey into a "foreign" territory.

To facilitate travel, the Philadelphia Neighborhood Tour offered a "passport"—a collection of discount coupons in a passbook whose cover showed a map of Philadelphia with passport stamps representing each of the city's ethnic neighborhoods: the Centro de Oro (the center for Latino life), Germantown (largely African American but with a well-known German immigrant history), University Village, Queen Village, Chinatown, Northern Liberties, Kensington, South Philly, and Center City. The neighborhood passbook differed from other coupon books because the participating stores were small and local compared with the larger, better-known stores that advertised in the standard coupon books. The 2006 passport read: "This Passport is your key to exploring some of what makes Philly . . . Philly."

To understand the city of Philadelphia required one to venture boldly within—to traverse small distances while crossing deep cultural boundaries. The concept of ethnic neighborhoods as foreign and unique ran the risk of turning the landscape and the routine interactions of its local residents into experiential commodities. The emphasis on the local history of these places, however, made the experience no more commercial than a public history course aimed at attracting outsiders to places that may have seemed "out of bounds"; it also served to attract business to local shops established by long-term residents, who wanted both to turn a profit and to make a statement about self-reliance, entrepreneurialism, and cultural pride.

Most of the tour's customers (71 percent) learned about the offerings by word of mouth or online.[7] Initially the marketing took place by word of mouth as the National Forum for Black Public Administrators, Teach for America, and the NAACP booked chartered tours to the neighborhoods. These early customers had a different sense of how the city should be experienced and enjoyed. Their organizational missions emphasize diversity, social justice, and multiculturalism, and these goals fed their desire to see the real Philadelphia—those communities in the shadow of the city's entertainment core. When I took the tour in 2006, the official visitor website for greater Philadelphia highlighted the Latino neighborhood as a place where one could sense ethnicity in the food tasted, the artworks displayed, and the rhythms felt:

El Centro de Oro (Philadelphia's Latino Neighborhood)
Latin soul, Latin flavor

Let the rhythms move you during your visit to El Centro de Oro, the heart of Philadelphia's Latino community. Venture north for an early sneak peak of Taller Puertorriqueño's Book and Craft Fair, a visit to Centro Musical, the state's largest Latin music store, and a salsa dancing workshop at Isla Verde, the neighborhood's hottest restaurant.[8]

Anyone familiar with the neighborhood knows that two of the community's best-known ethnic entrepreneurs founded the two businesses listed in that description. Rather than emphasize how homegrown the local offerings were, however, the description focused on the sensuality of place: what would be touched (crafts), done (salsa dancing), heard (Latin music), felt (rhythms), seen (crafts fair), smelled and tasted (Latin food). Tourists would use all of their senses as they experienced and attempted to understand the character of neighborhoods.[9]

People often time their visits to different neighborhoods according to events on their calendars. Taking a tour of the city's Latino district seems particularly appropriate during Hispanic Heritage Month. For those who have heard about Three Kings Day and want to see the procession along the neighborhood's sidewalks, a visit to the barrio is warranted. The annual neighborhood festival, Feria del Barrio, also offers a good opportunity to travel to this part of the city for a cultural event.[10] Such events resonate with the public because they help explain why people are paying attention to that particular neighborhood at a particular moment.[11] The same holds true for Hispanic Heritage Month, Black History Month, Christmas, and other times of the year deemed worthy of special consideration by societal consensus. During Hispanic Heritage Month in 2006, I decided to take two guided tours of the Latino district offered by different groups. First was the Philadelphia Neighborhood Tour, which departed from downtown at Fifth and Market streets, the center of the historic district where Constitution Center, the Liberty Bell, and Constitution Hall are aligned on three city blocks.

TOURING TIME

On a cool Saturday morning in October, I arrive at the point of departure at 9:30, three hours before the tour begins, to ensure that I am in the right spot. (Three days earlier I had purchased my twenty-seven-dollar tour ticket by phone using my American Express card.) Because all the major city tours depart from this site, some on double-decker red buses, others on the city's resurrected trolleys, I have to inquire which trolley or bus will be the one to board. That is how I learn that neither the GPTMC nor any other Center City organization plans or controls the ethnic neighborhood tours. I inquire about the Centro de Oro tour from a man wearing a Trolley Works jacket. He squints in confusion, so I add, "the Latino neighborhood." The area around his eyes softens. "Oh yeah, the Latin Heritage Tour. We don't run those directly, but if you wait along the wall I can call them and confirm when they leave." With his head turned away from me in profile, he speaks into his walkie-talkie. A nearly inaudible voice barks back, and he interprets the warbled message: The tour is scheduled to leave at 12:30, but I should be there a little early. He doesn't have other details about the tour because Trolley Works does not run it directly. The Philadelphia Neighborhood Tours office advertises the tour and provides the trolley for its use,

Children participating in the Three Kings Day ceremony at Taller. Photo by Tony Rocco.

but control of the tour remains with the community tour operators themselves.[12]

When I encounter one of the tour operators for the Centro de Oro at 11:45 a.m., she is wearing a peach overcoat—a Laura Ashley look—with her hair hanging straight though slightly curved at the base of her head to frame her face. Her fair skin could mean that she is Caucasian or Latina, and the ambiguity of her ethnic origins as well as the conventionality of her dress hint that the "decent" aspects of Latino neighborhood life will be well respected on this excursion. "You're a little early," she tells me, "but let me give you your passport." She explains that there are lots of good deals to be found with local mom-and-pop stores in the city's ethnic neighborhoods.

As I wait to see who else will join the tour, I wonder whether the light drizzle and threat of rain will keep people away. I await the trolley on the sidewalk and overhear the woman who had greeted me now talking with an older white woman who looked to be in her forties. "The community takes pride in having the trolley come through their neighborhood. You'll notice that people sometimes wave to the trolley. They're proud that outsiders are interested in them and in their culture." She also explains that the process of cultural tourism is dynamic, requiring the GPTMC to take into account how these neighborhoods are changing: "We've had to revise the South Philly tour, which used to be all Italian. Now there are so many other [ethnic] groups there [that] we have had to do some work to take into account these changes. In fact, I go to this great Chinese restaurant in that part of town." In other words, the ethnic designations on these neighborhoods reflect the lived experiences of the residents and the changing histories of the places they inhabit. These neighborhood tours in Philadelphia differ dramatically from the Chicago model described in David Grazian's *Blue Chicago*. Because the ethnic neighborhood is less constrained by legend than the particular blues clubs and their performers that Grazian studied, the tour leaders to Philadelphia's neighborhoods may more easily describe the dynamic nature of these places, letting neighborhood change and the facts that defy expectation serve as the inimitable value of the experience.

A TROLLEY RIDE THROUGH THE BARRIO

Two of the neighborhood's representatives greet us on the sidewalk: Joseph, our guide, and Bill, a community leader. Joseph looks to be in his upper twenties and is a PhD candidate in anthropology at Temple University. Bill looks to be in his mid- to late forties and is the executive director of the community development corporation. Both men have café con leche complexions. In the meantime, the woman who greeted us at the sidewalk has now been replaced by Erica, an African American woman representing the Philadelphia Neighborhood Tours program. Five tourists make up the group: two young Asian women who have come as a pair; two older (over-forty) white women who have come singly; and me, the lone African American tourist, in my mid-thirties. Joseph invites us to board the trolley, and as we leave Fifth and Market, he informs us that we are currently in Old City and will proceed directly to the Latino neighborhood, the Centro de Oro. As our trolley travels north along Fifth Street, the boundaries between the ethnic enclave and Center City become more physically pronounced. The change in landscape reminds me of Elijah Anderson's description of Germantown Avenue in *Code of the Street*.[13] From the city's core to its periphery, the types and names of businesses, the make and model of cars, the aspect of the persons walking along the street—all map on to the particular character of neighborhoods separated by ethnicity as well as economic and social conditions. Pointing to the first of many Puerto Rican flags hanging outside of a warehouse, Joseph announces, "As you can see, we are entering the Puerto Rican neighborhood."

There was no need to state that the flags served as the boundary; the remark "as you can see" acknowledges what flags do and how their sudden proliferation (along with the appearance of some Spanish-language

Paranda performers riding the trolley. Photo by Tony Rocco.

signage) marks the end of Center City territory. In order to connect with this "foreign" delegation, Joseph knows what the delegates will grasp without being told. Acting as the lead member of the ambassadorial team, Joseph understands that the delegates (audience members) have stepped onto the trolley with earlier memories and experiences that affect how they will feel about their current excursion. Leaving the familiar, "safe" zone of Center City and realizing that one has crossed a boundary where urban blight is evident could be an uncomfortable experience for the cultural tourists were it not for the skillful social performance of Joseph as well as of Bill, a cultural ambassador who says he is along for the ride.

Joseph gestures toward Bill, introduces him as the executive director of the Hispanic Association of Contractors and Enterprises (HACE), and asserts Bill's credibility as a native of the community: "Bill grew up in this neighborhood."

"Yeah," Bill says, growing animated as we approach the National Shrine of St. John Neumann, located in the Parish of St. Peter the Apostle. "Look. That's my church right there." Bill tells us that the shrine is named after the saint of immigrants. The pastor of the church helped Latinos adjust to city life by establishing a Spanish-language mass and by working to bring social services to the community. These are historical developments that

Bill knows about because of his biography, not because of a script handed to him by a team of marketers.

As we roll past Girard Avenue, Joseph interrupts Bill's discussion of the Virgin of Guadalupe with historical trivia tying mainstream narratives about American identity into his exposition of Philadelphia's Latino community. "When Teddy Roosevelt gazed on Girard Avenue in 1904," Joseph informs us, "he said that it was the future of American cities." The vibrancy of the immigrant inhabitants and the entrepreneurship they manifested served as a model for all U.S. cities and helped Joseph shape the story of Latino migration and settlement into a narrative of cultural inclusion. Even now, that vibrancy is evident, Joseph notes, in the redevelopment and revitalizations evident along Girard: "You can see lots of entertainment venues, restaurants, nice bars, and these recent developments are a part of Philadelphia's cultural reawakening." Joseph draws our attention to one restaurant in particular, whose façade has been given a fresh coat of paint. "You might notice that it has been painted recently," he says. "If you'd seen it before, you'd understand just how much the outside has been totally renovated."

Bill twists his neck to peer out the windows on our right. "You see that building there?" he says to no one in particular. "Those are going to be condominiums selling for about four hundred thousand dollars a pop." To the tourists on the trolley, high property values equal safety. Who would pay so much money, after all, to live in danger?

The trolley slows. A wall covered with bright graffiti comes into view, eliciting gasps from nearly everyone on the trolley. "As you see," Joseph says, acknowledging the group's sense of wonder, "the wall there has some really interesting graffiti. This is what you might call an outdoor [art] gallery, started by local graffiti artists. At first, the business owners were struggling to put a stop to all the graffiti, but then the businesses around here struck a deal with the guys who do the graffiti. Instead of getting all this random graffiti in the area, the graffiti artists host different exhibits here." The cameras flash. Joseph does not analyze the graffiti further—no need to tell the audience what the images are *supposed* to mean, no need to cook what best remains raw.

The psychological identification of the audience with the graffiti art depends on the ambiguity of meaning and the sense of collective, anonymous creativity that the graffiti conveys. "Yeah," Joseph concurs with one of the tourists, "it's pretty cool." In our first encounter with a large amount of graffiti, the tour's ambassadors transform negative narratives about urban blight into a positive script about urban renewal.[14] Joseph seems to confirm that graffiti is "a new way of bringing about a new order"[15] through the strategic deployment of signs, symbols, and language reinvented.

Later I would seek out one of the best-known graffiti artists in the neighborhood, Dan One, who started the wall, known as the Graffiti Hall of Fame, at North Fifth and Cecil B. Moore. When Dan One started doing graffiti in the neighborhood, he would create fake documents granting him permission from the particular business owner to paint the business's walls. Things began to change when a business owner whose wall he was painting drove up, complimented him on his work, and engaged him in a conversation about what Dan One intended to paint on the shop's exterior.

During our conversation, Dan recalled how the wall became a meeting place for graffiti artists, describing a contentious series of events:

From 1990 to '99, I had [that wall] on a lock. I would have my name, my name, my name, my alias. I would do the entire wall all the way, because you know the wall goes all the way around.... Other writers... would hate that this guy [me] has so much power!...

But see, they didn't know I had the advantage.... I worked at the community center. I knew people—the parents and the people that owned the properties. And on top of that, I knew the cops' schedule, because the cops would have a community meeting weekly at the community center, so I knew when they changed shifts and all that.

So it was easy for me to strategically plot myself [at a wall and write without getting caught]. And they [other graffiti writers] just didn't know that. You know, I left them that wall for them to fight each other over there. So now that's what they do. They don't hate me no more. They just fight each other over there: "Oh, you went over me," or "You did this!" You know what I mean?[16]

The wall serves an important function at the periphery of the barrio to mark a change in the cultural landscape. Several factors render the wall a distinctive component of the neighborhood's brand: the process by which it has emerged, its location near the entrance to the enclave, and its purpose as a creative vehicle recognized by local business owners whose properties are tagged. Graffiti becomes art, not vandalism, and the graffiti wall is an outdoor art gallery, not a property illegally tagged.

Back on the tour, as we pass Germantown Avenue, Bill points to an old warehouse. "Stetson Hats used to be there," he says. "You know Stetson hats, right? We had an abundance of manufacturing back in the day. Hat making. Cigar making. It was all here." Joseph explains that in the 1940s and later, when manufacturing jobs were plentiful, the Latino community thrived. Even when one looks at the housing stock along Fifth Street, one can see that these row homes look like any other row homes one might find in other parts of Philadelphia, even in Center City. Of course, the Puerto

Rican community had its share of troubles as greater numbers came to Philadelphia in search of good manufacturing jobs. Like others who arrived before them, the Puerto Ricans were sometimes misunderstood and were not welcome in some parts of the city. White flight opened up the row houses to facilitate the entry of the Puerto Rican migrants, but the community lacked political influence, and city services were scarce.

"Just look at the murals, there are so many in this neighborhood," Joseph observes. "These murals have a sense of place—a sense of Puerto Rican and Latino heritage. We are using art on these murals, in cooperation with the Philadelphia mural project, to develop community pride and to combat community blight." At Fifth and Berks, with Cousin's Supermarket at Borinquen Plaza and tropical mural scenes representing Puerto Rico on both sides of Fifth, it seems obvious to me that we are crossing an official (commercial) border into Latino life. After we pass the boundary line, a gray-haired, bearded fellow wearing a T-shirt and trousers waves to us from his front porch. Others along the sidewalk ignore our presence, but for some it seems that the sight of the Trolley Works is a thing to wonder about and smile upon.

The closer we come to Fifth and Lehigh, the more Puerto Rican flags and Spanish-language signs we see. On our right is a glass mosaic affixed to a building; underneath the mosaic are the words *El Barrio* and *El Corazon cultural del Barrio*, the cultural heart of Latino Philadelphia.[17] The mosaic depicts the anthropomorphic face of a bright yellow sun and a burning heart, candy-apple red. After we pass it, Joseph abruptly points it out. "You've missed it! That's the education center of Taller Puertorriqueño. Sorry about that. I'm so busy talking about the mural over there," he says, gesturing to his right as he faces us, "I almost missed the education center." By this time we have reached the corner of Fifth and Lehigh, and all can see the carnival scene on the northeast side of Fifth Street. "Now we are coming up on Taller, and the books and crafts fair is out on the sidewalk. We'll first go into Taller; then you'll be able to do some shopping on the sidewalk before we head over to Centro Musical and then over for lunch and a salsa workshop at Isla Verde."

THE HEART OF THE BARRIO

The trolley eases to a stop just past the busy intersection. Pitched canopies cover the handicraft artisans and other vendors lining both sides of the sidewalk, forming aisles to the left and right of the entrance to Taller Puertorriqueño. An outdoor sound system thumps samba rhythms. Seated on the two stools to the right of Taller's doors, men strum their guitars while adjusting the knobs on the amplifier. The lead guitarist plucks a few strings, then strikes the guitar's belly, playing nothing in particular, just tuning his instrument with a few phrases here and there. Towering over the other pedestrians on the sidewalk, two teenagers in carnival costumes tread carefully on five-foot stilts. As we step off the trolley, Joseph briefly introduces Carmen Febo, the executive director of Taller, who emerges from the crowd to invite us inside. Though obliged to walk steadily forward, up and in, each member of the tour group looks distracted, trying to catch a glimpse of what is to the right, to the left, above our heads, and behind us.

Inside Taller, we ascend the stairs to the Lorenzo Homar Gallery, named after a prominent Puerto Rican artist and printmaker, to view the exhibition titled "Living Traditions/*Tradiciones Vivientes*." At the entryway, an open book sitting on a pedestal invites visitors' comments. The white-walled gallery looks like any exhibition space one might find in Center City, and it has attracted a crowd of locals: a Latino man with his two children; a Latino couple and their daughter; a woman alone; a female staff member. The gallery serves the interests not only of outsiders but also by people in the community. Joseph's commentary subtly emphasizes the theme of the living arts, as two women on the tour ponder a brightly colored abstract design:

These designs are made by indigenous people on the island of Puerto Rico. They used to paint these abstract designs on their upper bodies as a ritual, [which] meant that both the men and the women were topless. When the missionaries came, they insisted that women could not walk around topless and that being half-dressed or almost naked was inappropriate, so the indigenous people were forbidden to paint these designs on themselves. In response, the local people transferred their abstract designs onto shirts and other bits of fabric, so this is what you are looking at now.

As Joseph suggests, people respond to their changing environment in order to survive. The judgment of outsiders about what is and is not appropriate sometimes threatens local cultural traditions, but the locals do not take these intrusions passively. Traditions are born, they mature, they regress and die, but they may also rise again.

For Bill, the artwork provides an opportunity to talk about his own experience as a young boy growing up in the countryside of Puerto Rico. "Wow, look at that," he says, pointing to a silkscreen. "It reminds me of my father." In the silkscreen, men wearing sombreros and V-neck shirts sit in a semi-circle around an oil lamp. One plays the guitar while the others sway and sing to the music. "I grew up in a big family," Bill explains, "and my father, he put us all to work on the farm. We were what some people [here] might call hicks." Bill's humble beginnings inform his evaluation of the art and how it speaks to living traditions.

Soon we leave the gallery and descend to the bookstore, where we browse the collection. "In fifteen minutes, we have to go to the next place, the Centro Musical, so let's get them out to the crafts fair on the sidewalk," Erica half-whispers to Joseph, reminding him that a schedule must be kept. Joseph has taken the stance of moving with our rhythms and our questions rather than with the preset schedule. He seems to be in no hurry to comply with Erica's instructions, but she does not insist on the schedule being kept. Only a few minutes pass before Joseph announces to the three people nearest him, "Well, we'll have to get on our way, especially if you want to do some shopping outside. The bathroom is here downstairs, and if you want to buy anything in the bookstore, there's time for that." As we leave Taller, one woman asks for information on future events at Taller; another makes a small purchase. Together we venture outside into the fair.

The vendors introduce themselves as artists and artisans and seem eager to talk about their handiwork. One paints images on peacock feathers and then frames the feathers. Joseph points at the *botánica* across the street, telling us that this is where "magic potions" are sold, then talks about the work of Benjamin Gonzalez, a self-described Latin urban artist who likes to modify traditional *vejigante* masks from Puerto Rico. As I observe how much at ease everyone seems on the crowded sidewalk, I begin to contemplate the social function of crowds. Neighborhood festivals, parades, and special crafts fairs bring outsiders into interaction with one another and with locals, giving visitors a sense of anonymity and safety in numbers.[18]

While on the sidewalk, I stay close to Bill as he casually relates the history of the neighborhood to an inquiring tourist who wants to know about the designs on the sidewalk. Bill explains that in the 1970s, themed sidewalks were created to give the business district the feel of the island. He proudly announces that his organization now has a $4 million grant and is raising $800,000 more to renovate the sidewalks, install attractive seating, restore storefronts, and plant a line of trees. The kinds of businesses that become established here matter, he tells us. He'd rather keep a building vacant than let in a check-cashing store, because that does not build wealth for the community. Joseph reinforces the message by pointing out the Watts Fitness Studio across the street: "The gym has been here for two years now. I didn't know if it would survive when it first came in, but [it's] still here. And on Friday nights when I've gone in, there have been lots of people working out." Bill agrees, adding that his organization is looking at bringing in a clothing store by a local Latino designer that would sell authentic shirts, dresses, and other clothing items. He's also looking for a Mexican restaurant to help integrate the different Latino populations in the area as well as some upper-end shops that represent the diverse cultures of the barrio. His stories of revitalization inspire one of the tourists to inquire about the organization's sources of support. "Do we take donations, you ask? Oh yes," Bill replies. "I will take money from anyone who will give it to me."

Now it is time for us to visit the Centro Musical, just across Lehigh Avenue. We pause before its storefront, even as Joseph and Erica attempt to usher us quickly inside. In the left window we see autographed black-and-white photographs of prominent Latino musicians; in the right we see a row of flags from various Latin American countries beneath a row of hand-crafted drums. Inside, one of the tourists finds a traditional instrument that puzzles her. The shop owner's daughter, who looks to be in her mid-thirties, encourages the woman to try playing the instrument. "No one will laugh at you here," she reassures the woman. "This is what it's all about." Bill joins in, offering an impromptu demonstration. "Five minutes left," Erica announces; then, as if on cue, the trolley driver throttles his engine just outside the entrance.

It hardly takes a minute to drive to our next destination, less than two blocks away. When we enter Isla Verde at 1:30 in the afternoon, we are the only patrons; the usual customers come later, at happy hour and on into the night. The bongos (two small drums joined side by side) and a conga turned on its side are set center stage. Five young women in white dresses are seated on couches lining the wall, awaiting our arrival. Seeing us, they stand and slowly begin to take their positions as the male musicians take their places. We are greeted by a five-foot-eight Blatino (Black Latino) man, who announces that his troupe will give us a *bomba* demonstration and that we will be asked to join in the dance. I sit close to Bill and listen to his comments. "That's Harry. He's my accountant," Bill tells me, referring to the greeter. The fact that the leader of the troupe also works as the accountant for HACE underscores Bill's strategy for promoting indigenous economic development. "I told the young man that if he was willing to go to school and get the right training, he could work for me," Bill explains. "I did the same with my vice president at the organization. She didn't have a bachelor's degree, so I told her to get it. I would help her as much as possible, but if she wanted to advance in her career and eventually take my job, she needed to finish her bachelor's degree. She did it." Bill's aside is cut short as Harry introduces the group and the cultural influences of the music.

"Welcome! What you will hear today has its roots in the Taíno Indians and the African slaves along with the Spanish—it is Columbus Day week-

Bomba dancers in action. Photo by Tony Rocco.

end, I guess—who lived in and mixed in the area where I'm from. That's why I'm so dark-skinned. You will notice that lots of us here are darker-skinned, but you see my cousin there, she's more of a light cocoa color. We are all Puerto Ricans, but my family comes from Loíza, where most of the African slaves got dropped off. So if you go to Loíza now, you see almost everyone is dark like me and you'll hear fast rhythms of the *bomba*.... We come from many different races and have many different colors. That's also reflected in our music, but in this [performance] group, all of us are re-lated—brothers, sisters, cousins, aunts, uncles, everything."

As the performers begin to dance and to pull us onto the dance floor with them, I notice that three members of the kitchen staff, along with the chef, have emerged from the kitchen and are bobbing to the music. These people have seen these performances many times, but they still come out to watch. The troupe's performance is not intended simply for us. It is also for them. It would have been easy to see the kitchen staff as shills in a con-fidence game who have come to cheer the marks. In the context of the tour, however, they were probably not supposed to leave the kitchen. They (in-advertently?) wandered onto the edges of the stage, beyond the metaphori-cal scrim into the audience's line of sight.

Before we leave for the trolley, one of the tourists crosses the street to go to Cousin's Supermarket, owned by a man of Arab descent who is married to a Latina. This supermarket is different from the one we encountered a few blocks away at Fifth and Berks and seems to break the stereotype of the poor ethnic community that has to rely solely on corner stores (*bodegas*) for groceries. "I want to buy some Spanish coffee that I can't find in my neighborhood," she explains. She does not ask about safety before her departure; she simply leaves after telling us why she is leaving and promises to return shortly. When she comes back, we take it as our cue to make our way to the trolley. Just before we board, Bill asks Erica whether we have time to visit the *casita*. "It's just right there," he says. Erica looks at her watch and sighs. "Sure," she replies. "It will only be for a minute," Bill assures her, motioning us to move away from the trolley and walk up the sidewalk about a hundred feet north.

As its name indicates, the *casita* is the frame of a little one-room house set in the yard of the Congreso de Latinos Unidos, a Latino service organization on American Street. Black-and-white photographs of community life, each semitransparent and three feet tall, line the *casita* interior on three sides. Members of the community have donated their personal photographs to be enlarged for the project, Bill tells us, and two of the photographs come from his sister's collection. The *casita* is open twenty-four hours a day, seven days a week. This openness accounts for the two smaller glass panes that are missing and for the little bits of graffiti embellishing a few of the panes. To replace one pane costs three thousand dollars, so once a pane is removed, an empty rectangle remains without hopes of immediate repair.

"That picture there reminds me of my mother," Bill says, his voice growing quiet as he looks at the image of a woman in her late forties with a light tan complexion and black hair. The woman's dress indicates that she is a seamstress. "You see, my mother couldn't find a job when we first moved here from Puerto Rico, so she took in piecework from Botany 500. She would sew sleeves onto jackets for twenty-five cents per piece. I would take my little red wagon to pick up the piecework and would take it back to her. We were a family of eleven. Then I'd take the finished work back to the factory and pick up the money."

While Bill is talking, Joseph eyes another photograph. "Look at the Casa del Carmen T-shirts the kids are wearing," Joseph remarks. Bill nods in agreement. "The Casa del Carmen is still around," Bill says.

One of the tourists raises an inquiring eyebrow. "Oh, yes," Joseph replies, answering the unspoken question. "Casa del Carmen is a social ser-

Artist Pepón Osorio in the casita outside of Congreso. Photo by Tony Rocco. Historical Society of Pennsylvania, Balch Collection.

vice organization run out of the Catholic church." No one remarks on the erect black penis drawn—by vandals, no doubt—onto the fiberglass plane just below a young woman's gaping mouth.

Back on the trolley, as we roll along Second Street, Joseph and Bill talk about the changing landscape. There is an empty lot that was contaminated by industrial toxins and now requires a million dollars to clean up. There is the community's recessed garden, whose location between two buildings made it a haven for drug users and prostitutes but which now boasts herbs and flowers planted by intergenerational teams of gardeners and bright murals painted by artists on the facing walls. There is the adjacent neighborhood of Northern Liberties, which used to be a poor and struggling community but now boasts $400,000 condominiums and upscale bars and restaurants. The men also speak of upcoming events and the future: Art Night on the second Friday of each month, which is followed by a networking party at Isla Verde; the tours of the community that are planned for next year. Come back, they say, and tell your friends *what it is really like here.*

A DIFFERENT KIND OF TOUR

Some groups come to the neighborhood for just that: to see what ethnic neighborhood life is really like in Philadelphia. These tourists, usually students, book directly with Taller for a tailor-made educational experience. Before embarking on a second tour of the area, I read the online description of the local neighborhood tour program, which highlights the cultural exchange one will find upon accepting Taller's invitation to "visit us"—extended jointly with Raíces.

TALLER PUERTORRIQUEÑO, INC.
and
RAÍCES CULTURALES LATINOAMERICANAS
Present
Visítenos: A Cultural Encounter

Taller Puertorriqueño, Inc. and Raíces Culturales Latinoamericanas have joined forces to present Visítenos: A Cultural Encounter, a series of tours, workshops and lectures that promote cultural understanding and appreciation of Puerto Rican and Latin culture. The initiative is aimed at schools, teachers and other interested organizations.[19]

Rather than highlight a pan-Latino identity, the web page distinguishes Puerto Rican from Latin American artists and Puerto Rican history from that of the larger Latino community. In addition to describing the mask

A woman tending a garden in Norris Square, where art and a community garden have replaced drug-dealing activity and trash. Photo by Tony Rocco.

painting, the web page advertises Puerto Rican *plena* dance workshops and notes that special workshops may be arranged with an emphasis on Latino culture—a residual category for anything not Puerto Rican: "other Latin American countries, other Latin dances, community murals, etc."

On the day of the tour, I join eleven college students and their professor, who disembark from a van onto the sidewalk in front of Taller. Daniel de Jesus introduces himself as our guide, serving as the cultural ambassador for the Puerto Rican community. We follow Daniel into Taller and gather around him just inside the entrance. Daniel explains the history of Taller and tells us that we are in the Centro de Oro, noting its distinction as a community with its own name and its own history. We learn that Taller started as a place to hold printmaking classes for youth and adults so that they could acquire marketable skills while learning about Puerto Rican culture.

The walls of Taller are adorned with colorful masks made on the island of Puerto Rico. "These are *vejigante* masks. Here you see the *santos*, the three wise men," Daniel notes. "The three wise men are important here in the Latino community for an event on January 6 that is probably bigger than Christmas for a number of families. It's called the Three Kings Day. Kids leave food and grass for the wise men on the sidewalk, and in exchange, the wise men exchange these offerings with a gift. It's a big deal." The event has its roots in Catholicism but is a "very Latino" affair, Daniel says.

Hoisting a music stand over one shoulder and a bag over the other, Daniel guides us out the door and takes us into the community garden between Taller and the corner gas station. After setting the music stand onto the grass, he explains that in 1994 the Mural Arts Project helped Taller put the first mural on its building, but as the mural became weather-worn the artists changed the background. Having reviewed one mural, Daniel picks up his music stand and proceeds to the next, a half-block away. We are a conspicuous crew as Daniel constantly turns his head over his free shoulder, keeping watch over his flock.

The outdoor walking tour ends at Taller's education building, a block south of Taller's main building on North Fifth Street. I remember the mural that adorns the front of Taller's education building, a vivid glass mosaic with Taller's motto, *El Corazon cultural del Barrio*, running underneath. When the mosaic was installed, as I learned later in an interview with Taller's executive director, Carmen Febo, some of the local residents studied it longingly before placing a hand on their own heart and then in the center of its jagged red core. Depicted in the mural above the mosaic, Daniel explains, are the Taíno people (the first inhabitants of Puerto Rico), the Africans, the white Spaniards, and their mixed offspring. We enter the education center and take our seats for the presentation on the history and politics of printmaking in Puerto Rico. Daniel sets his music stand down on the right-hand side of the screen positioned in front of the projector.

Daniel's PowerPoint presentation emphasizes the cohesiveness of the Puerto Rican community in the barrio; even the name of the art gallery at Taller, Lorenzo Homar Gallery, serves as a constant reminder of the obstacles that Puerto Rican artists (and by extension Puerto Ricans and other Latinos in the barrio) face in American society. The gallery's name is simultaneously an homage to an important Puerto Rican artist and, as we are about to learn, a painful reminder of the refusal of one of America's most significant cultural institutions to recognize his talent and, by extension, the value of Latino talent. As Daniel displays the prints of Lorenzo Homar, who was born in Puerto Rico but who moved to New York City as a young boy, he describes the printmaker as "the granddaddy of all these artists you see in the [mainland] United States."

American society was slow to recognize Homar. After his death in 2004, Homar's family offered to donate his prints to the Philadelphia Museum of Art, but the museum turned them down, Daniel says. His voice trembles as he relates the story and the insult inflicted not only on the artist himself but on the lineage of artists he represents. Rejection by one of Philadelphia's major cultural institutions, he points out, seems particularly unjust in light of the purchase of some of Homar's prints some years later by the Metropolitan Museum of Art. Hearing about the history of the Puerto Rican community's marginalization, and seeing the emotional energy it awakens in Daniel, draws the disconnected situations of individual tourists into the collective situation of the group. In the moment of unease when Daniel is stirred by the story of rejection, the marginalization resonates as real.

There is a danger that this emotional resonance could alienate tourists, who do not want to feel "bad" about being members of the oppressor class. But the educational mission of the tour enables the cultural ambassador to risk making the audience recognize the chasm between both worlds and their complicity in its creation. Indeed, during his presentation, Daniel invites this reflection when he exhibits a screen print titled *Vote* from 1968 and offers a personal context for understanding it. "My uncle went to Vietnam," he says. Like many Puerto Ricans seeking higher education, Daniel's uncle enlisted in ROTC to finance his schooling. The military typically offered to pay tuition as an enticement, Daniel explains, "but as soon as the Puerto Rican students would enroll, they would be sent to Vietnam." Daniel then exhibits a popular screen print from the 1960s that likens ROTC to Hitler's regime.

Daniel's discussion of Vietnam makes audience members fidget, and one person in particular seems to squirm. Is this the best way to promote cultural understanding and to attract new consumers to the enclave, I wonder. Then it dawns on me that the less concern Daniel shows for the psychological comfort of his audience (and thus for his economic well-being), the more authentic his presentation seems. Rather than give a neatly scripted, apolitical narrative, Daniel takes his educational mission to be one of trespassing the conventions of comfort that might be expected in a tour offered by the city.

To my left in the presentation hall, one of the students in the group looks uneasily at the print under discussion and at Daniel. She purses her lips and shakes her head in disbelief. Without pausing, Daniel continues his presentation. "Students burned down the ROTC building on campus in the mid-seventies," he says. Then he displays images of the Isla de Vieques protests without explanation. The professor in the group asks, "Can you explain Vieques a little more?" Daniel nods, then describes how the island municipality was used as a bombing test site by the American military and how the soil has been contaminated ever since.

"Wait a minute," protests the student, who cannot help questioning Daniel's representation of the facts. "A friend of mine has a house there... and she seems to be just fine."

In his reply, Daniel does not challenge the individual experience of the student's friend. Instead he offers information about the rate or levels of deterioration along key indicators, reporting that in the late 1990s there were high levels of radiation, cancer, and other medical conditions on the island. He concludes simply, "It is definitely contaminated." The tension in the room diminishes only after the hands-on printmaking workshop commences.

After the hour-long workshop, Daniel suggests that the students visit the *botánica* across the street. When the students ask what a *botánica* is, Daniel talks about the magic potions and other items the store sells.

"They have potions to get a person to fall in love with you, and candles and bath salts and statues. You can take revenge on an enemy or protect yourself from evil spirits," he says. "It's voodoo, basically, but it is like nothing that you will see anywhere else. It is quite an experience."

"Do you go there?" asks one of the students.

"I've been in just to look, but I don't use it for real," Daniel says. "My mother does not like that stuff. She hates superstition and witchcraft."

The students grow animated during the discussion of magic potions used in a *santaría*, which one of the students says she has "read about or seen in a documentary somewhere."

"But will I feel out of place there?" a student asks. Joining the questioner, the student who had been challenged on Vieques inquires, "Is it safe to walk?"

No one answers her question at first. Instead, Daniel looks at her as if the answer is obvious. Would he have suggested it were it not safe? "Yes," he says with a sigh.

"I'll go with you," offers a gentleman in the group.

"Me, too," offers bodyguard number two, a young man who made himself conspicuous by snapping his fingers after "me" and "too."

"You really won't have any problems," Daniel reassures them. I nod in agreement. The men seem giddy with anticipation of their venture to a place of spirits along a "risky" road. Like Dorothy, Toto, and their entourage off to see the wizard, the group apprehensively departs.

PERFORMANCE AND REGULATION IN THE "CULTURAL STOCK EXCHANGE"

Tours and parades require a great deal of organizational resources and planning as well as carefully orchestrated rituals to generate a performance that both the marchers and the onlookers can believe in. A standard approach to the question whether a tour or parade is "worth the trouble" might refer to the future profits to be earned from such public performances. In the case of the GPTMC, those future profits come in the form of return visits by tourists who spend their money in the ethnic neighborhood as well as positive publicity for the entire city as a unique cultural destination. Limiting one's scope to these economic profits, however, ignores the other forms of capital being exchanged—anti-stigma symbols, collectively held symbols spurring group solidarity, and political connections that can pave the way for government funding of other community projects.

Although some outside institutions have been tempted to hijack the neighborhood's cultural symbols for the sake of growing economic profits, they have met with resistance. Take the case of one of the neighborhood festivals I attended, the Feria del Barrio. In 1981, Gualberto Medina—then chairman of the Puerto Rican Day Parade and city councilman from across the river in Camden, New Jersey—had sought financial backing for the Feria del Barrio apart from its regular sponsor, Taller Puertorriqueño. Because the Puerto Rican Day Parade was so closely tied to the Feria del Barrio, Medina's attempts to curry favor with business leaders conflicted with the community's insistence on cultural autonomy. In a letter dated September 4, 1981, to Medina from officers of Taller Puertorriqueño, the institution threatened to remove the cultural foundations on which the festival and its parade were built:[20]

Dear Mr. Medina:

On Saturday, August 29, 1981 it came to our attention that a "Feria del Barrio" is to take place on September 20, 1981, or thereabouts. We are extremely concerned about the manner in which this activity has been organized and the method used to obtain funds.

First, let us give you a short history of how the idea of having "La Feria del Barrio" came about. In 1979 Taller decided to have an activity for the community-at-large to unveil a mural designed by Domingo Negron and painted by community youngsters. As a result of the positive reaction of the community, Taller decided to conduct this activity every year. Therefore, last year we successfully held "La Segunda Feria del Barrio," which was partially funded by Girard Bank. Since the activity fell within the first weekend of the Puerto Rican Week, we decided to allow having its name included in the publicity for the Puerto Rican Week activities. This year, however, Taller decided to hold this celebration of the talent of our youth and acknowledgement of our artists around el Dia de los Reyes Magos. In maintaining our culture and traditions, "La Tercera Feria del Barrio" will be specially dedicated to our children.

It is because of this history that we contacted you upon hearing of the alleged "Feria del Barrio" which is supposed to take place in September. Your response was that your group was approached by Girard Bank to organize "La Feria," that letters were sent to Taller to discuss the activity, that there was no response whatsoever from Taller and therefore you assumed that Taller was not interested in having the activity.

However, the reality seems to be that your group initially contacted Girard Bank, that you assured its representative that there had been communication with Taller, that Taller was not going to conduct the activity and that Taller approved your seeking of funds to have it.

This discrepancy leads us to believe that you have been making false statements about Taller and our position with respect to "La Feria del Barrio." Your solution of having a speaker from Taller in your activity, aside from being unacceptable, shows a lack of respect for Taller and indicates your ignorance of the significance of this activity.

The efforts made by Taller in prior years to develop La Feria must be taken into account and must be respected. As such, we demand that you DO NOT use the name "Feria del Barrio" for your activity and that all publicity reflect this change. "La Feria del Barrio" is, has been and will always be associated with Taller. If you agree with us that there should be more activities open to all segments of our community, then by all means have a celebration. However, we will not allow you to ride on our prestige, initiative, efforts and good name in the community to conduct your activity. Again, we want to emphasize that we do not object to your having an activity for the community in the community.

We hope that all the organizations in the community will continue working together for the betterment of our community. We expect, however, that the activities of self-expression of the different groups will be respected (e.g. La Feria del Barrio, El Desfile Puertorriqueño, El Festival de Hunting Park, The Annual College Conference, El Festival de San Juan Bautista, etc.). We, the Board of Directors of Taller Puertorriqueño, expect your prompt answer to this matter.

En Lucha,
Israel Colon, President
Socorro Rivera, Vice-President
Sol Vázquez, Treasurer
Board of Directors, TALLER PUERTORRIQUEÑO

Cc: Mr. Richard Tolbert
Vice-President
GIRARD BANK

Twenty-four days after Israel Colon launched the first missive from Taller to Medina, Socorro Rivera issued an open letter to the community roundly criticizing the appropriation of Puerto Rican heritage by outsiders for their own ends. The letter was as literary as its title: "Portrait of a Parade." And its point was clear: *What belongs to "us" will not be exploited. We will appropriate our own symbols in the manner and for the purposes we see fit.*

For his part, Medina argued in an unpublished statement that the dramaturgical performance of Latino culture served the material, political, and spiritual interests of the community. In order to battle economic and political troubles, he believed that one had to rely on one's cultural assets. He referred to culture as a commodity to be traded on the American cultural stock exchange for other resources: "It is our heritage which defines us as a people, allows us to offer a unique and precious product in the American cultural stock exchange, and will allow us to persevere regardless of the difficulties that the troubled eighties [with its high interest rates and inflation] may bring."[21]

Some social scientists place so much emphasis on how corporations and other capitalist entities transform the authenticity of neighborhoods into commodities that few ask what the neighborhood actors are doing about this proactively and reactively. Stories proliferate about how local actors lose ground in commercial markets, and sociologists and anthropologists studying the phenomenon have a penchant for giving voice to the victims of market processes who would otherwise go unheard. These protectors of the vulnerable sometimes go too far, mirroring the protectors of economic capital—denying the capacity of local people to pursue lives connecting cultural symbols and meaningful relationships with commercial market exchanges.[22] This is not to say that individuals and corporate interests will not try to treat culture as a commodity and rob its local producers of the "surplus value" of their labors.[23] Nor is it to deny that attempts to empower ethnic neighborhoods through cultural marketing might lead to the displacement of those neighborhoods' residents by higher-income outsiders who find the locale attractive or by powerful cultural institutions who deem some of the expressions of culture as a little too authentic to be marketable.[24]

In the capitalist democracy of the United States, corporate sponsorship signals social inclusion. Money acts as the universal door opener, regardless of religion, race, ethnicity, country of origin, or class, and the marketplace sends signals about the status of ethnic groups through money. Obtaining corporate sponsorship means that a rationally calculating organization has deemed a constituency, first and foremost, as existing and, second, as worthy of attention as a source of gain. The 1982 coverage of the Puerto Rican Day Parade in the *Philadelphia Daily News* demonstrates what corporate sponsorship means to leaders within the Latino community:

The Common Pleas Judge Nelson Diaz . . . acknowledged the presence of corporate sponsors for the parade, like the Anheuser-Busch brewing firm, and said the city's Puerto Rican population doesn't yet have "the political sophistication to use (the parade) as a forum to dramatize some of the problems we face in this city every day, such as housing and education. . . . It's like the black community 20 years ago," Diaz sighed. "We're marching and somebody else is paying the bill."[25]

Diaz hints that commercial markets allow Puerto Ricans to participate in the civic life of the United States and to demonstrate themselves as being like all other Americans. To make claims about being contributing members of society and to have those claims widely disseminated requires free-market mechanisms as much (if not more than) a political apparatus. Puerto Ricans were following in the footsteps of the black community, who understood that civil rights in the United States came through a demonstrated commitment to and advancement in the commercial marketplace.[26]

The engagement between culture and commerce involves negotiation, but the ability to advance one view or another depends on a set of collectively held beliefs about what is negotiable and what is not. Even the more economically and politically powerful actors acknowledge the claims that "weaker" parties make regarding the inappropriate uses of culture. Just as culture enables weaker parties to make claims on more powerful actors, so claims are made on culture. In the next chapter we look at how local actors create and maintain their art worlds as their music, dance, and material arts promote and undergo transformations in the barrio.

3 » The Art World of the Barrio

Sources of Attraction and Motivation

ATTRACTING AUDIENCES AND INVESTMENTS

"Machismo, does it not get in the way of the gentler arts?" The questioner, a thirty-something white man, is attending my presentation on how art and culture are helping to revitalize the Philadelphia barrio's commercial corridor. When I ask him what he means, he replies, "You know." Yes, I did know. Neighborhoods take on gendered characteristics, as effeminate (too much art and too freely expressed sexual identities) or hypermasculine (no art but lots of physical violence and defiantly expressed racial identities). How could an effeminate event such as an art exhibition succeed in a high-crime ethnic (and therefore macho) neighborhood, is probably what he was asking; and who would show up to *that kind of neighborhood* for an art event?

Art worlds in general attract a wide variety of people and institutions into their orbit, and the barrio is no exception.[1] An exhibition draws the artist's core set of friends and patrons into the neighborhood, some for the first time. People from foundations, private businesses, city agencies, and state entities that contribute resources to support the event will come to the barrio for opening night, and their exposure to the neighborhood may alter their perception of the type of place the neighborhood is, potentially affecting their evaluation of other projects being proposed for the community.[2] Business-to-business suppliers provide sound equipment, makeshift stages, large outdoor tents, and food trays as well as transportation services for the artworks. Printing services produce postcards and flyers advertising the event, and newspaper coverage provides publicity.[3]

Outsiders see how things are done in the barrio and how friendly people from the community seem to be at these art openings. They then tell their local networks of family, friends, and associates about how they ventured into a different world, lived to tell the tale, and enjoyed it enough for a return visit. These eyewitness accounts from an outsider to a set of outsiders soften the image of the community and change perceptions about what types of things "typically" happen in places such as the barrio.[4]

Art worlds can make insiders and outsiders alike perceive the neighborhood as a good place to invest time, energy, and money. A vibrant art world brings neighborhood residents in contact with the middle class, an interaction often missing in highly segregated, poor communities.[5] The ethnically diverse boards that govern the arts organization in the barrio are made up of middle-class outsiders and lower- and middle-class locals. As we will see, arts organizations act as cultural ambassadors, promoting partnerships and intercultural appreciation. Such organizations, whose main concern with outsiders is public relations, enrich local art worlds and by extension the neighborhood's commercial life.

LA COLECTIVA AND ART NIGHTS IN THE BARRIO

In 2003 David Mendez, Gil González, and Lucas Rivera founded La Colectiva and the Art Nights in the Barrio series to provide Latino artists with an opportunity to exhibit their work. They sensed that that the art world of Center City was closed to Latinos, and they wanted to do something about it. David, a fashion designer, explains how the idea was born. "I said to my friend Gil, 'Maybe we could do something like a First Friday [in Old City],' and he gave me a puzzled look like he didn't know what it was, so I took him down there and he really enjoyed it. And he said, 'David, we gotta do something like this.' ... The first art show we did was at his house. He had invited a lot of friends, and there were so many people who came. He said, 'There were strangers who came in off the streets.'"[6]

The First Friday series, although it inspired David, Gil, and Lucas, did not meet with great success at first. Photographer Tony Rocco recalls hearing stories of First Friday's early days from people he worked with at Cooperative Gallery in Old City. "When First Friday started, nobody used to go. I mean, they had to build critical mass. It would start off, they kept [at] it, and more people would come, and they would tell other people, and all of a sudden more people would go. They used to put out all these spreads trying to get people to come, and now they are trying to not put out food because people just never leave."[7] I learn from another community informant that for a long time, the area known as Old City was considered "a dump"—no one wanted to go there. By comparing the barrio with Old City, he suggests there is hope for the barrio.

As Gil González describes it, putting on Art Night is a complex affair that depends heavily on the generosity of business owners willing to do favors for the artists. Each time, Gil would walk up and down Fifth Street, asking businesses if they could help by letting them use space or equipment or donating food for the event. "They just did it without question, without even wanting anything back," he recalls. "There were a lot of people who *gave* to the Colectiva *a lot*. I'm amazed at how many people, really, from the artists to the institutions, just everybody."[8] The business owners are proud to see this type of event in their district. The capacity to mobilize resources based on social ties is social capital, and the donations of business owners and nonprofits to the art venture demonstrate the abundance of social capital in the barrio.

Over the course of a year I attended Art Night regularly to get a sense of its scope and to see the types of audiences that different artists attract. In the following sections I describe three visits: one in the fall, one in summer, and one in winter.

October

I arrive at Fifth and Lehigh at nine on a crisp Friday morning to get my bearings and observe preparations for the event. The air is thick with the smell of tar, as city workers wearing orange and yellow uniforms pour hot asphalt into potholes on North Fifth Street. The timing of the long-awaited roadwork seems deliberate, as if the city decided to spruce up the neighborhood just in time for the arrival of outsiders. Art Night is scheduled to begin at six o'clock, and barring last-minute delays, the street repairs should be done in time.

As I enter Pan Sabor, a Latin-themed and Puerto Rican–owned bakery, an employee greets me with a nod and continues his banter with a customer. The shop manager takes my order in English and asks if I want anything with my coffee. The nearby display case offers cookies named Taínos (after the people indigenous to the island of Puerto Rico) along with fresh pastries also bearing Spanish names; behind the counter sit fresh loaves of bread. I hear boisterous conversation behind me, and turn to see a bakery employee and customer adopt the roles of art gallery owner and potential buyer.

"Did you see the paintings? Did you see the paintings? Prepare yourself," the gallery owner exhorts, sounding like an anchor on ESPN holding forth on the antics of a mischievous player.[9] He pulls back a sheet, revealing a three-by-four-foot painting leaning against the wall—a surrealist watercolor of two naked women in a tropical forest, each resting an arm on the other's shoulder. Their brown hair with blond highlights hangs in ropes over their shoulders and rests on their ample breasts. Their lips seem to pucker, as though each were clamoring for a kiss.

"Damn. Damn!" says the buyer, sounding impressed.

From behind the counter, the bakery manager interrupts the role-play. "Yo, Jay! Why you ain't got these pictures up [on the wall already]?"

" 'Cause Ma told me to take 'em down."

"Those paintings have to go up."

"All right," Jay says, then continues his banter with the customer as he motions toward the other paintings leaning against the wall. "Man, that almost looks like two women together [sexually]."

The customer concurs. "You need to be at least eighteen years old to look at these," he says, and they both chuckle.

Owner Vic Negrón enters the scene from the rear of the pastry shop, sweat dotting his forehead. He has agreed to talk with me about what it is like to run a business in the Latino district. Vic applauds the idea of a book about "the little guys" like him who struggle to make a positive impact in the lives of their families and communities. While the media tend to focus on members of the community who land in jail or on welfare, Vic says, they ignore those who take financial risks and make personal sacrifices to set up businesses and hire people who might not otherwise have work. He looks approvingly out the window at the noisy road construction. "You know, some businesses around here complain that if you close the street, they not gonna get any business," he says, "but how are we supposed to fix the potholes if we can't close the street? You just can't satisfy some people."

Two men who entered the shop when Vic emerged from the back now join our conversation to register their views on the road works.

"A bunch of city workers, God bless 'em," one man says sarcastically.

"Sixteen of them motherfuckers, and for what?" the other chimes in.

"Yeah, we got a bunch of Mexicans out there fixing the street,"[10] the first one says. (I heard similar complaints from other business owners in the area, who were disappointed that local workers were not hired to do the repairs.) To have such a large crew of people "half-fix" a road only adds insult to injury. "We could do it ourselves for less money, but the city isn't going to pay for that," he laments. Vic excuses himself to check on something in the back of the shop, and the two commentators make their exit.

With the lull in conversation, I hear the sounds of *Jerry Springer* coming from the television that hangs from the ceiling in the far left corner. The show's bouncers were separating two women who had come to blows over a man. A Latina customer I had not previously noticed comments aloud to her female companion, "White girls will have an affair with the brother or the daddy [of their own husbands], but that wouldn't be us Puerto Rican girls. We know to go on to the other side of the 'hood and *not* [have an affair] in the same family."

Soon Vic returns and apologizes for not having more time to talk. His day is growing hectic with the stream of customers and the preparations for Art Night. "Here are my phone numbers, the business and the cell," he says, handing me his business card. "I really want to talk about this. I'm glad you're writing this book."

I spend some more time wandering around the neighborhood to observe the activities in preparation for the evening's art event, then drive home. That night I return to find the roadblock removed and both sides of Fifth Street paved jet black from Lehigh to Somerset. There are no signs directing me where to park my car for Art Night, an omission I find disconcerting, especially if the rumors are true that the neighborhood is unsafe. I was not the only outsider wondering where to park. As I left the art event that night, I overheard a conversation among three white people who seemed to be first-time visitors to the event. They were about to get into their car, and one of them said, "Well, looks like this was an okay place to park after all." Their car was parked on Fifth Street just north of Somerset and mine was parked just south.

Because Raíces and Taller anchor the intersection, I imagine how much more dynamic Art Night might be if people could park their cars in the lot at the corner, where a used car dealership seems to struggle with five vehicles for sale. Later I learned that this idea for the lot was discussed as far back as the 1980s, as a place for daytime customers wanting to park and shop along the North Fifth Street corridor.[11] The discussions ended in classic coordination problems between local merchants and city officials as well as difficulties in marshalling the resources to buy or lease the lot.

June

With the multitude of organizations and people involved in mounting Art Night, there is a sense of anticipation and purpose in the air. When I arrive around 7:30 on a summer evening, the first thing I hear is an Afro-Caribbean drum beat coming from the corner of Somerset and Fifth streets. I turn the corner on Somerset and see Raíces, where brochures listing the names of the artists, performers, and exhibition sites are propped on the outside window ledge. The blare of horns beckons me inside and up the stairs to the Talentos studio. There I see two rows of musicians, drummers in the front and horn players in the back. A woman dressed in red, white, and blue pivots as she dances; a Puerto Rican flag bearing the same colors is emblazoned on the back of her blouse. Twenty-seven spectators sit in the studio, and others spill out into the hallway.

When the band finishes the set, everyone pours out of the room and heads for the next exhibition venue. I follow them up to Taller, where I see a woman and two men seated at a table draped with a banner that reads, FO-MENTO/ESTADO LIBRE ASOCIADO DE PUERTO RICO/COMPAÑIA DE FOMATO (Economic Development/The Commonwealth of Puerto Rico/ The Puerto Rico Industrial Development Company). The woman, wearing a hat made of reeds, waits expectantly as I approach, while her male companions weave hats. I look at the jewelry on the table, and she says, "a mano," then, "made by hand." I ask how much the necklace and earring set cost, and she replies, "Treinta" (thirty dollars).[12]

I enter Taller and see Celia, who runs the bookstore. "Welcome. It is so good to see you back," she says, and we kiss each other's cheek. David Mendez recognizes me too and flashes a smile. He tells me about the dozen or so reporters from Spanish newspapers across the country who are attending Art Night at the invitation of HACE. They will probably have dinner at Isla Verde restaurant, an upscale yet comfortable place to entertain people in the neighborhood.

A band strikes up outside, and I step out to listen. People emerge from houses and nearby shops; drivers in no hurry are happy to slow down or stop, and passengers step out into the street, annoying drivers trying to pass. About seventy men, women, young boys, and teenage girls form a circle on the sidewalk; each takes a turn stepping into the circle to dance, then yielding to the next aspirant. The sidewalk has the feel of a carnival.

February

For *Terrazzo in Fallujah*, an exhibition by Damary Burgos, I expect the cold weather to dampen attendance, but the turnout is impressive thanks to the artist, who has brought her network of friends and admirers from Germantown and Mount Airy. The *Philadelphia Inquirer* reports that Damary wants to use her art to bring a largely white community of activists into contact with the Latino barrio. She thanks them publicly for driving down to support her.

As suggested by its name, *Terrazzo in Fallujah* focuses on art with a political theme. About seventy people attend the exhibition, and the crowd looks pretty diverse, with lots of people coming for the first time to Taller. Hanging on the walls are clothes bearing an image of the Iraq war taken from the Internet, inspiring Damary to talk metaphorically about the war as a stain in our own clothes that won't come out. She also tells us about Sherwood, a childhood friend of hers who died while fighting in Iraq. Sherwood's mother, Celeste Opala, holds up her daughter's 1987 high school graduation program, titled "Up Where We Belong," which was illustrated by Damary.

During the exhibition, Damary also talks about recent FBI raids in Puerto Rico against a pro-independence movement there. Referring to the neo-colonial situation of Puerto Ricans, who have had little voice in their political and economic development, Damary reminds her audience that the U.S. military uses the Puerto Rican island of Vieques for testing bombs without the islanders' consent. "We've lost forty-eight Puerto Ricans in Iraq," she announces, underscoring the sacrifices that Puerto Ricans make in supporting the military apparatus that mistreats their own homeland.[13] She says that "we as people of color" are in danger of losing our autonomy and the sense of joy and playfulness that comes from being free, and then she begins singing the children's song, "Miss Mary Mac-Mac-Mac," encouraging the audience to join in. The words are scripted in black on the gallery's wall for the exhibition:

> Miss Mary Mac-Mac-Mac
> All dressed in black-black-black
> She asked her mother-mother-mother
> For fifty cents-cents-cents
> ....
> The fourth of July-ly-ly
> ....

The children's song touches on the common humanity of young people joining together to jump rope and play patty-cake.[14] But with the war in Iraq, the political conflicts on the island of Puerto Rico, and the violence experienced in the barrio as well as other communities of color in Philadelphia, Damary argues that such innocence cannot long be maintained. Celebrations of freedom, such as the Fourth of July, are relevant for some, but not all. In her closing statement to the assembled audience, Damary notes the important role that programs at Taller play in kids' lives. She tells us that Taller helps kids find their niche in the world—a positive place, an alternative to the devil's playpen in the streets. "A mother's control can only go so far," she warns.

ART AND ITS AUDIENCES

The people who attend this cultural event tend to be well-educated cosmopolitans eager to visit the city's cultural frontiers. Some are middle- and upper-middle-class Latinos who are either curious about a place they left in the pursuit of upward social mobility, engaged in the Latino arts scene, or eager to support an event representing the cultural advancement of their ethno-racial group. Some community leaders hope that the focus on the arts and on the neighborhood's quality of life will lure upwardly mobile Latinos back to the neighborhood and that HACE's efforts to buy existing properties and construct affordable housing will reduce the threat of gentrification from outside the community.

Bill Salas of HACE observes that commercial and artistic efforts to serve the community are being coordinated more deliberately now than they had been before. During the past few years, he says, community development corporations such as his have become "much more supportive of arts and culture, and arts and culture [organizations] recognize that we're not the enemy.... There needs to be collaboration [with] the CDCs who are doing the physical development of the community, and we need to think of it a little more holistically."[15] There is no reason the Latino community could not have tastefully appointed restaurants with outdoor seating, coffee shops, art galleries, and performance venues as well as attractive streetscapes. There is no reason lofts and other housing suited for local artists could not be built so that a creative colony is firmly established in the barrio. Given the audiences attracted to Art Night and the ongoing transformations within the community, there is no reason these "barrio dreams" could not be realized. Art events provide dramatic markers of neighborhood change, as they suggest that individuals within the community have enough distance from the material necessities of life to tend to aesthetics. This "distance from necessity" functions as a distinguishing indicator of a place's special (desirable) character.[16]

The barrio's future depends in part on art, says David, who grew up in the community. "The whole idea of the art shows is to make a place for professional Latinos to go so they don't feel they have to leave the community to enjoy themselves," he explains. "We're trying to get people to spend here rather than... in places where [they're] really not welcomed." If the right services and amenities are provided, David says, Latinos will spend their disposable income in their own neighborhood. Some middle-class Latinos are starting to move back in. "A lot of Latinos who grew up in Kensington South who I've talked to really want to move back, wish they hadn't moved out. I know one executive director of one of the organizations who has moved back—he happens to still own the house he grew up in—so he's going to be moving back. Another Latino professional board member from one of the other organizations just purchased a house down the street." David marvels at the prices at which homes are selling. "I bought a property six years ago for ten thousand... and I know I can get at least a hundred thousand for it [now].... [M]y neighbor sold his house for seventy-seven thousand eight months ago. Two doors down, my other neighbor was selling [his house] this summer for a hundred and twenty thousand. He ended up getting a hundred and thirty-five thousand for it.... [I]t's weird."[17]

TALLER PUERTORRIQUEÑO

Like Gil, David, and Lucas, other Latinos have thought deeply about their own roles in the Latino arts scene. When a reporter for the *Inquirer Magazine* asked Carmen Febo why she, as a physician, was working part-time at a health clinic while serving as the executive director of Taller, she recalled how attending a concert at Taller helped her overcome her homesickness for Puerto Rico. "The arts are a much more integral part of everyday life in Latino culture than in American culture," she observes. "That's one of the reasons why, when Latinos come to this country, it's culture shock to the nth degree, because [back at home] the arts are incorporated in many traditions and ceremonies."[18] As a physician, she recognizes how a person's health (and the motivation to monitor and maintain their health) depends on feeling whole and happy. One sees this attachment to culture among children dressing up for trick-or-treat or among adults carefully preparing for holiday rituals. Carmen believes that individuals need to engage with the arts and with their own cultural traditions to maintain a sense of identity and humanity.

Taller's cultural center began in 1974 in a converted church parish house at Sixth and Venango streets. As Domingo Negrón remembers it, Taller was not the organization he intended to found. He began with the idea of setting up a business that would have a community development wing: "The noble idea was to set up this cultural entity that would house several micro-businesses from which eventually people would be trained to handle business transactions" such as bookstores and arts stores, he says.[19] That idea morphed into setting up a cultural center.

Carmen recalls how Taller and other community organizations emerged from the turbulence and creativity of the late sixties and early seventies: "The new thinking of the sixties, about activism and youth getting involved and progressive thinking and community participation and empowerment... [provided] the impetus that got a lot of organizations started like Concilio and Taller and the Young Lords and the APM [Asociación de Puertorriqueños en Marcha]," she says.[20] The arts and activism were one.

Johnny Irizarry, who became executive director in 1986, recalls years of crisis at Taller before he took his position. In the 1980s, he and his family

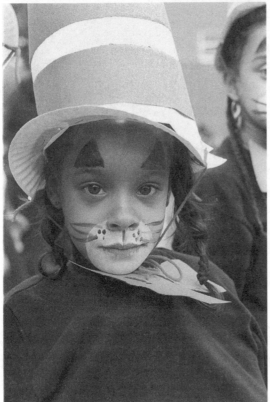

Puerto Rican girl and boy in colorful costumes. Photo by Tony Rocco. Historical Society of Pennsylvania, Balch Collection.

A girl dressed as a cat wearing a hat. Photo by Tony Rocco.

arrived from Puerto Rico (though he is originally from New York), and they moved to a neighborhood close to Taller. At the time, Taller had no staff and no volunteers, only a board of directors; they were anticipating a move to another location, but in the meantime, the original building "had fallen apart and was shut down," Johnny recalls.[21]

In 1986, Carmen Febo was the acting president of the board, and she persuaded Johnny to apply for the position of executive director. After accepting the job, he learned the enormity of the task that confronted him. "They'd given me a list of about thirty-three things," from filing back reports for the National Endowment for the Arts to bringing Taller up-to-date in its audits—"things I'd never really dealt with in the past," he says. (The National Endowment for the Arts requires that organizations document exactly how grant monies were used, who benefited, and what the various outcomes of the funding were.) Fortunately, he says, Taller had "a really good board—a lot of volunteers, a lot of energy." The new location, although not yet complete, was in good enough shape that programming could resume.[22]

Taller's programming has maintained a steady focus on local community concerns. Back in 1977 and 1978, two summer photography projects (*El Tercer Ojo* [The Third Eye] and *Positive Images*) sought to reinterpret the character of the Latino community to shed its image as a culture of poverty. Ten years later, Taller presented the exhibition *Two Faces: Gentrification of the Spring Garden Neighborhood and Its Culture Class* by Gil González, who grew up in the Spring Garden area and continues to exhibit his work at Taller. A brochure from the time gave this description of the photographer's background and message:

González has lived and experienced the circumstances that come with the gentrification of Spring Garden. As a witness to the change in the neighborhood, Mr. González has directly felt the racism and classism that the gentrification process has given birth to. As a professional, Mr. González cannot take photographs in his neighborhood without being harassed by police with threats to destroy his equipment.

González is specifically concerned with the generation of solutions to some of these problems. The first step is recognition and with this in mind Gilberto González through Taller Puertorriqueño brings to you "Two Faces."[23]

Although Taller, Raíces, AMLA, and other arts organizations have been active over the years, their presence has not been the defining feature of the neighborhood. Taller recognizes that its ability to attract audiences and funding depends on how the neighborhood is portrayed in the mainstream media. After Ted Koppel's "Badlands" report aired on *Nightline*, Taller had difficulty drawing audiences to its events in the barrio, according to Carmen. The *Nightline* report culminated in a series of newspaper and TV portrayals in the nineties depicting the community as a place where one was likely to be struck by gunfire or accosted by drug dealers. Characterizations like this pose "an additional barrier that you have to overcome," Carmen says.[24]

Johnny Irizarry recalls how the police would blockade the streets, permitting only people who lived in the community to drive through. He would hear stories of people being denied entry by police officers on the assumption that they were coming into the neighborhood to buy drugs. Mike Esposito, cofounder of Raíces, recalls one evening when he was stopped, asked for identification, and nearly turned away from the neighborhood.[25]

Despite the challenges Taller has faced over the years, Carmen notes that the volunteers and the staff are deeply committed to their mission and view their work differently from other endeavors. "Culture plays such a special place in people's perception of who they are," she says, and "at some level it's very emotional and it's very spiritual."[26]

Tony Rocco has experienced firsthand how culture attracts and motivates people to visit the barrio and become involved with organizations like Taller. As an undergraduate student at Temple University, Tony befriended students involved in the Latino students association on campus and, through them, came to know the neighborhood and become active in Taller. He explains:

Right after I had gotten involved with Taller, I started getting more interested in my background and my heritage. It was something I really didn't consider important before.... I thought it was a negative thing, being Colombian; I believed a lot of the negative stereotypes. Visiting Colombia changed my perspective. I got to see what it is really like, what an amazing country it is. How amazing my family and people around there are—you know, broke, but still the sweetest, most wonderful, giving people I've ever met, [both] Colombians in general [and] my family, of course. I came back kind of energized about Latinos. I was really loving who I was and wanted to learn more about it—wanted to support it and explore it.[27]

Both the country of Colombia and the Latino neighborhood in Philadelphia have reputations for violence, drugs, and poverty, but when one gets to know the people behind the statistics and the negative portrayals, one finds that the majority of residents are doing positive things and that their cultural heritage is worthy of celebration. Taller played a key role in helping Tony learn about himself and what it means to be a Latino: "You know, although [Taller] does concentrate on Puerto Rican culture and Puerto Rican heritage because of the name, and most Latinos in Philadelphia are Puerto Rican, they still reach out and include others. And they exhibit from other Latinos as well.... It is basically a cultural center for the whole [Latino] community."[28] The committee for the annual community festival Feria del Barrio dedicated the festival to Tony one year for his service to the community.

RAÍCES CULTURALES LATINOAMERICANAS

The personal stories of Yolanda Alcorta and Mike Esposito, cofounders of Raíces, offer some insight into their motivation for establishing the organization and operating it in the Philadelphia barrio. Yolanda's mother came from Guatemala, her father from Peru. They met in Brooklyn after her mother had won a scholarship from the Guatemalan government to come to the United States and learn English. Yolanda's father died ten days before she was born, and she and her mother eventually moved to a farm outside of Guatemala City.

After Yolanda's mother married an American man, the family moved to rural Elmira, Pennsylvania. She was initially worried that Yolanda might not be ready to enter kindergarten in her new American school, and she had reason to be concerned. "I didn't speak for three months upon arrival to the United States," Yolanda recalls. "I listened, I was immersed, but I said nothing. And then, just like that, I started speaking."[29]

Her mother helped her preserve her cultural heritage from Guatemala, speaking in Spanish with her at home and coming to the elementary school as a volunteer teacher of Spanish. "The teachers loved it so much that even though I went [on] to fourth grade, the third grade teacher asked, 'Oh, could you please come back?'" Yolanda says.[30] Eventually her mother taught Spanish in all the elementary grades and then was hired as the Spanish teacher at the junior high school.

In 1976, Yolanda moved to California. "It was the first time that I really felt Latina," she says. As she grew older, she found that being a woman (and a woman of color) in the sciences posed challenges to her career mobility. After obtaining a master's degree in museum education and working for the Mexican Museum in San Francisco, she followed her fiancé to Ann Arbor. "I went with him... and found myself working in the dining hall [*laughter*] because nobody would hire me, because my name was Yolanda Alcorta and I came from California."[31]

Yolanda earned her master's degree in botany from the University of Michigan, then applied for the PhD program in botany. She was not accepted even though she had performed well in the master's program. (A friend later told her that she was not accepted because women were seen as stay-at-home moms without careers.) With her master's in botany, Yolanda found a job in Philadelphia at Wyeth Pharmaceuticals, where she met Mike Esposito.

Mike grew up in Delaware County, the grandchild of Italian immigrants who lived in south Philadelphia. In 1980 he graduated from Saint Joseph's University, where he majored in international relations and minored in Spanish. As a Fulbright scholar, he studied political science at the graduate level in Bogota, Colombia, from 1980 to 1981. Upon returning to the United States, he obtained a master's degree in political science and took a part-time job teaching English as a Second Language in Chester to maintain his Latin American interests. "While this was happening, I was getting more and more interested in the culture and then specifically the music... and then eventually I started really, really getting passionate about folklore," he recalls. "I also learned a little bit about the community dynamic—about how groups form, why they dissolve, what goes on to keep them together, and what splits them apart." Mike went back to Colombia as a teacher in 1987–88, then returned to the United States "more determined than ever to get involved in the community in a cultural way." In 1991, he met Yolanda. "Our initial thought with Raíces was to develop performances that would showcase the variety in Latin American culture by taking the groups and juxtaposing them within the space of a performance," he explains.[32]

Mike and Yolanda envisioned Raíces as a loose network of cultural performance groups, with the organization providing the main hub for coordinating collaborative performances.[33] In this way, Raíces would add value by getting existing groups into more prestigious venues, helping new groups find gigs, and mounting collaborative performances that no single group would likely coordinate on its own.

When the organization was founded, it did not have an office in the neighborhood or anywhere else. It operated virtually, coordinating with performance groups to find rehearsal space and performance venues. Once it acquired office space at the intersection of North Fifth and Somerset, Raíces provided a cultural home for local artists, who could drop in for a jam session; a space for after-school, weekend, and summer programs for adults and children; and an epicenter for Latino culture that represented all nineteen Latin American countries, in contrast to Taller's founding emphasis on Puerto Rico.[34]

Mike stresses the importance of bilingual performances in which the history and cultural significance of a dance or composition are explained first in Spanish and then in English. Although he recognizes that the majority of the people in the audience speak English, he knows that they will wait patiently to hear the Spanish. He also knows that the audience expects to see well-known performances and might be less comfortable with folk performances that are authentic and traditional but unfamiliar to a majority of U.S. citizens. Mike says that Raíces likes to conduct a "systematic overview of cultures that are in their various stages of 'health and development,'" putting, for example, "a dance form native to the Virgin Islands called the Quelbé... on the same footing as a Calypso.... We want every manifestation to have that opportunity to grow and survive."[35]

Programming is a difficult task, and things do not always go according to plan. Through trial and error, the organization has learned that the historical experiences of different cultural groups lead them to attach different meanings to concepts that may seem otherwise straightforward. For example, when the organization wanted to put together a performance demonstrating Latin Americans' struggle to adapt to American society, the idea was rejected for two reasons. One was that its title, La Lucha (The Struggle), had a Marxist connotation, "so that put people off," Mike explains. "And number two, they probably sensed that they weren't necessarily ready to do the dramatic part of it, ... the acting part," he says.[36] Although academics and cosmopolitan museumgoers celebrate "the struggle" of the immigrant and the artist alike, these struggles are read differently by the people directly engaged in them. A struggle can take on unwelcome political or social overtones, particularly if it suggests that a person or ethnic group is having trouble "making it" on their own. Thus one cultural group may celebrate la lucha while another denigrates it. Opportunities abound for miscommunication.

Another source of conflict lay in trying to represent the various Latino cultures and not focusing exclusively on Puerto Ricans, though they are the majority in the neighborhood. The magnitude of the challenge manifested itself in the organization's attempt to replace the long-serving executive director and cofounder, Yolanda. Would hiring a Puerto Rican make non–Puerto Rican Latinos think that the programming would be dominated by Puerto Ricans? Would hiring a Mexican American send a similar message? The board members at Raíces were sensitive to how the ethnicity of the executive director might be perceived by various artists and other stakeholders, but the board was also sure that so long as the new executive director seemed committed to the organization's mission, concerns about the person's ethnicity would be allayed.

The board decided to hire a Mexican American woman from Texas who was ready for a new arts scene. Veronica Castillo-Pérez likes to tell the story of how she packed up her home, rented a U-Haul, and drove herself from

Austin to Philadelphia to begin her new job as executive director. She remembers arriving at Raíces only to discover that the outside funding for her salary and health insurance was not forthcoming. Veronica was invited to stay with longtime board member Monica Rodrigo, and soon thereafter she began to take charge of the organization's resources, cutting up extra credit cards, renegotiating the terms of the organization's accounts at the local bank, and reestablishing ties with the various performance groups in the network. As the entire board, the performance groups, and the local business owners pulled together, so too did outside funders. Raíces was saved.

Raíces depends on voluntary contributions from people in the community as well as corporate sponsorship. At an art opening and fund-raiser for Raíces, the board members contributed food for the reception and contacted local businesses for help; Raíces also received the support of people working in other community organizations. Isla Verde, whose owner also owns the building in which Raíces operates, contributed food, along with El Bohío and Tierra Columbiana restaurants. Veronica recalls how people pulled together to help her with the silent auction: the owner of Centro Musical donated a guitar, and artist and Taller staff member Daniel de Jesus donated a dozen paintings.[37]

Veronica observes how friendly and helpful Carmen Febo and others at Taller were as she began work at Raíces. Indeed, Veronica nominated Taller for a Governor's Award for Excellence in the Arts, putting another organization before her own. When I ask why she did it, she replies, "They've been here for such a long time and have done such important work. It's about time."[38]

While interorganizational ties have been strong, so too have the social ties within these organizations, which have served as bridges to opportunity outside of the barrio. Lisa Linn de Barona, a board member at Raíces who works at the Wharton School at the University of Pennsylvania, helped to secure support for the silent auction from the university's Latino students association. Lisa also proved instrumental in identifying and applying for marketing assistance through the graduate consulting program at the Wharton School. Other board members have a diverse set of ties to people within and outside of the community, and these ties bring resources to the organization as well.

Over lunch at Tierra Columbiana, Veronica tells me how the organization makes a difference in the lives of local people.

The exhibit that Raíces just did came from this woman Anna, who has two small kids. She lives in a house just in the lane behind Raíces. She approached me and told me that she had something to show me. Apparently Anna had been doing art on her own at home for many years, but didn't know what to do with it. She'd never had an exhibition. She began painting after she . . . got some free passes to the Philadelphia Museum of Art, and that's where she became inspired.[39]

Veronica is pleased that Anna felt comfortable enough to come into the Raíces office and talk informally about her passion for art. Anna's success in obtaining her own exhibition reflects how much the local arts organizations serve the needs and ambitions of local talent while attracting artists and exhibits from outside of the community.

At Raíces I have encountered lots of local musicians who describe it as a cultural home, a place where they could unwind and play. One morning, as I arrive at the neighborhood just before eleven, Johnny Cruz and his cousin spot me standing outside Raíces, ready to knock on the door. Johnny clearly feels at home as he hands me a flyer and encourages me to attend next weekend's *descarga* (musical jam session). "Bring your family, your friends, everybody you know." I don't recognize him at first, nor he me. (We met in 2005 when Johnny and his wife, Aida, were conducting a workshop on Puerto Rican folk music for middle-school children at the Free Library of Philadelphia.) He and his cousin descend into the lower level of Raíces to get bongo drums and set up on the sidewalk for an impromptu performance, as is their weekend custom. Standing on the sidewalk, Johnny tells me that when people say "Puerto Rico," they must speak "from the diaphragm," from deep within. A passing police car serves as his cue for a demonstration. Johnny raises his arms toward the sky to form a V and calls to the police officers, "Puerto Rico!" They respond with an equally jubilant *honk-honk-honk*. Johnny and his cousin laugh.[40]

Johnny also performs with Aida, the lead vocalist who plays the maracas; she works for the school district and helps to schedule and arrange performances for Raíces. Monica Rodrigo, the current president of the organization's board, takes great pride in the fact that Johnny and Aida have been with Raíces through thick and thin. They help keep the doors open just by showing up, inviting friends and passersby to visit, and opening their throats to sing.

ARTISTAS Y MÚSICOS LATINO AMERICANOS (AMLA)

Latin American musicians are Philadelphia's caged birds, says Jesse Bermudez. He should know: back in the 1980s, Jesse experienced firsthand the poor working conditions faced by Philadelphia's Latino musicians. He and his band members "would go to a club, say, at about eight o'clock in the evening and not leave until 3:30 in the morning and do about five sets, and the owners were only paying twenty-five dollars per man"—less than minimum wage. Jesse began to meet with leaders of thirteen salsa orchestras on Monday nights at Saint Boniface Church to discuss their plight; eventually the group grew to include 125 musicians. Jesse believed that the musicians needed to go on strike until their working conditions improved, but first he had to gain their trust.

Before I formed AMLA [in 1982], there had been individuals who tried to form music organizations and then had exploited the artists, okay? So exploitation was in the minds of the artists all along. "Is Jesse another one of these guys?" Because the last guy that tried to do something before me did a big event, made a lot of money, and he disappeared. Nobody ever saw him anymore. . . . I just had to go and *show* that I was different. . . . [W]e used to throw events and dances; and boom, boom, boom, when it would be all over with, we'd sit down and divide the money. Everybody got paid and everything was in order. So then after that, the issue [of distrust] didn't exist anymore.[41]

By 1986, La Asociación de Músicos Latino Americanos, as it was originally known, launched the Latin School for the Performing Arts (LSPA), offering music classes in the basement of Taller. In 1990 the organization moved to Fifth and Somerset, where Raíces is currently located, and remained there for ten years. In 2000 Councilwoman Maria Quiñones-Sanchez helped AMLA obtain the firehouse a block away. From the firehouse, AMLA began to host the Philadelphia Neighborhood Tours, but the beautiful old building came with high upkeep costs: "It was an old firehouse, and all of the heating system and the pumps were like from the 1800s or whatever, and we kept investing money and trying to get them fixed, but after a few years that we were there, we couldn't [do it] anymore."[42]

By 2005, the organization did not have a physical office in the barrio, and Jesse began to operate it from his home. The following year he formed a partnership with the Reverend Luis Cortes, of the social services organization Esperanza, and renamed the organization Artistas y Músicos Latino Americanos. AMLA has shared Esperanza's facility at 4261 North Fifth Street ever since.

In 2008, AMLA began broadcasting a radio show on Saturday mornings from Centro Musical, a well-known musical instrument shop and a popular hangout for Latino artists. Jesse and Wilfredo originally approached a local radio station about doing the show because the station was not featuring local artists. Ultimately they decided to launch it themselves with their own funds and received significant support from Councilwoman Quiñones-Sanchez.

The program has a short segment called "Your Government," in which Councilwoman Quiñones-Sanchez is a fixture. The rest of the show focuses on Latino musicians, with an emphasis on Philadelphia-area performers. Jesse is especially pleased with the community's response to the radio program:

When we ask folks for something, immediately you'll see them coming into the record shop. One time we said, "It's a rainy day, and boy it would be a great day for soup." And would you believe that about an hour later this guy comes up on a motorcycle and brought a big pot of soup? And I mean, it's like, we know that people are listening because they are responding. When we ask them for food (we're getting ready to do another food drive), they come and they bring food or whatever it is [we ask of them].[43]

Since its inception, however, the program has had limited success in keeping business sponsors, Jesse tells me, because whenever the show attracts new advertising, the radio station swoops in and offers the business a better deal.

AMLA's programming and fund-raising efforts have met with competition from another quarter as well. As multiculturalism has gone mainstream, it has been picked up by large non-ethnic arts organizations, creating a number of challenges for smaller local arts organizers such as Jesse.

When the whole concept of multiculturalism came in, someone at the Ford Foundation called me up because they wanted to pick my brain. And at that time I said to myself, "Oh my God! We have a problem coming down the pike." And we did.... [Now] I'm competing with the Annenberg Center; I'm competing with everyone else and their uncle for dollars for something we've been doing in the community forever.[44]

No longer could communities of color count on reliable flows of funds for annual programs, because those programs could now be mounted by well-known arts institutions with million-dollar budgets and trusted financial administrators. The Mellon Jazz Festival, for example, used to come into all of the communities in Philadelphia, and smaller nonprofits such as AMLA and the Philadelphia Clef Club of Jazz and Performing Arts looked forward to the festival every year because of the resources it brought. Jesse recalls producing a festival with 10,000 people in attendance, but then the Kimmel Center for the Performing Arts entered the fray with its new focus on more multicultural programming, and Mellon gave all its funding to Kimmel. As

Jesse sees it, "If I wanted to present this Latin band now and the Annenberg Center wants to present it or the Kimmel Center, [underwriters are] going to give the grant to the Kimmel Center, because the first thing they're going to say is, 'They're a bigger institution, they're going to handle my money better'... so you're right back to square one again."

Mainstream arts and music organizations do not always understand how Latino music should be presented, Jesse observes. The appropriate way to experience some forms of music is not by sitting in one's chair, tapping one's foot quietly (if at all). It is by allowing one's body to move to those rhythms in a gathering where others are also freely participating in the music, whether dancing at their seats or stepping out into the aisles. The performance spills out from the stage, and its power derives partly from the audience's response. Jesse explains how mainstream music organizations fail to understand these dynamics:

I remember the first time that the Mann [Center for the Performing Arts] produced Celia Cruz. I was there on that show because I put a 27-piece... orchestra together to open up the show.... It was a tribute to the late great Marco Rizzo.... We had a tremendous show that day. At the Mann, they were all upset because people were standing up in the aisles, and they were dancing and stuff like this. And they [the Mann] were very upset about that, because, you know, you're not supposed to be standing up or dancing in the aisles at the Mann.... I tried to tell them, I said, listen, you're presenting a certain kind of music that does a certain thing to its audience. You can't [tell people to sit restrained], you know what I'm saying?[45]

This sense of frustration with mainstream arts organizations speaks to how different social groups appreciate and respond to music in different ways. Musical value does not exist solely in the pitch of the voice or the composition of the notes; it is generated in the interactions and the psychological identification between performers and the audience.

Likewise, the ideas for projects that arts organizations propose are not "good" in and of themselves; their viability depends on the identity of those offering the ideas. As Jesse observes, small ethnic arts organizations that partner with larger organizations may be prized for their ideas and cultural traditions but not trusted to handle their own finances. This became apparent to Jesse when he first proposed that Philadelphia mount a neighborhood tours program similar to the one Chicago did. Jesse approached Wachovia Bank with a solid funding proposal, but he was told that the bank did not engage in those kinds of ventures. He later gave the proposal to his partner organization, which approached the bank two months later and

Stilt walkers in front of Taller's mural. Photo by Tony Rocco.

(Facing page, top): Former curator of Taller staffing a face-painting booth at the Feria del Barrio. Photo by Tony Rocco. Historical Society of Pennsylvania, Balch Collection.

(Facing page, bottom): A Raíces performer entertaining kids on the street at the Feria del Barrio. Photo by Tony Rocco. Historical Society of Pennsylvania, Balch Collection.

was granted the requested funds. These experiences have taught Jesse that he and others in the Latino arts community are "the small fish being swallowed by the big fish," but he insists that the work is too important to lose heart.

Arts and culture provide nourishment for the community, and this nourishment is especially important in the barrio. Jesse takes pride in the quality of education that AMLA offers through the LSPA. Although some students struggle to do well in their courses due to language barriers or issues at home, Jesse argues that talented students should be given an opportunity to develop as musicians and artists even if their grades are not what they should be. LSPA students and graduates have won the televised *Star Search* competitions and the NJN Tito Puente and Celia Cruz awards; they have performed regularly with the Fania All Stars and the Eddie Palmieri band; and they have joined Beyoncé's band of instrumentalists. A long line of Latino artists comes from Philadelphia—including Grammy nominee Papo Vazquez, Isidro Infante (the last musical director for Celia Cruz), and Jose "Papo" Rodriquez (who performed with Poncho Sanchez)—but the recognition that Philadelphia's Latino community receives for its high concentration of musical talent remains scant.

SEPARATE WORLDS

As we shall see in the next chapter, the art world of the barrio sometimes overlaps with the business community, yet the two are commonly thought of as occupying separate spheres of activity. During Art Night, many merchants close their shops at five o'clock; the audiences usually show up specifically for the art, perhaps stay for a snack, and then leave the neighborhood. The challenge for Art Night is to act as an anchoring event, drawing audiences to the district not only to engage with the artists but also to become more familiar with the local commercial offerings. Bill Salas of HACE says he hopes to bring in a large upscale Latino restaurant directly onto North Fifth to complement Isla Verde on American Street. Perhaps, he says, such an addition will provide the kind of cultural anchor the district needs to attract consumers from other parts of the city.

The art world of the barrio differs from the art worlds evident in parts of the city where neighborhoods suffer no social stigma and where the poverty rate is much lower. Both Yolanda and Veronica spoke to me about the challenge of working with artists who do not own a car and do not live near a reliable form of public transportation. When Raíces books a performance in a part of the city or county that is difficult or impossible to reach by public transportation—not an uncommon occurrence—a staff member or volunteer has to take the artist to and from the venue. The artists and other performers within the network have their day (and sometimes their night) jobs, so scheduling rehearsals also proves challenging.

Perhaps one of the most difficult things for outsiders to understand is how much the community is imbedded in the artistic world. Carmen Febo recalls discussions among board members of Taller over whether to hand over the Feria del Barrio to other community organizations so that Taller could focus more of its attention on the traditional tasks of an arts and culture organization. For fifteen years, Taller had worked with AMLA in mounting the event. The event does not make money for Taller and drains the organization's resources. Economically speaking, Taller should have withdrawn from it. The staff and volunteers of Taller simply work longer hours without compensation in order to break even on the Feria. Why continue an economically costly activity? Carmen Febo explains that Taller could not just stand off to the side—to do so would contradict "our efforts and our mission and our vision"—so the Taller board decided to stick with it.

The art world of the barrio is remarkably different from the mainstream art world, yet has been deeply influenced by it. When the Philadelphia Museum of Art hosted the exhibition *Tesoros/Treasures/Tesouros: The Arts in Latin America, 1492–1820* in fall 2006, it seemed that Latino cultural heritage was finally being recognized by one of the most prominent museums in the world. But the connection went beyond that of institutional recognition. Anne d'Harnoncourt, then the director of the museum, had made an effort to reach out to the Latino population. The news of her death in 2008 quickly circulated via e-mail, one correspondent writing that she "was a real friend to our community." Though worlds apart, there were bridges of goodwill linking the minority art world to the mainstream.

My intent in illuminating these linkages is to reveal the different ways they influence public discourse about the Latino community. Aside from the social ties that Latinos in the barrio have to people and organizations outside of their neighborhood, there are *symbolic* resources—collectively held stories, images, rituals—that the barrio dwellers cultivate, and those resources affect the kinds of ties they are able to establish with outsiders. Even when the same *volume* of monetary and other material resources flows into the neighborhood, the *qualitatively different purposes* to which those resources will be put and how outsiders will earmark those resources depend on the way these outsiders perceive the character of the place. The way that locals perceive their community likewise influences the actions they take to improve their businesses and other community concerns.

4 » Ringing the Registers

Entrepreneurial Dreams

THE PRICE OF AMBITION

Maintaining a good cultural scene in the neighborhood requires investment. Food and space must be donated for exhibitions and performances; funds must be provided for tents, stages, sound systems, and publicity. Do these expenditures translate into economic profits for local merchants? How does their cultural attachment to the neighborhood influence their financial investments and participation in local endeavors? The answer to the first question may not be within our reach. But the answer to the second question is, for it can be found in the personal experiences of entrepreneurs and in the problems confronting their neighborhood and their city. The timing and conditions of their entry into the business district, coupled with the overall health of the community and of the city, shape the entrepreneurs' expectations and guide their investments.

Before delving into the lives of the pioneers, the offspring who have succeeded them, and the newcomers who arrived during different time periods, I would like to tell the story of one of the neighborhood stars. Reinaldo "Rey" Pastrana went from having nothing to being one of the biggest property owners in the district and one of the most daring proponents of reinventing the district's image. In his story one finds the promises and pitfalls of ethnic entrepreneurship and neighborhood change.

On the evening of October 20, 2005, Rey's political mentor, Councilman Richard "Rick" Mariano, was seen entering the tower observation deck of City Hall. Mariano was about to be indicted on fraud and money laundering charges, and newscasters suggested that he was contemplating suicide. Firefighters across the street were preparing for a possible plunge, and the television reporters for a good story. Mariano had been doing deals across the city, issuing licenses and facilitating large-scale real estate deals for people who could make the councilman feel their appreciation by paying his bills and performing in-kind favors. If the rumors were true, Mariano had not behaved differently from other city politicians in granting (unlawful) favors for favors. The remarkable thing was the carelessness of his behavior and the desperation he displayed upon discovery.

Like spiderwebs, as Balzac once quipped, the laws had snared a few flies but seldom deterred the vermin from passing through. One such small fly was Rey Pastrana, who had been an active promoter of large developments in his community. During Feria del Barrio the previous month, Rey had stood on the outdoor stage at Fifth and Lehigh, waiting to be recognized as Person of the Year for 2005. A man of vision, Rey had developed Plaza Americana at the corner of Lehigh and American streets and anchored it with an upscale restaurant, Isla Verde Café. The plaza served as an oasis in the barrio and a sign of things to come.

Rey opened Isla Verde on December 8, 2004, just three days before the monthly Art Night. With a price tag of $1.6 million, Isla Verde made no secret of its ambitions. The restaurant was named after a city in Puerto Rico, and its self-described South Beach menu recalled the fashionable strip in Miami. Isla Verde attracted the attention of Craig LaBan, the food critic for the *Philadelphia Inquirer*. "This sleek spot, with a fine young chef, is a bit of South Beach in North Philly," read the subtitle to LaBan's story. His review focused on how Isla Verde fit within the context of the Centro de Oro, the community's business district, and what it symbolized for the rebirth of the barrio:

We could easily be sitting in a high-style lounge near Old San Juan, listening to the background rhythm of lapping waves. But then the man turns.... Suddenly, Cousins Supermarket comes into view.... Fringed with barbed wire and a weedy vacant lot, this corner of American and Lehigh is an unlikely spot to discover a trendy lounge such as Isla Verde.... Isla Verde could be a hot spot in South Beach. [And] the promising young chef, Juan Carlos Rodriguez, would be at home in any Center City bistro. But Isla Verde is definitely something new for the barrio.... Owner Reinaldo Pastrana... thinks the time is right for an upscale anchor to the neighborhood's rebirth.[1]

The restaurant attracted businesspeople from the hospitals nearby as well as from Temple University a few blocks away. This was a place where one could meet business partners for a meal or drinks in one's own neighborhood. Rodriguez, the executive chef, is a native of Puerto Rico; he attended the Art Institute of Philadelphia's culinary program and gained valuable experience cooking at the exclusive Alma de Cuba in Center City and the Hyatt Park at the Bellevue. With Chef Rodriguez running the kitchen, Isla

Verde promised high quality from someone trained in the best of Center City dining.

Such ambitions cost a great deal of money. The restaurant was housed in a building that had originally been owned by the E.F. Houghton Company but had sat vacant once heavy industry moved out of Philadelphia. The building required a $130,000 environmental study before it could even be reopened. Its fair market value was $400,000 in 2001, but the city council, at the behest of Councilman Mariano, passed an ordinance allowing it to be purchased at a below-market price. Pastrana purchased the property for a quarter of its value and paid only a quarter of the cost of the environmental study. Less than two weeks after the ordinance went into effect, the favors began. On December 19, 2002, Rey Pastrana paid $1,812.60 for Councilman Marino's gym membership fees at the Sporting Club at Bellevue; two more gym membership payments followed, one on January 14, 2004, and the other on December 20, 2004. Rey had paid about $5,400 total for the councilman's gym membership.

Rey was sentenced to two and a half years in prison. About six months after his release, I sat down with him for dinner at Isla Verde to talk about what had happened and to find out more about this man hailed by so many in his community. When I asked him about his conviction, he described himself as a pawn in a much larger game; prosecutors thought he knew more than he did about Mariano's connections and dealings, he said, and wanted to pressure him with a harsh sentence so that he would tell them all they hoped to hear. "It was a bullshit case, and I just wouldn't cooperate. They wanted me to talk nonsense about other folks, and I didn't know what they were talking about."[2]

Rey's conviction dealt quite a blow to the Latino enclave he had worked so hard to revitalize, and business owners varied in their opinion of his behavior. Some entrepreneurs regarded him as a hero who had helped them set up their own businesses and had offered reduced rents to newly established enterprises, but they were quick to add that they did not condone what he had done. Others viewed Rey's actions as a setback for the community, worrying that it confirmed outsiders' assumptions that those who make it in the enclave do so by operating outside of the law and that the "street mentality" of doing whatever it takes to get one's way taints even the respectably self-employed. Still other business owners saw Rey's conviction as further evidence that when Latinos or other minorities work hard to get ahead, they invariably confront roadblocks erected by the government and other so-called protectors of the public.

Unlike most business owners in the district, Rey had connections to the highest levels of city government. Moreover, his operation was not a mom-

and-pop shop but a small empire of businesses that included a favorably reviewed restaurant, an economic development corporation, a real estate business, and a beer distributorship. The week before we met, Rey was finalizing plans with Congreso de Latinos Unidos, the Latino service organization, to build a $16.5 million charter school in a plaza that Rey owns.

Isla Verde has been "a grand slam" for the community, in Rey's view. Before he built Plaza Americana, the corner of Lehigh and American "was like the Badlands," Rey says. "It was a dead end up here. Crack heads, prostitutes, drugs, drug dealing. Dark. You know, dirty."[3] "The Badlands" is not a popular term with community leaders, but there is broad recognition of what the term represents. With legitimate commercial activity came more positive media attention to the barrio.

Rey's success is notable given his origins. In 1981, he obtained about $18,000 from his grandfather, mother, and uncle to buy a beer distributorship on the 2700 block of North Fifth Street. The rest of the money for the license came from the previous owner, whom Rey paid back within about six months of starting his business. Rey recalls how working longer hours and extending short-term credit to shady club owners gave him a competitive edge in the market.

Beer distributors were only open to five o'clock, but I stayed open on Fridays and Saturdays till twelve midnight. I was doing more business from six o'clock till midnight [with] the Joey Montanas and Scar Faces of the world, who had clubs and bars [and who] would call me and say, "Hey, Pastrana, I'm going to send over a buddy of mine. You know, forty cases of Corona, forty cases of Heineken, I'll pay you later, OK?" And I'd say, "Please, OK, I need the money." And they used to come in and take care of me. I was a kid. I was twenty, twenty-one years old.[4]

At the same time, white flight was under way in Philadelphia, and Rey purchased properties for ten or fifteen thousand that would later be worth at least ten times that amount.

While white flight created some new opportunities in the barrio, redlining continued to pose barriers for business owners seeking loans. It was hard to get financing, and for projects such as the Plaza Americana, it was challenging to find the right tenants. Rey had always thought that the plaza would be an ideal place for a bank to locate, given the size and the needs of the population, but most banks saw the area as a struggling "immigrant" community. Outsiders saw the community as being "Puerto Rican, Latino, ghetto," Rey explains, as if an ethnic identity for the community made it synonymous with "ghetto." Then came a breakthrough.

We contacted Jefferson Bank, and they came up here. The president met with me, and he stood on the mound of dirt, ... and he said [in a voice like the comedian George Burns], "Hey, kid, hey, kid. You want to build this here? I admire you, kid. You get this done, I want this corner right here."...

And me, being ballsy like I am, I said, "Well, you can't get it because Dunkin' Donuts has this spot." Bullshit, because Dunkin' Donuts had nothing. I just wanted to feel this guy out.... And it worked, man, because at that time in 1995, ... when everybody else was getting six, seven, eight dollars a square foot, I got thirty dollars per square foot. And guess what, he didn't even blink. That branch is one of the busiest branches. Jefferson got bought out by Hudson Bank; then they got bought out by TD Bank; now they may merge with Commerce Bank. It's still a very, very busy branch.[5]

Rey points to his own success as proof that one can give back to the community without turning one's profitable enterprise into a welfare hotel. He also contributes to the community by regularly hosting fund-raisers for Taller and other causes, but he does it in ways that do not endanger his business's profitability. He recognizes that he is able to contribute to the Latino community through his commercial success and therefore does not make hiring or other decisions based solely on the fact that some people have fallen on hard times.

One of his big complaints is that some Latino organizations that started in the barrio have moved to Center City, where they pay high rents and where their expenditures do not flow back into the barrio. He asks, "Why should the largest Latino newspaper, Al Día, pay rent on JFK Boulevard in Center City? What good is the Hispanic Chamber of Commerce outside of the barrio? The business owners who need the services of the chamber most may be first generation with limited English-speaking abilities and probably feel intimated by the magnificent foyer of the Bellevue [where the Chamber is now housed]."[6] These people at the Hispanic Chamber, Rey rails, are behaving like wannabes. To earn real respect from outsiders, he says, one has to be true to one's community and one's self: no apologies, just see what's possible and seize it.

Rey's speedy ascent to commercial stardom may have been his undoing.[7] When Rey was convicted, the enclave in north Philadelphia had only begun to experience its rebirth, and much of it hinged on the new wave of businesses, such as Isla Verde and the Peter Watts Fitness Studio, that would fit comfortably in the heart of a Center City neighborhood. Rey and other business leaders realized the importance of shaping how outsiders viewed the business district by strategically placing higher-end, middle-class amenities within it. These business leaders also realized the importance of how they viewed their own enclave and how they acted upon those visions. These visions and the actions they inspired animate this chapter.

WHEN AND HOW THEY ENTER THE BARRIO

As I interview other business owners in the Centro de Oro, I notice how they respond differently to my questions about why they decided to locate their business there and whether they thought that arts and culture were effective means for revitalizing the district. Some business owners express optimism about the future and see arts and culture as engines of economic revitalization. "The Golden Block will shine again," says one, using the former name of the district. The presence of arts and culture signals the investment of local artists and businesses in improving the business district; it also invites the interest of cosmopolitans with an affinity for the ethnic arts. Such signals fuel expectations among the business owners about what should and should not happen along the Golden Block. Drug dealers conspicuously working the street corner and bits of trash rolling along the sidewalk like dandelion puffs are not acceptable in a district that calls itself golden. These business owners believe that as people within the business district awaken to its possibilities, remembering what it had been and dreaming of what it could be again, their day-to-day business opportunities would improve.

Other business owners are less sanguine. Rather than gold, "silver or copper" might offer more accurate descriptions of the district, they suggest dryly. Although they share a belief in arts and culture as drivers of local economic development, they fear that the district would do too little too late. They have grown weary of broken promises, and they expect little help from outsiders such as the mayor, foundations, or banks. They are waiting to see demonstrable improvements in their own economic livelihoods before placing their trust in the economic miracles that arts and culture have reportedly wrought in other business districts. Right now, their cash registers do not ring as a result of these arts and culture initiatives. These merchants have less faith in the district's possibilities and are less willing to participate in community improvement efforts.

Whether business owners see their district as golden or tarnished correlates with the timing of their entry into the neighborhood (a cohort effect), how favorably they view the district's art events and cultural initiatives, and to what extent they participate in these group initiatives. Old-timers (those with thirty years or more in the corridor) mostly recall the halcyon days of the Golden Block and talk about how the gold will shine again. Newcomers who first encountered the corridor during its golden years are more hopeful than those who did not. Both talk about how the gold is tarnished and lament the lack of street cleaning, but the hopeful ones believe, like the old-timers, that better days are ahead.[8]

THE PIONEERS AND OTHER OLD-TIMERS

What people remember about the barrio and how they assess its future depend on how long they have been there. There are the pioneers, some of whom we met in the first and second chapters of this book, who were the first to arrive along North Fifth Street when many (but not all) of the white business owners of Eastern European descent and their Jewish colleagues began to leave the neighborhood for "safer" environs. White flight opened up "brown" opportunities as Latinos purchased properties at rock-bottom prices and set up lucrative businesses. Aside from the pioneers are those longtime residents who came after the district was established in the late 1970s and early 1980s. They too saw the district in its heyday and can envision a return to fiscal health and social prosperity. As we meet four of these entrepreneurs, we will come to know their business histories and their reasons for participating (or not) in neighborhood revitalization efforts.

The Spirit Woman

When Maria Acevedo came to Philadelphia in 1963, she was fleeing an unscrupulous business environment in New York City. Born in Puerto Rico to small farmers, she was attracted to *Santerismo*.[9] In her younger years, she migrated to New York City and opened her first spiritual arts shop, but after being in business for less than a month, she found herself surrounded by copycats. Philadelphia had no *botánica*, and the North Fifth Street corridor had some vacant properties at the right price, so she decided to pack up and move. She set up shop in a Fifth Street building that had formerly housed a sewing facility for men's dress shirts. The place needed work, so she did the physical labor necessary to prepare the *botánica* for business. "The house had no floor," she tells me. "She put everything in," her grandson adds. "It was all cardboard." Maria takes pride in her initiative, determination, and grit. Even now, forty-five years later, she still climbs a small ladder to pull products off the tall shelves for her clients. "She works six days a week, from seven in the morning till five o'clock in the afternoon, and she's eighty-eight," her grandson notes.[10]

Maria's grandson responds to my question about the function of the *botánica* in the community by emphasizing how much his grandmother's wares help people in different ways. He leads me to a wall of red, green, blue, yellow, and purple candles bearing images of saints on the front and instructions on the back. Each candle is lit during prayers for a specific purpose or outcome, such as winning a court case, being cured of a disease, blessing a house, or invoking the protection of a guardian angel.[11] During our interview I see that the shop does a good business selling candles. The proprietors remember what their regular customers have purchased in the past and inquire about how it worked for them. Everyone buying candles is purchasing more than one, apparently replenishing their stock. When business slows and we resume our conversation, the grandson emphasizes that the intent is to help people in a unique way that is fully compatible with Christianity. The image of Jesus Christ appears on the candles they sell, and both the grandson and his grandmother say that Christ is at the center of all they do.

The shop has been in the barrio for a long time, and the proprietors see no reason to move. Their clients and suppliers know exactly where to find them. Maria and her grandson know their neighboring business owners, some of whom Maria has seen grow up to take over the family business. Most important, they survived the hard times of the mid-nineties, when some business owners decided to move or close. Now, as they see improvements being made in the neighborhood, they watch with the satisfaction born of perseverance.

The efforts to clean up the neighborhood began in 2003, when streets were cleaned, garbage cans were placed on the sidewalks, and storefronts were painted. (These improvements coincided with the commencement of the Art Night in the Barrio series.) The Acevedos appreciate these improvements, but they do not participate in such efforts. When I ask Maria what kind of support she received from others when setting up her business, she tells me that she did not get any help (nor did she seek any) from people "out there."[12]

The Artist Entrepreneur

Domingo Negrón, a silkscreen printer, decided at the outset of his career to become involved in promoting social, cultural, and economic development through his work. After serving in Vietnam, Domingo attended art school, where he studied graphic and advertising arts. He wanted to establish his own business, so he purchased a building on North Fifth Street. It was then that he stepped back to assess the purpose of his life and his work. He felt that it was time to do something that would satisfy both his dreams of owning a business and his desire to give back to the community. One way to accomplish this dual goal was to set up apprenticeships with young people who could gain marketable skills in the graphic arts business while learning about the tradition of Puerto Rican graphic arts. Toward that end, Domingo joined up with college students and other young people, and together they founded Taller Puertorriqueño. "I re-routed my idea of setting up a business into... community development via Taller," he says.[13]

Domingo sees no separation between the worlds of business and culture. Indeed, he believes the latter is made more sustainable and truer to itself through the former. At Taller, the idea was to have the success of the business side pay for the organization's nonprofit activities and thus insulate it from the whims of private foundations or government agencies. The activities on the cultural side would be more attractive to youth in the community, who would recognize how an immersion in culture and an insistence on cultural pride could pay off economically.

From the barrio's inception in the sixties and seventies, Latino artists have occupied a shared sphere with the business district. Artists such as Domingo and Wilfredo Gonzalez, the owner of Centro Musical whom we will meet below, run businesses, business associations, and neighborhood revitalization efforts. Indeed, in 1975 Domingo left Taller to become the inaugural president of the Fifth Street Merchants Association.

Now, when Domingo ponders the challenges he faces in his printmaking business (founded as Graficas 5000, now called Gran Enterprises), one of the first that come to mind is hiring the right people for the job. From his time at Taller onward, Domingo has aimed to train people in different areas so that they would have the experience and versatility needed to be effective in the workforce. People in the barrio are willing to work for him so that they can earn extra cash or acquire skills in graphic arts, advertising, or office management.

I have waves of people that leave here and that come back and I still give them a job. A lot of the people that I work with here have other jobs, but... they're always looking for extra money.... I hired a seventy-five-year-old woman who does sewing for us.... And then I have a high school kid who loves to come in after school and work with the computers, and he's learning and he's doing very well with that.[14]

Domingo sees his business as a purpose-driven entity that provides a haven for people in the barrio no matter their age or level of experience. He is careful not to let his altruism run his business aground, but he also knows that a small sacrifice on his part can make a big difference in the lives of the people he hires, even if he receives no material reward in return. Some of the workers Domingo adopts are later hired by companies outside of the barrio who pay higher wages and offer better benefit packages than Domingo. As he improves their lot, they leave, and while others might see this as a "loss" in view of the time and energy Domingo has invested in these workers, Domingo sees it as the very reason he makes the investment.

There seems to be a cohort effect, Domingo tells me in so many words, in the level of progress the barrio's residents are making. He carefully distinguishes the cohort effect (based on the timing of arrival in the barrio and one's life stage) and the generational effect (one's age) to explain how the fate of barrio residents has changed.

Fortunately, a lot of our kids are going to college and graduating and getting the better jobs, so that's where we are right now. We're in a generational [change], not by years, but by waves.... I consider myself second generation; my parents were first. And that first generation... came to [the] neighborhood and struggle[d].... My kids, you know, are going to college, graduating from college, and who knows whether they'll come back to the neighborhood.... I think that people from that second-, third-generation struggle will probably not come back. Whereas the people that are middle class, they will come back, so it is sort of like reverse. I think it's that whole mystique of who you are, who your subconscious Hispanic thing is, that [makes] you want to experience [the barrio].[15]

He has witnessed an interesting reversal of fortunes, whereby the Latino kids who grew up in the barrio because they could not afford to escape it want to leave it as soon as they can, but the middle-class Latinos who grew up in the suburbs want to experience life in the barrio, and some are relocating to the up-and-coming areas on the barrio's edge, within ten minutes or so of Center City. These people represent different cohorts who have experienced the barrio at different historical periods; they either feel drawn to its mystique or are thoroughly disillusioned with the prospect of progress.

Domingo is under no illusions. He knows that he might be able to make more money were he to concern himself less with hiring people from the neighborhood and teaching them marketable skills. Domingo might also earn more were he to move his business to a different part of town, but that is not what is most important to him.

I wanted to have a clear conscience, that I... don't take advantage of people, that I'm not a thief, that I pay my bills.... I want to create a model that my kids will follow. And I won't be a rich man, but I will be a person that will be remembered.... [T]here are people that consciously have made an effort to take a chance, and it's paid off; it's worked out for them or for the neighborhood or for both. And that's [a] rarity. You don't [often] see that.[16]

The decision to contribute to the community need not mean that economic payoffs have to be sacrificed. For some entrepreneurs and community leaders, it has been possible to benefit financially from working in the barrio while contributing to the barrio's development. These pioneers and old-timers have taken a chance, forgone immediate financial rewards, and contributed to the transformation of the barrio.

The Music Man

Another Vietnam veteran, Wilfredo Gonzalez, decided upon his return stateside to buy Centro Musical from his father, who had established the Latin music store after the family moved from Puerto Rico to Philadelphia. But getting a loan for the purchase price was not easy: banks did not view small enterprises as worthwhile investments, and Wilfredo lacked the collateral to obtain the loan. Wilfredo's brother-in-law stepped in to help by getting a loan on Wilfredo's behalf through the Navy Federal Credit Union, and Wilfredo repaid the loan.

Wilfredo attributes his business success in part to the changing demographics of Philadelphia. As the Latino population has grown, so too has the demand for Latin music. The neighborhood population was mostly working class when Wilfredo arrived, but Latinos have been moving in steadily. He attributes some of the positive changes he's seen to the work of HACE. "Right now, we're trying to rebuild the whole area, and HACE is trying to do the best they [can], and different organizations [are also involved], which I like," Wilfredo says. "I think this area in the future is going to be very productive towards business and the environment.... I think there's going to be big improvements in this area."[17] Working with HACE, Wilfredo has been able to bring artists to his shop to paint a new mural across his storefront and to engage in other improvements.

Like the *botánica*, Centro Musical draws people from miles around. "This store is well known," he says, noting that out-of-towners make a point of stopping in when they are visiting the city. "The Centro Musical slowly has [been] built [as] a part [of] the community, and I'm proud of it."[18] His pride shows in the investments he has made in his storefront and the care he has taken in arranging the interior, almost as if he were curating an exhibition.

Wilfredo has contributed his time and some material resources to the local arts organizations and continues to do so; he has also participated in

Men socializing at Centro Musical. Photo by Tony Rocco.

HACE's efforts to increase parking spaces in the business corridor and to shape the physical image of the barrio's future. Wilfredo's efforts have not gone unnoticed: his likeness can be seen on the mural outside of Raíces at North Fifth and Somerset. Yet for all he has done in and for the community, Wilfredo and others like him are slow to take credit. I became aware of many of their contributions not from them but from other community members and newspaper stories.

The Dry Cleaners

Max Izaguirre came to the United States from Guatemala in 1962, settling first in New York and then, in 1976, moving to Philadelphia. In the barrio he worked at a dry cleaning plant, and when the owner decided to move to Germantown, he offered to sell the plant to Max. "The old owner said to me, 'You do everything in here, anyway, so why don't you just take over the business when I leave?'" Max recalls. Because Max would have had trouble getting a loan at the bank—"in those days, banks were not lending to... small business owners"—and because of the owner's trust in Max, he made arrangements for Max to buy the dry cleaning business from him over time.[19]

Max recognizes that some of his personal struggles are tied to public perceptions about where he works. Outsiders hold an image of the neighborhood and its residents that is collective rather than individual. A drug-infested neighborhood becomes a label equally applied to law-abiding and lawbreaking individuals by virtue of where they live and work. Max recalls just how pernicious this perception has been among members of the Philadelphia police force. "I was personally told by a lieutenant from the Highway Patrol that everybody in North Philly was, *is*, a drug dealer. And that's wrong.... You know, you can't assume that everybody is a drug dealer. Hell, there's good and bad in every neighborhood, in every race, but we changed that [perception] a little bit.... There still is some [stereotyping], but not as bad as it used to be."[20] While recognizing that outsiders stereotype people within the Latino community, Max also compares non-white (ethnic) neighborhoods with "white" neighborhoods as a way of indicating what attributes a good neighborhood should have. "If you go to white neighborhoods, you see the difference. They're just clean. A lot of their buildings are well maintained, and [shop owners] don't park the cars in [front of their shops], because they value the customers."[21] Amplifying the last point, Max notes that local business owners could solve the parking problem simply by agreeing not to use the parking spaces in front of their businesses so that customers can come and park easily. His points of reference are successful shopping areas in the city that he describes as clean, well maintained, orderly, convenient, and white.[22] These categories become inculcated in the minds of the entrepreneurs themselves even as they fight against dominant, overarching depictions of their business district.

Still, Max remains optimistic about the barrio's prospects. He has bought five buildings in the barrio and wishes he had bought more. His daughter owns a flower shop nearby. His son worked in the dry cleaning business for a while, then decided to open a bar. His other kids are active one way or another in business, he says with satisfaction. He and his wife have been involved for a long time in the neighborhood business association, and he showed me some architectural sketches of what the association plans to do with the sidewalks, the official gateway entrance to the barrio, and some of the storefront designs. It will take some time, he says, but he can envision a successful future.

THE OFFSPRING

Just as the historical experience of the pioneers and the old-timers affects their vision of the future and their tolerance for setbacks, the experiences their children and grandchildren have as the progeny of business owners in the barrio affect their attachment to place and their willingness to contribute to improving the business district. The offspring are at a different stage of their lives, and they feel the need to prove themselves. Their forebears were successful, and they feel the need to establish their own worth independently. This leads them to strike a balance between being concerned for the collective efforts to improve the business district and being engaged in their individual business's efforts to survive in a competitive economic environment. One of the first things they tell me is the fact that they have taken over the business from their parents, who like to spin tales about what life was like "in the beginning" when they (or their own parents) arrived in the district and started the business from scratch. These heroic tales buoy the offspring through hard times and offer them tangible evidence that the economic condition of the barrio can change for the better.

The Third Pedro

"I'm Pete. We're all Pete—me, my father, my grandfather...—and we're all entrepreneurs."[23] The Varona Beer Distributorship has been in the barrio for about thirty-three years, but it was not the first business that members of the Varona family had started. Pete's grandfather came to the United States from Cuba and established one of the first Latino stores in the neighborhood, Pete tells me. By the time Pete's father was ready to strike out on his own, Pete's grandfather was running a supermarket and acting as landlord for several commercial properties in the area. When Pete's father decided to become a beer distributor, Pete's grandparents gave him the money he needed to open his own business; now, at the age of twenty-two, Pete himself is running the business. The history of his grandfather's migration and his own experience growing up in the barrio inform Pete's understanding of what the neighborhood is and what it could be.

Both Pete's father and grandfather are full of stories, especially when Pete complains or suggests changes in the way the business is conducted. Mimicking his grandfather, Pete says, "'I came from Cuba and everything, and I didn't have nothing,' you know the whole song." The grandfather likes to tell Pete about the first building he bought in the barrio, at 2960 North Fifth Street, where the beer distributorship got its start. "'2960—I was *there*, [with] no water, and at that time [*voice goes up*], I paid five grand, you know,'" Pete recalls.[24] As his grandfather and father remind him of their sacrifices, they tie those hardships and triumphs to a particular place, a particular street address.

Pete's grandfather also reminds Pete of the injustices suffered in the old country, under Fidel Castro. After fleeing from Cuba, Pete's grandfather moved to Orange, New Jersey, just outside of Philadelphia, and then to Philadelphia. Pete tells me that his grandfather owned a farm in Cuba before it was wrested away by Castro (who is always referred to as "Fidel"):

You see, this is how Fidel was. He took all his stuff. I think [Fidel] left him maybe one butcher shop, I don't know. I don't even think he left him with a butcher shop because you can't eat meat. You can go to jail for eating meat over there. You get, like, a crazy amount of time in jail. If you get caught, you could get like five, up to ten, years for killing a cow, because you're starving.[25]

Pete flips to a blank page of the notepad he uses to keep track of the different types of beers sold that day. He draws a circle and splits it in half. "They don't just take half," he explains, and divides the circle again into fourths.[26] The intensity of his grandfather's experience cannot be told in words alone; it also evokes an image.

Lest his grandfather be confused for the "wrong" kind of Cuban, Pete emphasizes that his grandfather fled the island *before* the Mariel boatlift:

Pete: He came before, way before. Remember when Cuba sent over all those people in the eighties?

Author: The Marielitos?

Pete: Yeah, they sent all the delinquents over here. All the riff-raff, all the trash from Cuba, they sent them over here.

Author: I remember reading about that.

Pete: There's a lot of them around here still. They weren't all bad, but you know, more than half of them were killers and all that shit, but yeah, my grandfather came way before that.[27]

After I said it, I regretted my use of the word *marielitos*, considered by some a derogatory term for the 1980 exodus from Cuba, during which the mentally challenged and the criminally indicted were sent to the United States as a "gift" from Castro. The Mariel boatlift changed the positive opinion that many Americans had of Cuban refugees and ended the significant economic benefits reaped by ethnic entrepreneurs doing business in Miami's Little Havana.[28]

When I ask Pete whether he participates in any of the efforts to revitalize the district, he sighs and tells me about the other businesses that he has to run and the time constraints that he faces.[29] He remembers the painful consequences of leaving the business once, closing it briefly to take care of personal matters. One of his regular clients, a bar owner, had run low on beer and urgently needed a replenishment. Because Pete had closed shop briefly, his client went to another beer distributor, who beat Pete's prices and made the client question whether Pete and his family were charging too much.

Even with these challenges, Pete asserts, "I always wanted to do this. This is my dream. I'm living my dream.... I wouldn't change my job for the world. You can come in here sometime, and we be joking all day. All day joking. You know, I got a good crew here." He summons a fellow wearing a baseball cap who had been operating the cash register and moving cartons while Pete and I stood talking over stacks of beer cases in the middle of the store. "Yo, Shorty!" Pete calls out. Earlier I had assumed that "Shorty" was one of his regular employees, but Pete tells me during this impromptu introduction that Shorty just "comes by to help" from time to time and to keep him company. "He likes to come help out because when he hit some hard times, we were there for him. We're a family here."[30]

The Friendly Pharmacist

Another member of Pete's cohort is Chadd Levine, the twenty-six-year-old owner of the Fifth Street Pharmacy. His father and two partners started the business in 1976, attracted to the area by its low overhead and good profit margin. The group of three opened this pharmacy along with five others across the city. About two decades later, when the barrio was suffering from record violence and a flourishing illegal drug trade, Chadd's father bought out his other business partners and became the sole proprietor. An economic decision to establish the pharmacy in the barrio soon led to a more complex, socially entangled enterprise.

As a community pharmacist, Chadd (like his father before him) has built strong relationships with local customers. Chadd knows them by name and knows what medications they are taking, who their doctors are, and in some cases what they did last week or last night, what they cooked for dinner, and how their kids are doing. "If you go to a Rite-Aid or a large chain," he says, "you won't get that."[31] His social ties with clients and the size of his pharmacy distinguish it from a franchise. While both aim to generate economic profits, the community pharmacy does so by catering to the local population.

Two years before I interviewed Chadd, other business owners had told me who the longtime entrepreneurs were. Chadd's father was certainly among them, but with his retirement, business had declined. Chadd confirms the reports I had heard. The community members were looking not just for a good pharmacy but for a social connection with the pharmacist.

They knew "the old man," but they did not know the pharmacist who was hired on a temporary basis while Chadd finished his studies. After obtaining his degree in pharmacy at Temple University, Chadd was ready to rebuild those connections, and his efforts bore fruit.

Chadd expresses a sense of obligation and commitment to the well-being of the barrio. "It's very important for me, having grown up here, to give something back to them, because I feel indebted to them.... My father was very successful, down here specifically, because of the way these people responded to him. And I am very grateful for that," he says.[32] Chadd has joined the committee coordinated by HACE to add parking spots for clients and shoppers during business hours, and he has floated ideas with other business owners to designate a day when they all stand in front of their businesses and hand out flavored ice to local kids. He is eager to "give back" to the community that has been welcoming to him and his father before him.

Chadd believes he may have a special role to play in helping to advance the goals of the enclave. The district does not receive as much recognition as it should for being the center of Latino life in Philadelphia, he says. The average person on the street—the average person in a business suit in Center City, that is—wouldn't be able to tell you where the Latino district is, wouldn't even know the cross streets. Chadd suspects that this lack of recognition may have something to do with the messenger. "Maybe it takes someone of a different race... [coming from] me, being a Caucasian male, it might be more widely received. And let's be honest, there's bias, there's racism no matter what you do, and you can't beat the fact of that, but if you have someone like me speaking as an advocate for an area like this, that may have a greater influence, you know?" He and some of the other business owners have even discussed submitting an advertisement to the *Philadelphia Inquirer* that features the Centro de Oro and emphasizes its unique character. He feels that something needs to be done to overcome some of the biases that Latino people face in Philadelphia. As a Jewish guy, he says, he has had some experience with dealing with bias, but the racist notions that some people have about Latinos blinds them to the human kindness, cultural richness, and the potential economic opportunities in the district.[33]

As a second-generation business owner in the district, he has fond memories of the way things were when he was growing up, and he wants to see the district return to the way he remembers it. "These streets were flooded [with business]. I mean there used to be an enormous, enormous club over here [next door].... This really is what I equate to the center for Latino culture. This is the Center City, the mecca, for the Latino people. And that's a cool thing."[34]

The Disappointed Son

To protect his privacy we'll call him "Dee," for "disappointed." He's at least ten years older than Pete and Chadd, but he's the son of one of the pioneers. He works for his father and also runs his own business projects in other parts of town. He has seen his father's business decline in the nineties and then improve in the years since, but it has yet to return to the same level before the downturn. Dee believes that efforts to promote the arts and to revitalize the community need to answer some key questions: How do these efforts improve the entrepreneur's bottom line? Are these art shows "ringing the registers"? Will the attempt to make the storefronts and the sidewalks look "Latin American" attract clients to the district who are coming to spend money rather than casual tourists who make a ceremonial purchase out of a sense of obligation?

Dee anchors his understanding of what is possible in the Latino district, and what opportunities have been missed, by comparing its history and its challenges with those of other districts he has worked in. Dee knows, for example, that entrepreneurs in those other districts have much less difficulty acquiring financial capital. The businesses in the Latino district are expected to satisfy a much higher standard of collateral for obtaining loans, and although redlining may not be an official policy, the same outcome is achieved informally. When a small-business owner from the barrio seeks a loan, Dee says, the banker's reaction goes something like this: "Well, we need your tax register for five years, *blah, blah, blah, blah, blah.* We need you to fill out this application that's ten pages long, and then we need you to, you know, put your blood on this pencil. You can sign the page." Faced with all these obstacles, entrepreneurs "throw up their hands and say, 'Well, I'll just shut my shop and go find a job.'"[35]

But bankers are not the only ones at fault. Dee also lays the blame for the district's slow progress at the feet of the local business owners and community leaders. If other neighborhoods have progressed after grappling with difficulties in the late eighties and early nineties, he says, the Latino district should be able to experience a similar trajectory. His disappointment underscores his belief that although the Latino commercial district has much potential, some of the biggest obstacles to progress are "his own people" within the district.

Dee volunteers for various efforts to improve parking and to attract investment into the community, but he seems to do so out of a sense of duty. He worries that the use of arts and culture to attract business and investments might fail because of the material constraints on the arts sector in the barrio. How can the Latino district compete with other areas of the city offering numerous art galleries, coffee shops, and restaurants with out-door seating? Blunt in his pessimism, Dee declares, "If I was a tourist and I went to the JFK Plaza and got my ticket [for a neighborhood tour], and got on the little trolley to come up here, I'd be like, 'What the heck is this? It's terrible. It's a mess.'"[36] Making the situation worse is the community leaders' insistence on imposing licensing and permit requirements on all businesses regardless of size, which adds to the cost of doing business, Dee says. For small establishments to flourish, they need to be left alone or be given access to capital, he believes.

Among the second-generation entrepreneurs I interviewed, Dee is exceptional in his pessimism. Like Pete and Chadd, Dee remembers the "good old days," but unlike them he focuses on how much business he has lost and how little the corridor's leaders have done compared with those in other parts of the city. Dee does not work primarily in the Latino business district, whereas the other two do. With their spatial "isolation" from other parts of the city and their intense interactions in the enclave, Pete and Chadd experience moments of "rediscovery"—spontaneous reminders of the enclave's rich history and its future potential. Ironically, the more interactions that Dee has with other business districts, the less satisfied he is with his own. Engaged in constant comparisons, Dee does not develop a standard of how "success" might look here independent from the way it looks elsewhere. As an exception, Dee helps prove the rule: different cohorts have different perspectives on the current and future status of the business district, depending on when they first encountered the district and the conditions of both their encounter and their continued exposure.

THE NEWCOMERS

Newcomers to the district come for a variety of reasons and have varying expectations of what working there will be like. For those attracted to the barrio for its reputation as the center of Latino life in Philadelphia, the difference between hope and reality is jarring. What they encounter is not exactly what they expected to find, and signs of progress do not come fast enough. Some of the new entrepreneurs I interviewed first encountered the barrio as children visiting relatives or on a shopping trip. They witnessed the barrio in its heyday and saw themselves partaking in its revival. Others came to the barrio without such expectations and accept the district for what it is—a place experiencing a revival whose nonmaterial attributes (cultural symbols, food, friendliness) compensate for those things it still lacks (better parking, higher foot traffic, greater recognition among consumers across the city of Philadelphia).

A street vendor selling fruit in the barrio. Photo by Tony Rocco.

The Woodcarving Musician

I first met Robert Smith-Shabazz on the busy sidewalk outside Taller during its annual Arts and Crafts Fair (his work appears in a photo in chapter 1). Robert was sitting with a conga drum, a tenor saxophone, and a small table that displayed his woodcarvings. That day, Bill Salas also stopped by to ask Robert about his business. At the time, Robert was working out of his home on Diamond Street, where he had little exposure to foot traffic. Bill invited Robert to think about moving up to North Fifth Street in one of the vacant buildings between Taller and Raíces. Robert said he lacked the capital for starting up a business in a commercial space, but Bill assured him that HACE was committed to bringing in the "right kinds of businesses" (not a check-cashing business, not a pawnshop) to the district, and here in this block of North Fifth, any business engaged in the arts would be welcome.

Bill and Robert struck a deal. Robert agreed to put "sweat equity" into his new business. Similar to a Habitat for Humanity home in which the new resident contributes labor to building the house, some Centro de Oro businesses get their start by having the new business owners work on the interior and exterior of the building to prepare it for occupancy. The entrepreneur's labor serves as equity—an investment in the business that defrays start-up costs. Bill also leases some of the HACE-owned properties in the Centro de Oro district on a sliding scale, understanding that new businesses earn less in their initial years and are therefore less able to pay higher leasing rates before becoming established.

One of the ways that Robert provides sweat equity for his business is through his contributions to the business district as a whole. At the time of our interview, he is participating in HACE's clean streets initiative by sweeping up trash from the sidewalk, and he's wearing a cap and polo shirt sporting the Golden Block motif: a radiant sun with a plea to keep the Centro de Oro clean. Part of his motivation is altruistic. "It's almost like... the Christian service of foot washing, to be humble to do a job that most people don't want to do," he says as he works. But Robert also realizes how important clean streets are for the district's reputation. "How can we call ourselves the Golden Block if we have trash on our streets? So that's why I'm out here. We are out here to show people and to show other business owners that keeping the sidewalks and the streets clean is important."[37] The initiative sends two important messages. The first, directed toward existing business owners and local residents, is inspired by the history of the district and the evolution of its name. If the area was formerly known as the Golden Block (El Bloque de Oro) and is now hopefully called the Golden District (Centro de Oro), the area's residents must act in a way that supports the label. The second message, directed toward outsiders such as visiting consumers, city officials, private investors, and foundations, is that the landscape and storefronts say something about the kind of people who live and work here and about their culture.

The Trash Obsessed

When the district's name does not match up with its day-to-day realities, a sense of righteous indignation results. Another newcomer I interviewed, who prefers to remain unnamed, recalls coming to the district as a child to visit her relatives. The neighborhood was a lively place, she says, with busy shops during the daytime and a thriving nightlife. "It really *was* the Golden Block back then."[38] This memory attracted her to the district, but when she arrived, it was not what she thought it would be. She is frustrated because she thinks that not enough has been done to highlight the unique cultural elements of the district. She also believes that there should be more parking, more frequent trash collection, and a more visible police presence. She keeps hearing about how the streetscape is going to be improved, but she hasn't seen it happen yet. "Too much talk, [and] not enough action," she says. Pointing to a pole outside her shop window, she suggests that it be painted brilliantly. The street should have the feel of a carnival, full of folk art, she says. In the meantime, she does not consider this the Golden Block. "Because now, in the Golden Block, . . . you can see trash and garbage. . . . This is the Trash Block now."[39] Her negative view of the barrio that day might be exacerbated by the appearance of loose paper and soda cans blowing about the sidewalk. But as she talks about what is wrong with the barrio, it is clear that the standard she compares it to is an ideal, a paradise lost. Perhaps her dismay reflects, in part, an unconsummated desire for a paradise regained.

THE ARTS AND COMMERCIAL LIFE

Some of the business owners I interviewed see the culture of the district as the reason they decided to establish a business there and as a strong attraction for outsiders. But no consensus exists on the extent to which art events affect the profit margins of local businesses. Because there is no anchoring arts or performance space to draw large groups of consumers into the district on a regular basis, it is hard to see the distinct role that the arts play in increasing a business's profits. This is especially the case when art events occur after business hours or when art audiences do not stay in the community after an event even when shops are still open.

In contrast, when there is a large community festival with live street performances, the power of art to increase foot traffic in the district is apparent and the role that the arts play in keeping commercial districts vibrant seems obvious. Daytime festivals are typically free of violent incidents and demonstrate the community's capacity to be as safe as any other place in the city. It is this capacity that gets woven into the narratives that business owners tell about the Centro de Oro. When the community shines, there are bright colors and national flags waved enthusiastically; there is music, the sounds of drums, string instruments, and booming voices; there is dancing, bodies calling and responding to the congas. There are reminders of the community's capacity to create.

These entrepreneurs' narratives are heterogeneous. They differ by generation and by experience, but as we will see in the coming chapters, these narratives told by entrepreneurs often reflect what it means to be a constructive member of society and what behaviors threaten civil society. Narratives help us justify how we have acted in the past and how we *should* *act* in the future. Narratives that help business owners frame what type of commercial district they are located in and what type of neighborhood it anchors can either hasten positive transformation or hold it back.

5 » Stigma, Status, and Staging

The History of a Reputation

It was, after all, "one of their own" who wrote about the neighborhood's troubles in the papers and who so vividly portrayed them in his novel *Third and Indiana*. Journalist Steve Lopez (perhaps best known for *The Soloist*, starring Jamie Foxx and Robert Downey Jr.) wrote in the 1990s of the barrio's gang-infested streets, where drugs were sold as openly as tomatoes at a farmer's market, bullets popped like firecrackers on the Fourth of July, and big-bellied teenagers too young to mother but old enough to give birth strode the sidewalks.[1] With his Latino last name, Lopez could venture to say what others dared not utter, namely, that a culture of poverty had created an alternative reality in which the lives of young people were expendable and commonly spent. This reality was anchored in the Badlands, a stigmatized place whose pollutions needed to be contained. The indicator of stigma was not poverty but rather the combination of poverty, ethnicity, and violence. Deindustrialization, segregation, and drug epidemics became hallmarks of the barrio, and community development leaders along with marketers had to figure out how to manage the stigma.

In ethnic urban settings with high poverty levels, rebranding efforts are especially vulnerable to mishaps and unforeseen circumstances because the neighborhood is not given the benefit of the doubt by outside audiences. Discredited and easily discreditable places are hailed as lucky success stories when all goes well, but in the event of an unfortunate incident (even if it is a fluke), such places are thought to be reverting to their natural states. By contrast, in a "good" and not easily discredited place, a shooting or the sight of a junkie injecting heroine into his veins is either a fluke or an unusual, but controllable, happenstance.

In *Branding New York*, Miriam Greenberg describes how location consultants emerged in the 1960s as corporations recognized that the location of their production and distribution facilities could augment their profits by virtue of the characteristics consumers attributed to those places.[2] At the same time, city and regional planners began to reshape their locales to highlight their most appealing characteristics. Location consultants became even more important in the 1970s, as New Deal–style policies began yielding to free-market approaches to city development. Image consultants adeptly bundled the city's visible attributes into a coherent image intended to attract consumers who were eager to experience the city scene firsthand.

Each city, and each neighborhood within the city, has a set of reputational attributes that marketers can use in their campaigns. Neighborhoods with murals have a different artistic quality than neighborhoods with graffiti. Artists in both places have staked claims to outdoor walls; however, in the first case, the public authorities praise the artists for contributing to society; in the second case, the authorities and the property owners they protect deride the graffiti artists as damaging private property and dampening the community's civic spirit. Even two neighborhoods with the same number of public amenities may qualitatively differ in the ethnic character of their inhabitants, the types of festivals publicly celebrated in their streets, and the manner in which people within the neighborhoods are seen by image analysts.

Ultimately, public opinion about the inhabitants of a place will determine what messages about that place resonate with mainstream audiences. Public opinion itself depends on the history of settlement of a particular group within the city and on the differential impact that large-scale economic changes have wrought on different parts of the city. Public opinion is also informed by major events and social epidemics that sweep across and become symbolically anchored in a particular locale.

PUBLIC OPINION

Our review of public opinion begins at the national level, both to understand the general public's attitude toward Puerto Ricans and other Latinos and to learn how an urban ethnic community is branded to appeal to the broader public. According to a survey conducted by the National Opinion Research Center in 2000, most Americans do not think that Puerto Ricans have made significant contributions to the country (table 2). Only 21 percent of those polled stated that Puerto Ricans have made important contributions—nearly tied with Vietnamese and Muslims. In contrast, 53 percent stated that Italians had made important contributions, and about 52 percent said the same about Blacks. The leading group who are thought to have

TABLE 2. Attitudes toward Peoples of Different Races, Nationalities, and Religions Who Have Settled in the United States, 2000

	Make Important Contributions to the Country (%)	Make Some Contributions to the Country (%)	Make Few Contributions to the Country (%)
English	76.5	20.6	2.9
Jews	58.6	35.5	5.9
Italians	52.8	41.3	5.9
Irish	52.7	39.4	8.0
Blacks	51.5	37.3	11.2
Japanese	44.8	40.0	15.1
Chinese	42.8	43.9	13.4
Mexicans	31.1	46.8	22.1
Puerto Ricans	21.2	48.4	30.4
Vietnamese	21.0	44.7	34.4
Muslims	20.8	42.9	36.2
Cubans	18.7	41.9	39.3

Source: Survey by National Opinion Research Center, February 1–June 25, 2000. Retrieved April 17, 2008, from the iPOLL Databank, The Roper Center for Public Opinion Research, University of Connecticut, http://www.ropercenter.uconn.edu/data_access/ipoll/ipoll .html.

made important contributions to the country are the English (about 77 percent) followed by the Jews (59 percent). As we shall see when we probe the local public opinion polls, many Philadelphians saw the Puerto Ricans as a minority group clamoring for welfare handouts and engaging in antisocial behaviors, a perception that would help explain why some Philadelphians did not want to have them as neighbors.

In the past, negative attitudes toward Puerto Ricans manifested themselves in physical violence, particularly against those who tried to move outside of their ethnic enclave. In the mid-1950s, at least half of the Puerto Rican population lived in one of three areas, each ranging from five to nine square blocks, in lower north, central, and south Philadelphia.[3] One night in 1954, a group of white men forced their way into the home of a Puerto Rican family who had moved to a neighborhood at Seventeenth and Vernon streets, outside the established enclaves. The men carried weapons and ejected the family from their home. In the wake of the attack, the newly formed Commission on Human Relations of Philadelphia enlisted the help of research analysts to determine "to what extent... Puerto Ricans [were] accepted by their neighbors."[4]

The analysts examined three levels of interaction between Puerto Ricans and other Philadelphians: marriage, social clubs, and the workplace

TABLE 3. Social Interaction between Puerto Ricans and Non–Puerto Ricans

		Non–Puerto Rican Americans (n = 102)	Puerto Ricans (n = 205–209)
Do you think that (Continental)* Americans willingly admit Puerto Ricans to close kinship by marriage?	Yes	24.5%	26.1%
	No	44.1	42.5
	Don't know	28.4	30.4
	No response	2.9	1.0
Do you think that (Continental) Americans willingly admit Puerto Ricans to their clubs as personal friends?	Yes	21.6	25.7
	No	52.0	47.6
	Don't know	23.5	26.7
	No response	2.9	—
Do you think that (Continental) Americans willingly admit Puerto Ricans to their streets as neighbors?	Yes	20.6	46.9
	No	57.8	37.7
	Don't know	20.6	15.0
	No response	1.0	0.5
Do you think that (Continental) Americans willingly admit Puerto Ricans to employment in their occupations?	Yes	41.2	80.0
	No	33.3	11.2
	Don't know	23.5	8.3
	No response	2.0	0.5
Do you think that (Continental) Americans would like to exclude Puerto Ricans from this country?	Yes	41.2	44.0
	No	25.5	31.1
	Don't know or no response	33.3	24.9

Source: Strobach, "The Attitudes of Philadelphians towards Their Puerto Rican Neighbors," p. 62.

* "Continental" is included only for Puerto Rican respondents.

(table 3). When speaking to non–Puerto Rican Americans, questioners asked whether they thought Americans felt comfortable having their close kin marry a Puerto Rican. About one-quarter of the respondents said yes, but a greater percentage said they didn't know. A similar proportion held for Puerto Ricans when asked about "Continental Americans" (non–Puerto Rican Americans). Where the two groups differed most markedly was in their assessment of how open Americans are to having Puerto Ricans as neighbors. Only about 21 percent of non–Puerto Ricans said Puerto Ricans would be welcome, compared to 47 percent of Puerto Ricans. More than 40 percent of both Puerto Ricans and non–Puerto Ricans polled in Philadelphia felt that Americans would like to exclude Puerto Ricans from the country.

The reasons for exclusion lay in the impressions non–Puerto Ricans have of their Puerto Rican neighbors. The non–Puerto Ricans polled in Philadel-

TABLE 4. Perceived and Reported Forms of Recreation by Puerto Ricans

	Reported by Neighbors (n = 58 people; 81 activities)	Reported by Puerto Ricans (n = 109 people; 703 activities)*
Listening to the radio, watching television, listening and playing music	28.4	45.5
Going to movies	2.5	18.5
Sports (watching or playing)	0.0	10.4
Dancing	4.9	11.9
Informal get-together	4.9	8.5
Drinking	13.6	0.0
"Lounging"	38.5	0.0

Source: Commission on Human Relations, *Puerto Ricans in Philadelphia*, table 7-1, p. 56.

*The number of people is not specified in the report's table for Puerto Ricans, but the number of activities they listed is specified. This table assumes that all Puerto Rican respondents answered the question.

phia believed that Puerto Ricans differed from them in terms of language, cuisine, clannishness, noisiness, dress, and cleanliness (of person and/or home).[5] Three of these differences—language, food, and dress—could show up for any non-English-speaking ethnic group. The other three, however, refer to behavioral characteristics regarded as undesirable. To be clannish is to ignore the general good of civil society for the sake of the family unit; to be noisy is to disregard the personal space of others; to be unclean is to pollute oneself, one's household, and one's neighborhood.

The ethnic attributes of a Puerto Rican neighborhood are made manifest through public consumption and recreation. But as table 4 demonstrates, the level of participation in leisure activities is viewed quite differently by Puerto Ricans and their non–Puerto Rican neighbors. No Puerto Rican respondents identified "lounging" or drinking as one of their leisure activities, yet about 39 percent of non–Puerto Ricans stated that their Puerto Rican neighbors enjoy lounging and about 14 percent said the same about drinking. Similarly, 12 percent of Puerto Ricans identified dancing as one of their leisure activities, while only 5 percent of non–Puerto Ricans identified it as a Puerto Rican activity. Puerto Ricans saw themselves as moviegoers, but non–Puerto Ricans largely did not. As far as Puerto Ricans were concerned, their favorite pastime was gathering informally in each others' apartments, listening to the radio, watching television, and listening to music, but their non–Puerto Rican neighbors saw them as loitering outside bars and drinking. Meanwhile, a small group of white people polled in the Mount Vernon area believed that misbehavior by neighboring Puerto Ricans had eroded their community's positive qualities. Out of fifty-eight respondents in the Mount Vernon area, 13 percent believed that the neighborhood had gotten dirtier, 17 percent believed that there were more street fights in the neighborhood, 16 percent believed that families were leaving the neighborhood, and 11 percent believed that the neighborhood seemed to be more crowded.⁶ It is ironic that a small group of white people felt that their neighborhood was becoming more crowded although families were moving away; this highlights the mismatch between neighborhood conditions and people's perceptions of them.

A VIOLENT RECEPTION

In 1960, the Commission on Human Relations of Philadelphia conducted a series of hearings that revealed the unwelcome environment that Latinos and Blacks encountered in the city's housing market. In some working-class neighborhoods such as Fishtown (which now abuts the Centro de Oro and has a growing Latino population), being mistaken for a Puerto Rican or a Black was enough to prompt a mob gathering outside one's home, as one Portuguese family discovered. At a hearing on December 19 of that year, George Schermer, the executive director of the Commission on Human Relations, called on Dennis Clark, the supervisor of the Housing Division of the Commission, to describe the incident:

Captain Powell of the 26th Police district called our office to report that on June 6, crowds had gathered at the intersection of Belgrade and Earl Streets. This is where the Fernandez family had rented a second floor apartment over a grocery store. The grocery store window had been broken. Eggs had been thrown, and a very vocal and unruly crowd had gathered, expressing resentment at the fact that the Fernandez family had moved into the area. They believed that the Fernandez were either Negroes or Puerto Ricans. The Fernandez family is of Portuguese background.... On June 7 and on June 8, crowds also assembled. By June 8, the Fernandez family was sufficiently intimidated that they decided to move out. On the evening of June 8, I witnessed the crowd demonstrations as the family moved out. The atmosphere was quite tense, and luckily the family was able to move very rapidly, or the crowd situation could have gotten out of hand.

One very sad feature of this case is the fact that the owners of the apartment and the manager of the grocery store, both Mr. and Mrs. George Dub, were people who had come to this country after having had very tragic experiences in Europe. They were in concentration camps in Germany during the war, and as the result of having rented to the Fernandez family, Mr. and Mrs. Dub were compelled to close their business at this address and to relocate at another address in North Philadelphia.[7]

During the incident police arrested several people, including Mrs. Dub, who had brandished a firearm to scare off her attackers. It became apparent during the hearing that Puerto Ricans and other people of color faced hostility from working-class whites, who denied them access to homes in white neighborhoods and who threatened to punish any white family that attempted to help persons of color.[8]

Later in the summer, when the Figueroa and Torres families, both Puerto Rican, attempted to move into the same block, they encountered a similarly hostile crowd, milling around and readying for battle, outside the mysteriously padlocked premises. "Eggs were thrown, and the Puerto Rican family was threatened, and they were unable to unload their furniture and were prevented from occupying the property," Clark testified.[9] Two months later, a Native American family, of the Cherokee Nation, attempted to move into the Kensington neighborhood on Memphis Street. A local resident visited them and asked what race they were. They stated that they were American Indians, but he thought that they were lying and left the premises to stir up mischief. He began by stopping passersby and pointing back to their apartment, but the real trouble started after he succeeded in flagging down a car teeming with young white men, who obliged by throwing rocks and racial epithets. After the police arrived to calm the crowd and a local resident displayed to the crowd the family's birth certificate indicating that the family was indeed "American Indian, not Negro, as rumored," the crowd dispersed.[10]

Although the rejection of Puerto Ricans had been violent, the presence of Puerto Rican businesses in the community offered a reason for hope. These entrepreneurs did not need access to bank loans for large capital expenses, and they could start up and maintain a business with little help from outsiders. As the Commission on Human Relations noted, their industriousness could help dispel negative attitudes toward Puerto Ricans generally and demonstrate that Puerto Ricans were good, hardworking people striving to succeed in their new home:

In the denser Puerto Rican neighborhood almost every retail establishment is run by Puerto Ricans. (This is what has been described as the heritage of the American Administration. The American occupation of Puerto Rico introduced a number of influences from the mainland: today one hears that Puerto Ricans know much more about installment buying than other Latin Americans.)

The first sign of Puerto Rican movement into a neighborhood is the bodegas, owned and operated usually by a husband and wife. There are now about 80 bodegas in the Puerto Rican community of Philadelphia. Also not hard to find are the Spanish-style barbershops, of which there are many, catering to Puerto Ricans and other Spanish-speaking people. The list may be continued to include notary public's offices, dental and medical offices, print shops, motion picture theatres offering Spanish movies, combination bookstore-newsstands (Spanish style, of course), where a mixture of Spanish-language magazines, books, newspapers, phonograph records and sometimes perfumes, souvenirs and other rare items may be found, all the way down the line to beauty parlors, photo-studios, bars and restaurants, bakeries, laundries, etc.[11]

As far as the Commission on Human Relations was concerned, these positive aspects of the Puerto Rican community resulted from the American occupation of the island. Rather than seeing entrepreneurship as an aspect inherent in Puerto Rican culture, the report portrayed entrepreneurship as an exceptional activity that could bloom in the "new world," suggesting that the poor socioeconomic conditions of Puerto Rican residents might be overcome through hard work, individual initiative, and an appreciation of the American dream.

INTERVENTIONS

In 1974, as the country prepared to celebrate its bicentennial, Philadelphia received a great deal of attention as the cradle of American democracy and as a city with a vibrant civil society. That year, a marketing study conducted by the firm of Hammer, Silver and George Associates for the Spanish Merchants Association gathered various statistics about the Fifth Street trading area and projected how the district would change over the following six years.[12] (The Spanish Merchants Association represented Latino business owners throughout the greater Delaware Valley, whereas the Fifth Street Merchants Association represented only the business owners from the North Fifth Street corridor and its immediate vicinity.) Nelson Díaz, then the association's executive director, summarized the relevant findings:

- The Fifth Street trading area had a population of 56,900, which would grow to 58,400 by 1980.
- The number of households stood at 16,400 and would reach 17,000 by 1980.
- Average household income was $8,900 in constant value dollars and would rise to $9,300 by 1980.[13]

As part of the bicentennial preparations, the federal government directed financial and technical resources to local business associations that championed the entrepreneurial spirit embodied in mom-and-pop stores. The federal Economic Development Administration, along with the city's Redevelopment Authority and Office of Housing and Community Development, selected the North Fifth Street corridor and three other commercial districts to participate in a new revitalization program, formed to establish neighborhood business associations and to help develop a coherent, attractive identity for the districts in time for the bicentennial.[14]

In 1975, an article in the Philadelphia *Bulletin* reported on the changing fortunes of the district.[15] Back in the early 1960s, wrote reporter Joe Davidson, shop owners were primarily of German, Irish, and Jewish stock. Then the population of Puerto Ricans along Fifth Street, north of Lehigh and south of Indiana, began to grow. As Latinos moved in, many of the white ethnics moved out, according to Domingo Negrón, the inaugural president of the Fifth Street Merchants Association.[16] In a typical pattern of ethnic succession, Latino entrepreneurs concentrated in an area where property values had fallen after the sudden exodus of white business owners. Once the entrepreneurs took advantage of the reduced prices and bought up the vacant properties, demand for property in the area returned, pushing property values back up.

In the *Bulletin* article, Oscar Goldfarb, director of the Philadelphia Neighborhood Revitalization Program, likened the progress of North Fifth Street to an "acid test" that showed a positive outcome.[17] Michael Muñoz, owner of La Famosa department store, told Davidson that he benefited directly from the upswing. When Muñoz arrived in the district seven years earlier, business was slow and he owned only one building. Now he owned five buildings, "so you can judge for yourself," he said.[18] Elmore Johnson, executive director of Hartranft Community Corporation, observed that what is good for business is good for neighborhood: with a healthy business sector at the neighborhood's center comes growing stability in the neighborhood itself.[19] Still, a number of civic organizations were taking a wait-and-see approach before building new housing in the neighborhood, Davidson reported. If the business district succeeded, they would build, but not otherwise.

Negrón expressed optimism about the new curbs, sidewalks, and trees along with off-street parking and mini-parks that the revitalization program would help bring to the area. Some of the business owners operating in the corridor before the Latinos arrived, however, saw things differently. Sarah and Samuel Schaff, who had been in business for forty-five years and owned six stores in the North Fifth Street corridor, told Davidson they

TABLE 5. Property Uses, 2700–2900 North Fifth Street, 1977

Ground-Floor Uses of Properties	Number	% of Total Uses
Residential	22	17
Commercial	75	58
Industrial/wholesale	3	2
Institutional/city	5	4
Parking lots/gas and auto sales	3	2
Vacant buildings	21	16
Vacant lots	1	1

Source: Philadelphia Architects Workshop Survey, 1977, found in Historical Society of Pennsylvania, Balch Collection, MSS 118, Box 1, Folder 7.

would rather see more money invested in police protection and business improvement loans. "Who needs trees?" Samuel asked. "What good is... beautiful pavement [when] business is deteriorating?" Although property values increased, problems remained: "Newspapers blow down the street and trash litters the curbs. Parking is a major problem and the cobblestone roadway can make driving a headache," he said.[20]

Still, by 1977 the revitalization effort seemed to be paying off in low commercial vacancy rates and a varied mix of businesses. As table 5 demonstrates, a survey conducted by the Philadelphia Architects Workshop showed that most of the properties served commercial purposes (58 percent), and a smaller number were used as residences (17 percent). The remainder were for industrial or wholesale uses (2 percent); institutional or city-owned buildings (4 percent); parking lots, gasoline stations, and auto sales shops (2 percent); and vacant buildings or lots (17 percent).

Another survey, conducted the following year by the Spanish Merchants Association, came up with somewhat different numbers.[21] The biggest difference between the studies lay in the number of properties included in the count: 192 in the Spanish Merchants Association report and 130 in the Philadelphia Architects Workshop survey. This difference stems partly from the fact that the Spanish Merchants included one more city block than did the Philadelphia Architects. The greatest similarity between the two studies is the reported percentage of commercial properties (57 and 58 percent, respectively). Notably, the vacancy rate is nearly double in the Spanish Merchants report, suggesting that the last city block excluded from the Philadelphia Architects survey included a number of vacant properties, or that the architects' survey underreported the number of properties in the corridor. These discrepancies also suggest that the Spanish Merchants may have overstated the degree of economic hardship and the size of the existing entrepreneurial drive.

MANAGING THE IMAGE OF THE STOREFRONTS

In the late 1970s the attempt to transform ethnic difference into a branded advantage was well under way. Records kept by the Fifth Street Merchants Association indicate extensive conversations with cultural brokers from city hall and with architects working to promote local economic development.[22] The discussions centered on framing the impression that the neighborhood gave outsiders by making the storefronts themselves represent the neighborhood's ethnic identity. In its 1977 survey, the Philadelphia Architects Workshop assessed characteristics of the existing commercial storefronts and found that only about half of the storefronts had projecting signs and less than one-quarter had wall signs (table 6).

In 1978, the architects developed storefront design criteria as part of the revitalization plan for the Fifth Street corridor. They noted the importance of "ethnic pride and solidarity" among shoppers and merchants in the commercial district, as well as the effect of "theming" the landscape, on the reported sales among local enterprises:

The commercial corridor addressed in this booklet is a shopping strip along Fifth Street, extending some three blocks north from Lehigh Avenue in North-Central Philadelphia. It has been described as a neighborhood commercial center, serving the largely Hispanic community of over 60,000 people which surround it. The strength of this corridor is at least in part a result of the ethnic pride and solidarity of the shoppers and merchants here....

The site improvements consist of the replacement of existing sidewalks with multi-colored, patterned sidewalks, the installation of new curbs (with curb cuts at corners for the handicapped), trees, bollards, trash cans, parking meter supports, telephones, and the painting of sidewalk vault covers and utility poles. Work on these improvements began in 1976, with the first phase completed early in 1977. As a result of this phase work, there was a 10% increase in business (as reported by the Spanish Merchants Association).[23]

The ethnic pride apparent to the architects resulted partly from the absence of opportunities for Latinos outside of their enclave. Latinos had been shut out or ejected from other neighborhoods in the city, and many came to see the commercial corridor not just as a market where goods were bought and sold but also as a representation of their identity. Latinos who owned businesses intended to pass them down to their offspring. Some shops clearly catered to Latinos, selling products with Spanish names. The commercial district represented some of the best the Latino community had to offer, both to itself and to society more generally.

TABLE 6. Characteristics of Commercial Fronts, 2700–2900 North Fifth Street, 1977

Characteristics	Number of Stores	% of Total
Wall sign	17	23
Projecting signs	36	48
Door signs	66	88
Recessed doors	45	60
Awnings	26	35
Long fronts (spanning two or more addresses)	14	19

Source: Philadelphia Architects Workshop Survey, 1977, p. 4, found in Historical Society of Pennsylvania, Balch Collection, MSS 118, Box 1, Folder 7.

The architects held a series of meetings with the shopkeepers about their ideas and preferences for redesigning the business corridor. The architects' report offered the following observations:

1. Merchants felt the street lacked an image or strong identity. There was no uniformity in appearance, type of store, or product sold. Although the shopping area had an ethnic base, there were no strong features to identify it as such.
2. The merchants felt the most important factor in increasing patronage was better signs. The merchants were undecided between replacing existing wall signs with a uniform sign band or simply a clean-up/fix-up of existing ones. There was, however, strong preference for the replacement of existing projecting signs with new ones of coordinated size, position, and materials, but with distinctive shape.
3. All merchants desired a logo and name for the commercial strip.
4. The merchants desired an architectural image that balanced uniformity of design with diversity of appearance. They wanted to elaborately redecorate their storefronts using decorative brick, stucco, tile, or shingled pent eaves [narrow roofs supported by a beam jutting out from a wall]. Painting was also mentioned as an important first step.
5. Finally, the merchants wanted to keep the cost of improvements below one thousand dollars, with most preferring an investment of one hundred to five hundred dollars.[24]

The report included diagrams of existing businesses such as Hill's Photo Center and Diaz Meat Market with some architectural upgrades, to give a sense of what the redesign would look like. The architects also provided do-it-yourself instructions for building a pent eave, creating Plexiglas window signs, and obtaining city permits.

Following this report, a group of local business owners formed a storefront committee and teamed up with the Philadelphia City Development Corporation (PCDC) to learn more about best practices in storefront design. In a memorandum from the PCDC to Fifth Street businesses, Dane Wells, manager of the PCDC's Neighborhood Commercial Revitalization program, tried to explain how important customers' impressions are for the economic prospects of their businesses.

PHILADELPHIA CITY DEVELOPMENT CORPORATION

TO: Storefront Committee
FROM: Dane T. Wells [DW initialed in ink]
DATE: 22 September 1978
SUBJECT: Committee Operations

... Look down your street, what are your fellow merchants telling a prospective customer with their "storefront language."... Why the big deal about storefronts? Small items like increased customers, sales, profits—that's all. For the corridor it is important that when a potential customer steps on the street that they are impressed, feel comfortable and confident. Otherwise, selling [to] that person is an up-hill fight. For the individual store, a customer's first impression comes from the front. They will believe that behind a shoddy storefront lies shoddy merchandise. Logical isn't it?[25]

Storefront design continued to be a topic of debate well into the next decade. In 1987, Luis Mora, the acting director of the Spanish Merchants Association, launched the Store Front Improvement Seminar at the association's office on North Fifth Street. During a slide show of storefronts along the North Fifth Street corridor, Mora pointed out that some signs gave only the name of the owner. Locals would have known what the shops sold, but for outsiders such signs were meaningless. He also showed drawings of redesigned awnings that would do a better job of enticing customers and protecting against bright sunlight and sudden downpours.[26]

DEINDUSTRIALIZATION AND JOBLESSNESS

During the late 1970s and through the 1980s, local entrepreneurs started new businesses, employed local people, and dreamed of a prosperous future. The Puerto Rican community, however, was hit hard by changing structural conditions in the economy. In 1976, an article in the *Bulletin* described in compelling terms the peculiar predicament that Puerto Ricans faced in Philadelphia:

The Puerto Rican is a foreigner in the United States who came from a protectorate of the United States. Racially, he is a Spaniard, an African, an Indian or a combination of all three. He came late to the mainland, mostly since the end of World War II.... He came at a time when traditional avenues of employment traveled by earlier immigrants were closed. Light industries were leaving the big cities, taking jobs for the unskilled with them. The political patronage system, whereby earlier immigrants got city jobs, was being replaced by [the] Civil Service. The Civil Service Tests were in English. Labor unions made sure that all but the most menial jobs in the private sector were kept for their own members.[27]

Had Puerto Ricans settled in Philadelphia before the deindustrialization of America's cities, they might have followed a path similar to other immigrant or migrant groups. They could have started at the bottom of the ladder in a local factory and worked their way up the ranks. The hard work of the parents would have manifested itself in the opportunities available to the offspring, who would be members of labor unions working in jobs with benefit packages that included health care and retirement. The timing of Puerto Ricans' arrival in Philadelphia, however, meant that they faced a different set of opportunities relative to immigrant groups who had come previously.

It is no secret among social scientists that various ethnic groups have been channeled into particular types of jobs. There is a general perception that certain types of people are good at doing certain types of things. Not only do employers rely on their prejudices about what types of workers are likely to have the right kinds of "soft skills" (such as the ability to get along with others and a willingness to work hard), but these workers will be recruited easily by virtue of their social ties to other workers already on the job.[28]

Marta Tienda, a sociologist studying the incorporation of various Latino groups in the United States, examined how Latinos fared between 1970 and 1985. While Mexican Americans did well in the labor market despite their lack of education, the same was not true of Puerto Ricans: their economic well-being declined generally in that period, falling precipitously in the latter half. "Puerto Rican family income declined by 7.4 percent in real terms during the 1970s and by an additional 18.0 percent between 1979 and 1984," Tienda reported.[29] (By comparison, African American real family income rose slowly in the 1970s before falling by 14 percent in the 1980s.) Tienda found that Puerto Rican men tended to work in areas where employment opportunities were shrinking and that Puerto Ricans lived in areas where the most severe economic dislocations were occurring.[30]

Historian Carmen Teresa Whalen, who has studied the experiences of Puerto Ricans in Philadelphia, emphasizes how social scientists, policy makers, social service workers, and the media have portrayed Puerto Ricans as suffering from a "culture of poverty."[31] She quotes Nathan Glazer and Daniel Patrick Moynihan, who believe that Puerto Ricans and African Americans living in the worst urban neighborhoods lacked "a strong family system" or a "network of culture, religion, art, [and] custom" that would give "strength and grace and meaning to a life of hardship."[32] This portrayal of Puerto Ricans as victims of their own ills had an important impact on what the city's leaders thought could and ought to be done to improve their condition. As the notion of a culture of poverty took hold, Whalen writes, "Puerto Ricans gained the dubious distinction of being among the first to be cast as migrating in search of welfare benefits. From this perspective, Puerto Ricans could not be labor migrants because they lacked a work ethic and desired welfare dependency. The obstacles that confronted Puerto Ricans stemmed not from a new urban environment, a tight job market, or discrimination, but rather from their own cultural deficiencies."[33]

Even people who came into the Puerto Rican community to offer assistance believed that a culture of poverty pervaded it. In a set of handwritten notes to Luis Mora dated December 23, 1986, a white community development worker offered the following observations:

Unfortunately, economic development is impeded by 1) the morass of illiteracy, low self-esteem, drugs, teenage pregnancy, absence of work ethic value system, probably some kind of psycho/physiological deficiencies, 2) available money, 3) outside human talent which is sadly lacking....

GOAL

To help merchants of Fifth between Lehigh and Indiana double their gross sales volume by the end of 1988 (Two years)....

OBSTACLES

1) Merchants are utterly unskilled.
2) Merchants do not know or are unwilling to believe they are unskilled.
3) Merchants blame their poor sales on uncontrollable variables—*not themselves*. As a result, they are unwilling to be sincere about the need for self-improvement.
4) The physical plants are deteriorated and/or are too small....
7) The entire market is weak—there is no draw into the neighborhood.

8) I think the plethora of agencies has created a climate in which hundreds of do-nothing programs litter the landscape and contribute mightily to the sense of hopeless, negative, hostile arrogance that pervades the air.
9) I think the community leadership politically contributes to a sense of impotence.
10) I do not feel there is any spirit of "in union there is strength."[34]

For this outsider, intent on helping Puerto Rican businesses succeed in Philadelphia, the obstacles to development lay within the control of the merchants themselves. If only "the culture" would enable these individuals to act in solidarity to solve common problems and if only the business owners would listen to the advice of well-meaning outsiders, the community might thrive. This focus on what individuals ought to do ignored large-scale shifts in the economy that increased joblessness and thereby decreased the sources of legitimate disposable income.

Macroeconomic changes also affected the physical landscape of Philadelphia's neighborhoods. In the barrio, large factories were shuttered, and some stood half-demolished. As factories were closed and employees were let go, small businesses providing goods and services to those workers also suffered. The jobs that left the barrio were not replaced by legitimate work, and the resulting void began to be filled by the drug trade.

THE CRACK EPIDEMIC

As deindustrialization progressed, the crack epidemic spread across America's cities. A 1985 news program on CBS, *48 Hours on Crack Street*, informed 15 million viewers of crack's detrimental effects to both individuals and communities; NBC News followed suit with *Cocaine Country*. By 1989, President George H. W. Bush joined the conversation from the Oval Office. In the popular imagination, crack became associated with the ghetto. Crack whores, the crack babies they birthed, and the crack heads with whom they socialized were the objects of public scorn.[35]

The social character of the epidemic made inner-city neighborhoods undesirable places to visit. People living in these neighborhoods recall how drug dealers walked the streets with impunity as the police would drive by but not disrupt obvious drug sales. The neighborhood's easy access to the highway meant that people could drive in quickly from the suburbs, purchase drugs, and then drive away. Because selling drugs was so widely documented in the Latino neighborhood and because a relatively poor, ethnic neighborhood is easily discredited, the crack epidemic was seen not as an

The Quaker Lace building at Fourth and Lehigh, destroyed by arson in 1994, had been shuttered by deindustrialization; the site is now the location of Julia de Burgos Middle School. Photo by Tony Rocco.

external force that had besieged the Latino neighborhood but rather as a reflection of the community's internal deficiencies. For the community to break the reputational hold that the crack epidemic had on it, the epidemic itself had to wane. Because the epidemic waned across all cities at about the same time, the drug problems of the barrio clearly were societal rather than the fault of particular individuals or a particular cultural orientation. The epidemic itself, however, influenced those who, intentionally or otherwise, branded the barrio's image for the broader public.

In a paper published by the National Institute of Justice in 1997, Andrew L. Golub and Bruce D. Johnson reported a decline in crack cocaine use among people who were being arrested and tested for drugs. In Philadelphia, a rapid decline was reported starting in 1989. Overall, about 73 percent of people arrested in 1989 tested positive for cocaine or crack, but that proportion fell to 49 percent in 1996. Among young people being arrested, the rate fell from 70 percent in 1988 to 21 percent in 1993. A slower decline took place among Manhattan arrestees generally (70 percent in 1987 and 62 percent in 1996), but among youthful arrestees, it fell from 70 percent in 1988 to 22 percent in 1995. In Chicago, the overall rate hovered around 58 percent, but the rate among young people fell from 49 percent in 1993 to 22 percent in 1996.[36] Of course, policing practices might have affected the perceived decline in cocaine use among arrestees, especially since some of the people selling were not also using it themselves and since the police allowed some areas of the city to operate outside of the law, with drug sales happening in plain sight.

Operation Sunrise, initiated in 1998, attempted to turn the Latino neighborhood into a gated community so that people from the suburbs and other parts of the city could no longer use it as their drive-by drugstore.[37] The Philadelphia police modeled Operation Sunrise on a strategy implemented by the New York City Police in Washington Heights. Gun violence there dropped sharply after police erected barricades and monitored who went in and out of the neighborhood.[38] Philadelphia Police Commissioner John Timoney launched Operation Sunrise in the Kensington and Fairhill neighborhoods, but the reaction to the initiative was mixed.[39] Neighborhood residents wanted the drug dealing to stop but remained deeply suspicious of the police, fearing that they would arrest and assault the innocent along with the guilty. (A few known incidences of police brutality, particularly one in which a youth was shot in the back, fed these suspicions.)[40] And, as described in chapter 3, the operation not only kept drug buyers out of the neighborhood, it also kept out people trying to attend art exhibits and cultural performances. Some community leaders worried that Operation Sunrise reinforced the notion that any neighborhood meriting such extreme containment was probably no good to begin with.[41]

SOCIAL CONDITIONS AND CULTURAL CONSTRAINTS

As the crack epidemic waned, the cultural economy took off, not only in Philadelphia but also in Chicago, New York, and a host of other cities whose downtown neighborhoods were becoming safe enough to attract middle- and upper-middle-class inhabitants. The number of cultural firms and cultural providers doubled or tripled in Philadelphia between 1996 and 2003.[42] As industrial jobs left the city, cultural jobs entered the scene. This shift should have translated into more opportunities for local development across the board, especially in places with cultural heritage sites or with clusters of cultural producers considered important by the general public.

To what extent cities and neighborhoods benefited from the booming interest in cultural heritage depends on collective understandings so deeply held that their effects are often taken for granted. As we discover in chapter 6, these collective understandings fall along binary lines, with the sacred pitted against the profane, the good neighborhood against the bad. This binary understanding influences how people engage in neighborhood revitalization efforts.

Most cities have a well-known anti-model neighborhood, and the city's residents refer directly or indirectly to the anti-model to establish why and how model neighborhoods should be prevented from falling into chaos. The barrio remains at risk of being the anti-model neighborhood, despite the efforts of community leaders and business owners. As demographic patterns shift and new discredited populations enter Philadelphia, the barrio may be able to rise in the hierarchy of neighborhoods as another population occupies the lowest rungs of the city's society, but its anti-model status prevents it from rising on its own merits. The barrio's leaders, artists, and merchants must wage a constant symbolic battle to demonstrate that they live or work in "a good place" with unique cultural treasures and a *civil* society.

6 » Character on Parade
Cultural Constraints on Neighborhood Branding

In chapter 5 we saw that there are social and structural constraints on how a neighborhood can be represented. Now we will examine how public ceremonies such as the Puerto Rican Day Parade help to fix the shifting meanings about what it means to be Puerto Rican and what it means to be Latino.[1]

By witnessing and participating in the preparations for the Puerto Rican Day Parade, I learned about the implicit and explicit messages that community members send to the rest of the society and to each other about what it means to be Latino. In 2005, Yolanda Alcorta, executive director and co-founder of Raíces whom we met in chapter 3, persuaded me to march in the parade itself. Happy to offer help wherever needed, I volunteered to drive some of the young marchers to the event as a way of seeing how things happen backstage without disrupting the usual operations of the group. Circumstances, however, did not permit me to keep my distance.

"We need a *caballero*," Yolanda declared. "Most people want to play the role of the *vejigantes*, not the Spanish conquistador." The *caballero* is one of the roles in the *bomba* and the *plena*, as they are practiced in Loíza, Puerto Rico. In the parade, the *caballero* represents the Spanish conquistador, the *vejigantes* the Moors. *Vejigantes* don a loose-fitting jumpsuit with batwings and a cape; each wears a mask made from a coconut husk with three horns (two red and one yellow) jutting from its crown and long yellow fangs piercing its open mouth. Dancing to the beat of the *bomba* and the *plena*, the *vejigantes* attempt to scare away the *caballero* by shaking their rattles—sticks about two feet long bearing fist-sized paper sacks filled with beads.

Ironically, Yolanda assigned the role of white European conquistador to me, a black man. Was Yolanda trying to tell me something? I suspect that the irony was not lost on her, either. Her husband is African American and her sons' complexions are darker than hers. She, along with several other people I came to know in the barrio, told me that I could easily pass for Latino. Being fully covered by the mask and the costume of the *caballero* would help me pass even more easily, since I would not speak and the people around me would act as if I were a fellow Latino participant. (I speak Spanish with hesitation and with too much correctness.)

"I'm happy to fill in wherever you need me, but I've not been coming to any of the rehearsals, and the parade is in, what, two weeks?" I half-heartedly protested.

"It'll be easy," Yolanda reassured me. "And two weeks is enough time for what you'll need to do. Just have fun with it."

On the day of the parade, I stood around during the rehearsal and wondered whether I would be given instructions more specific than "just dance on the edge of where the performers are, pass out flyers, and pull a few people in to dance with you." I had arrived at a few minutes before 1 p.m. at the Raíces office on Fifth and Somerset. Upstairs, the teenagers and their preteen counterparts were giggling as they put on their costumes. The boys were trying on their *vejigante* outfits while speaking in low voices with one another, bursting with laughter at their own jokes. Yolanda warned me that my mask would be hot, so for now I did not need to wear it. She wanted to see if the *caballero* outfit needed to be adjusted. There was no need, for the costume was a perfect fit.

Maribel Lozada led us to the parking lot behind the Julia de Burgos Bilingual School on the city block behind Raíces. That's where I heard parents of the younger performers and other adults emphasize that the parade is a place where Puerto Rican traditions are put on display and where participants have an opportunity to demonstrate their integrity and respectability to the wider civil society. One of the performers, a teenage girl, wore golden earrings with her name etched in the ring's lower curl. It seemed to me that her earrings were about a third of the diameter of a Frisbee. One of the older women at the rehearsal took the young woman aside to discuss whether the earrings were appropriate jewelry for the parade. In the meantime, even greater attention was being given to the decorations on each of the dresses the females wore.

As I watched the group rehearse, one of the mothers leaned toward me to tell me about the dresses and her concern that they be decorated properly and treated carefully. "My grandmother used to sew all those dresses, and she made sure the ruffles were *even*," she said, speaking more loudly as if to everyone nearby. Then she joined two other mothers a few feet away who were complaining about one of the girl's dresses, which lacked the red ribbons that should have been stitched on the front.

Mafalda Thomas-Bouzy, one of the choreographers who heads Kuumba, an African and Caribbean dance troupe in Philadelphia, told me more about the dances and about the ribbons stitched onto the girls' dresses. "You see, the *bomba* and the *plena* are plantation dances. The dances incorporate the African side of the culture. First, the locals wanted to do what they saw the Spanish doing. You see that with the more 'dignified' dances. Then the dance breaks into thrusting with the butt out and the people just a-shaking it. That is much more of the African side. We didn't have silk and all the fancy things back then, but we wanted our dresses to be adorned, so we tied little ribbons on them so that they could be seen on the under-dress whenever we lifted our skirts." Mafalda smirked as she described the multiple messages the oppressed could send through the innocence of dance. "That's right," confirmed a woman with blond hair who was listening to Mafalda. "The beats in this music and African beats all come from the same place," she told me after identifying herself as a Puerto Rican whose lineage is likely a mix of African and Spanish blood. "Most of us [are mixed]."

The performance continued over our chatter, the men beating the drums while the women and young girls pumped their torsos. Our attention soon turned to the performers, and our conversation ceased. During one of the breaks, the girls tried to join the boys in a pickup game of basketball. This act drew loud protest from the mothers, who feared the girls might sully their dresses before the parade the next day.

"Remember," one of the mothers told the pouting girls, "*they* are all watching you tomorrow. The parade will be in the newspapers, on television. You have to show them *who we are*. You have to show the pride and the beauty of our culture."

Another mother interjected, "You know what they say about us. Now is your time *to show them wrong*."

A year later, I observed the parade from the sidelines. I arrived at the bleachers just before noon beside the main stage on the Benjamin Franklin Parkway on a Sunday. About one hundred or two hundred feet away from the bleachers, I saw a table that displayed copies of *Al Día* newspapers with the front page bearing the headlines "Hispanic Firms are Growing at Three Times the Average Rate for All US Firms" and "The Other Latin Face." Also on the front page was a prominent picture of the Philadelphia Museum of Art's new exhibition, titled *Tesoros/Treasures/Tesouros: The Arts of Latin America, 1492–1820*. Such headlines emphasized the economic and cultural contributions of the Latino community.

Girl in City Year sweatshirt marching in the Puerto Rican Day Parade. Photo by Tony Rocco. Historical Society of Pennsylvania, Balch Collection.

Beside the newspapers stood rows of café con leche in small cups and a large blue thermal carafe. I almost failed to notice the miniature golden arches on the carafe. A McDonald's worker asked whether I wanted hazelnut or vanilla, then handed me a cup of hazelnut coffee along with a coupon that read, "Introducing McDonald's Iced Coffee… Need something hot? Any size hot coffee, 69 cents." I took my coffee and walked the short distance to the bleachers to sit.

A number of families—most of them adorned in the red, white, and blue of the Puerto Rican flag along with a small flag or its image on their clothes—had already gathered near the bleachers. A man and a little girl who appeared to be about nine years old sat beside me. The man was probably her grandfather; his back was hunched high and his cane was tilted away from his body at a forty-five-degree angle. Speaking to no one in particular, he said, "The rain will not fall." He waved toward the sky, as if shooing away the drizzle. "It's just a little drizzle and it is coming from over there, not from straight above us. The wind is bringing it here." His explanation seemed to mollify the little girl, who remained silent, smiling but fidgeting in place.

Another man with a female companion came and sat beside them. "It's almost twelve," he observed, speaking apparently to the old man and his daughter as well as anyone else who cared to listen. It did not seem that the two knew each other because there were no names exchanged, nor were there hugs or handshakes. They were strangers drawn to the same civic event and engaged in small talk.

"You know they're not going to start on time; they never do," the newcomer's female companion replied. They both chuckled, along with the grandfather sitting beside them. After sitting for about twenty minutes, I began to walk along the edge of the parade to witness the variety of floats and hear the people riding the floats chant slogans of ethnic solidarity. Most of the messages were in English or in both Spanish and English. Rarely was a message shouted in Spanish that was not immediately translated into English. In one particular instance, it was clear why there was no translation. The message expressed outrage and solidarity over the FBI's killing of a Puerto Rican activist the year before.

Soon afterward I ran into Maria Mills-Torres, a board member at Taller, and asked her about the protest. She told me that the FBI had assassinated Filiberto Ojeda Ríos, a leader of the pro-independence movement in Puerto Rico. About two years later, I told Daniel de Jesus at Taller about the protest and mentioned that it was never translated into English the way some of the other chants at the parade had been. Daniel knew immediately what

I was referring to. Standing near an exhibit by artist Miguel Luciano at the Lorenzo Homar Gallery, Daniel told me about the assassination:

This is a piece called *Machetero Air Force-One*, and it's an homage to Filiberto Ojeda Ríos, who was a major leader for the independence movement for nationalists in Puerto Rico. They considered him to be the Puerto Rican Che Guevara. He was assassinated by the FBI in 2005. They literally barged into his house, military style, and they killed him. And people were just enraged. They had no idea what was going on. Why did this happen? And why was it this man, out of all people? The thing about the *independistas* is that they have, to some degree, [been] considered terrorists just because of events back in the mid-fifties.[2]

Although Daniel did not say so explicitly, he suggested that in the government's eyes, being suspected of terrorism was reason enough for execution. As I learned later, pro-independence activists had no doubt that Ojeda Ríos's death was intentional.[3] Still, the last thing the Latino community wanted was for their parade to be associated in the English-language press with the destructive elements of chaos. Newspaper coverage of the parade did not highlight this particular procession.

Newspapers covering the parade present an image of the neighborhood's character. In this chapter we will review the coverage of the barrio by the *Philadelphia Inquirer* and the *Philadelphia Daily News* in order to understand what the public characterization of the barrio is. Embedded in these mainstream publications are code words for what constitutes a good neighborhood as well as its opposite.[4] Some neighborhoods are depicted as possessing a civic spirit, as being tidy, clean, safe, and sociable; others as the epitome of an uncivil society, as disorganized, dirty, and violent. These narratives provide a glimpse into the deeply embedded constraints on how neighborhoods can be believably represented to a mainstream audience.

The challenge we face is to think through how neighborhoods change and how unseen (nonmaterial) factors constrain those changes. I suggest that we think about the nonmaterial constraints as cultural codes that alert members of society to places of safety by virtue of their difference with places of danger—places of habitation for the respectable members of civil society versus ghettoes of unrest for the troublemakers, the lawbreakers, and the welfare dependents. Ethnic neighborhoods often serve as the antithesis of the ideal urban neighborhood. In *Racism without Racists*, sociologist Eduardo Bonilla-Silva highlights how the public discourse about good and bad people cloaks racial stereotypes in seemingly nonracial, acultural attributes. The emphasis on universal values, individual choice, and free markets in American society means that neighborhoods may be viewed as bundles of attributes that individuals evaluate based on their own idiosyn-cratic preferences.⁵ Paying close attention to the language that is used to talk about different city neighborhoods helps us better understand the dis-guised racism as well as the cultural codes that limit what mainstream so-ciety members believe about a neighborhood's potential for transforma-tion and growth.

In *Language and Symbolic Power*, Pierre Bourdieu exhorts us to consider language as both a communicative tool and an instrument of power. The language of the daily news does more than relay information about what has and will happen in the city. The newspapers serve as the "unbiased" authorities assessing the attributes of neighborhoods and their residents. Language operates like an economic market: there are producers, consum-ers, distribution channels, and negotiations over what will ultimately be said and how much weight such utterances will be given. As we review the mainstream newspaper coverage of the Latino community and its public events, we begin to see a binary depiction of mainstream versus margin-alized neighborhoods. This binary depiction follows what Jeffrey Alexan-der and Philip Smith call the ritual structure of society,⁶ with the domi-nant favorably portrayed and the dominated unfavorably cast. How the mainstream press has cast members of the Latino community in "bad" roles over the years and how the codes tagged to the neighborhood have changed over time correspond with three narratives. In the first, the bar-rio is a place where hardworking immigrants and other good ethnics pull themselves up by their bootstraps and strive to become patriotic capital-ists. In the second, the barrio is plagued by social problems that must be contained so that the rest of society is not contaminated. In the third, the barrio is a struggling community whose artistic and cultural riches might help it in joining the city's upwardly mobile neighborhoods.

THE "HARDWORKING IMMIGRANTS," CIVIL SOCIETY, AND THE AMERICAN DREAM

In the 1980s, newspaper reports about the Puerto Rican Day Parade also fea-tured descriptions of the Latino neighborhood and its residents, framed as a place where immigrants arrive and struggle for a better life. In a 1983 *Philadelphia Inquirer* article titled "For Area Hispanics, Celebration amid the Struggles," reporter Russell Cooke seemed to give the parade a pass-ing mention despite the story's headline: "This is the week each year when the area's Hispanic community celebrates its victories in that *classic immi-grant experience*. As part of the annual Puerto Rican Festival Week, [a series of events will be] *capped with a colorful parade* through Center City on Sunday."[7] The rest of the article focused on the struggles of Puerto Ricans and other Latinos vis-à-vis "the classic immigrant experience" of arrival in the land of opportunity, where one could overcome the odds to achieve the American dream. After supplying the reader with statistics about how one-fifth of the Latino population was unemployed, how a large percentage of Latinos from the barrio spoke only Spanish, and how their residences were spatially concentrated in one-tenth of the city's area, Cooke described the Latino neighborhood.

To gaze into the heart of this community you would have to stand at, say, Girard Avenue and Seventh Street and look as far north as Roosevelt Boulevard, a distance of about 45 blocks. Three areas have the greatest concentration: West Kensington, eastern North Philadelphia, and Hunting Park. *In its rough geographic center is a jewel: the so-called Golden Block commercial district along North Fifth Street*, where Spanish is spoken by storeowners, and Latin music and the smells of Latin cooking greet shoppers.

Generally, the farther north a Hispanic family lives in this community the better off it is, officials say. In the south the problems of joblessness, housing deterioration and crime increase—and hope declines.

But not always. Walk into Monserrate Feliciano's small bakery *in the heart of the Golden Block*. . . . They live above the store with their 19-year-old son, James, who is a Temple University student. And they have few complaints.

"So far, we make enough to live. We have no debts; everything is paid up," Mrs. Feliciano said.[8]

In this place there were both successes and failures. The Latino population depicted here was heterogeneous, with decent, hardworking, entrepreneurial families alongside the idling and the unemployed. An unemployed man actively sought work and did not consider himself to be too good for dirty tasks. He explained, "I was walking almost without shoes looking for a job because I wanted work. . . . I'm willing to do anything. I don't care if I have to clean toilets. I want to work."[9] Not everyone was desperate, particularly those living in the Golden Block. The community's ethnic entrepreneurs and its manual laborers worked hard, lived modestly, and tried to create better opportunities for their offspring.

A number of other newspaper reports on the parade referred directly to the main streets in the barrio. In 1984, a *Philadelphia Inquirer* article titled "For Puerto Ricans, a Day of Pride" ended with a reference to Fourth and Berks streets (at the edge of the barrio), where a carnival scheduled to begin just after the parade had to be canceled because the proper licenses were not obtained from the city.[10] Two years later, an article titled "Puerto Rican Fest Floats Out in Style" described a float bedecked with flowers that had been cultivated in a lot at the same intersection of Fourth and Berks.[11] The article noted that the "small" display of flowers resulted from a large civic effort: "The flowers were cultivated in what was once a vacant lot at 4th and Berks streets. That lot became the first of about 150 lots that were turned into floral showcases through a joint community effort aided by the Urban Gardening Program of Pennsylvania State University's Cooperative Extension Service."[12] The same article also referred to Third and Somerset streets, where a community carnival opened the night before the parade.[13]

Newspaper articles written in the 1980s emphasized the positive contributions of Puerto Ricans and other Latinos to American society and likened the tastes of Latinos to those of other Americans. In a 1983 article in the *Philadelphia Inquirer*, one Latino leader stated the theme succinctly:

"There is a wealth of individuals in this community who have done well, and they're living the American Dream. They like the Eagles and the Sixers and the Flyers, and they're no different from anyone else," said Puerto Rican–born Maximo Santiago Jr., who runs the Hispanic Outreach Office of the City Commission on Human Relations.

"We have everything to be proud of," he said. "You go out to the Southwest and look at the Rio Grande; it isn't named that way because of the Indians. We played a vital role in this country."[14]

In an article written in 1986, Diego Castellanos, president of Puerto Rican Week, extolled the contributions of Latinos in the classroom, in law enforcement, and in the private sector and the positive effect they had on race relations: "Puerto Ricans have demonstrated that a melting pot is possible, that people of diverse racial stock can live together in harmony, respect and love."[15] The *Philadelphia Daily News* noted that the twenty-third annual Puerto Rican Week festival celebrated "in the festival backers' words, 'Hispanic Contributions to the City of Brotherly Love.' For parade grand marshal, Gualberto Medina... the good times and good vibes represented 'a lot of positive energy' that, if harnessed, 'could be turned into kinetic political energy.'"[16] In a 1987 *Philadelphia Inquirer* story, a thirteen-year-old boy named Ismael Jones explained, "This is a Puerto Rican parade with Puerto Rican people, but it is not just for us, it is for everybody."[17] On the occasion of the parade in 1989, Mayor W. Wilson Goode remarked, "Philadelphia is a city of many ethnic groups. It's a microcosm of this world. It's important that we recognize that we are strong because of our diversity."[18] In 1990, a local businessman and former president of Concilio, Candelario Lamboy, emphasized that the Puerto Rican Day Parade should be seen as an affirmation of how the Latino community proudly constituted an integral part of the city and had much to contribute to society: "We are very proud to be a part of the city," Lamboy said. "We like to show to the city of Philadelphia that we have much to offer. We like to show that we are people from all walks of life."[19] During the next eight years of newspaper reports about the Puerto Rican Day Parade, however, there were few references to the contributions that Latinos have made to society.

The newspaper reports from the 1980s depicted the Latino community as contributing to society and as working constructively to solve its own problems. Cooke's 1983 *Philadelphia Inquirer* article observed the Puerto Rican Day Parade's dual role as a public relations event and as a forum for making demands on city government.[20] Cooke reported that on the day of the parade, as Mayor William J. Green made his formal proclamation for Hispanic Heritage Week at City Hall, a group of about seventy-five people took the opportunity to highlight the need for more bilingual officers on the police force. Cooke viewed the lobbying effort as a rational use of a public event—the one time in the year when demands from the Latino community were more likely to receive broader and more intense media coverage.

In a 1982 *Philadelphia Daily News* article titled "Puerto Rican Celebration a 'Party Day,'" reporter Gene Seymour depicted the parade's Latino audience and its marchers as proud "immigrants" who "achieved like other immigrant groups," waving the Puerto Rican flag and printing it on their clothes and on their bodies, and joining in a ritual of solidarity.[21] "Paul Santos, of North Philadelphia, typified the approximately 100,000 Hispanics lining the parade route. Not only was he waving a Puerto Rican flag, but he was wearing jewelry on his hat and jacket that depicted varied forms of the Puerto Rican national symbols."[22]

In 1990, the *Philadelphia Inquirer* ran a headline for the twenty-seventh annual Puerto Rican Week Festival Parade, "A Celebration of Latino Heritage; 5,000 Turn Out for Puerto Rican Week Parade." The article captured the sense of solidarity engendered by the Puerto Rican flag as one of the paradegoers from Camden marveled, "Did you notice how many people are carrying Puerto Rican flags? Everybody's carrying a flag." The article further noted how "some cars and vans had no adornment other than the Puerto Rican flag."[23]

Three years earlier, the newspaper had portrayed the parade not as a pan-Latino event of celebration but as "A Day for Puerto Rico," and the reporter described the similarities between the Puerto Rican and U.S. flag: "[The Puerto Rican flag] has three stripes, two white ones, and a blue triangle in which rests a lone star."[24] The article also explained that the Committee for a 51st State was arguing for the incorporation of Puerto Rico into

Puerto Rican and United States flags draped across girls at the Puerto Rican Day Parade. Photo by Tony Rocco.

the United States as a state rather than a commonwealth, a status it has held since 1898. The Puerto Rican Week Festival brochure that year explained why such emphasis was being placed on statehood for Puerto Rico and the similarities between the two flags: 1987 was the thirty-fifth anniversary of the Puerto Rican constitution and the bicentennial of the U.S. Constitution.[25] The brochure recalled the history of Philadelphia as a "cradle of democracy" built by immigrants, and that history resonated in the newspaper coverage of the parade.

Another theme that surfaced in newspaper articles of the 1980s was the significance of the decision to pledge allegiance to the United States. In a 1982 *Philadelphia Daily News* article, the decision was cast as combining the best of both worlds. The newspaper quoted New Jersey educator and parade organizer Diego Castellano, who wrote an open letter to Latino youth on the occasion of the parade:

"Part of the price [previous generations of Puerto Ricans in this country] had to pay to share in the American dream included renouncing their heritage, silencing their mother tongue, disguising their names, and surrendering their values." But because of progress by that generation, today's youth, Castellano advises, "have options to choose the best of two worlds . . . Pedro is as American as Peter . . ."²⁶

But there was also some ambivalence about what "having options" would mean, especially for people who became completely "melted" into the American melting pot.

"We are a very different kind of immigrant because we are U.S. citizens and because we have not had to go through that process of mourning our country, and then getting on with life," [Mrs. Thillet] said.

It is easy to return to Puerto Rico—flights are as low as $99 from Newark International Airport, a popular departure point for Philadelphians who want to save a few dollars. Families routinely return for a year or two, then come back here—and that sometimes prevents them from putting down roots.

"They never quite feel comfortable here or there," Mrs. Thillet said in an interview last week. "They say to me, 'Where do I feel more comfortable? I feel more comfortable when I'm in the air in the plane and I don't have to make any decisions.'"²⁷

In this account, the Puerto Ricans in Philadelphia were not completely at home anywhere. The options available to them meant that they did not initially fall into the classic assimilation pattern, but the article generally suggested that Puerto Ricans would eventually follow the path of other immigrants who found themselves feeling at home in the new land.

In his 1983 Philadelphia Inquirer article, Cooke described the streets of the Latino community in North Philadelphia as "grim" and "narrow," lined by "deteriorating row houses."²⁸ In this struggling community, a social worker described how a mother reproached her child for not being mentally retarded. Had the child failed the examination for mental competence, the mother would have been eligible for welfare payments. In the mother's attempt to remain dependent on the public purse, Cooke argued, the mother eclipsed the opportunities for the next generation. She was, in short, the worse kind of welfare queen—a depiction closely tied to the Black urban poor.

The depictions of the parade in the 1980s mention the problems of welfare dependency, drugs, and urban poverty in only a few places, and they appear alongside positive depictions of the neighborhood and its struggles to combat these corroding forces. A 1988 Philadelphia Inquirer article titled "Puerto Rican Pride Braves the Rain" quoted the observations of Edwin Delgado, a resident whose family moved from Puerto Rico to Philadelphia twenty-five years earlier: "In a community that is battling drug abuse, high drop-out rates among its youth and other problems related to poverty, Delgado said, the parade serves as 'a sort of stimulant for the community. It gives us that motivation to continue the struggle in Philadelphia.'"[29] These more balanced depictions, however, did not last.

THEY COME TO TROUBLE AND TO DESTROY

By 1993, the newspaper coverage of the Puerto Rican Day Parade no longer included both the positive and negative aspects of the Latino community. Just as the parade served as an opportunity for problem solvers to address the need for more bilingual police in the 1980s, it now served as the arena for hooligans to wreak havoc on the Latino community and its host city. As we shall see, newspaper coverage referred to Latinos as troublemakers and "knuckleheads" who liked to get drunk, behave in a disorderly manner, and generally "act like fools"; likewise, the troublemakers were sometimes referred to as lawbreakers charged with offenses ranging from drag racing to murder.

The troublemaker theme was likewise applied to Latino advocates fighting on behalf of their community. Wilfredo Rojas, the president of the National Congress of Puerto Rican Rights, threatened to disrupt the parade if the city did not adequately address the police brutality that led to the shooting of Radames Bonilla for an alleged carjacking. Rojas had assembled about two hundred protesters, including ACT UP members and African American activists, to highlight the fact that the police shot Mr. Bonilla in the back as he fled. With William "Will" Gonzalez, the executive director of the Police-Barrio Relations Project, Rojas called for a review board to investigate the circumstances of the shooting. Some of the parade organizers saw Rojas and Gonzalez as unnecessarily disrupting the parade. Ramonita Rivera, chairperson of the Puerto Rican Week Festival Committee (which organizes the parade) in 1993 and president of Concilio, feared that a protest against Mayor Edward Rendell and the police force during the parade would "make us look like we are a bunch of hoodlums."[30] But Rojas disagreed. "We are not necessarily disrupting anything. We are letting the mayor know we are upset. [Rivera and other critics] are jumping to the conclusion that we are a band of unorganized rebels."[31]

In the mid- to late 1990s, newspaper coverage of the Puerto Rican Day Parade began to connect activities of Latino "hoodlums" with the exuberance generated by the parade. A 1997 *Daily News* article titled "Violence Mars Puerto Rico Day" described a chaotic situation forcing "peaceful citizens" to "dive for cover" as some people "carried the festive mood [from the parade] into North Philadelphia."[32] In the West Kensington area, the

paradegoers' charity: "People not only reached into their pockets for a buck or two... they pulled out fives, tens, and twenties, aggressively reaching for volunteers who were soliciting donations along the parade route."[45] The voluntary associations soliciting assistance for those confronting *natural* (as opposed to human-made) destruction became the focus of attention; indeed, the article made no mention of violence or antisocial behavior and quoted no one who feared that violence might tarnish a festive day. Still, an *Inquirer* article published weeks earlier had run the headline "Police, Latino Leaders Want a Trouble-Free Festival: They Announced a Plan to Help Keep Things Calm in Festivities after the Puerto Rican Day Parade."[46] The magnitude of the hurricane had offered some respite from the narratives of chaos, violence, and externally imposed control. But the public was still being reminded that even during times of civic engagement, all hell might break loose.

THEY REBUILD AND RESTORE

The general tenor of the news reports changed in the days following the September 11 attacks. As the nation was consumed by the sources of chaos emanating from outside of the United States, Puerto Ricans and other Latinos seemed more "American" than they had in previous media reports. Coverage of local events celebrating Hispanic Heritage Month (which begins September 15) noted the change in tone. One *Philadelphia Inquirer* article reporting on the festivities ran the headline "At Hispanic Heritage Month Events the Mood Is Somber." The Latina quoted in the article, Lisa Navarret, was from a national, not a local, Latino organization: "This is not a time of celebration. People, rightly so, are focusing on how they can rebuild New York and Washington and restore America," she said.[47] Pennsylvania Governor Tom Ridge was answering the call to serve as the head of the newly established Department of Homeland Security and thus would not be on hand for the parade's opening ceremonies. The parade participants would subdue their usual liveliness out of respect for those who had lost their lives in the attacks and in recognition of the country's nascent struggle against terrorism. Rubi Pacheco-Rivera of Concilio remarked, "I know about two groups that would normally play music on their floats [at the parade] who decided not to, and another sponsor will not have a salsa band on its float, just kids."[48] Curiously, the phrase "Puerto Rican" did not appear in the article, not even in association with the parade. The article focused on the pan-ethnic labels "Hispanic" and "Latino," noting that Congress established Hispanic Heritage Month in 1988 during a time on the calendar that captures "the independence days of Mexico, Costa Rica, El

Salvador, Guatemala, Honduras and Nicaragua, as well as other annual observances."[49] Now that the Puerto Ricans had become Latinos, they could engage in their civic duty to defend and restore their adopted American homeland as pan-ethnic citizens.

In 2002, the parade was one among a list of activities happening the same weekend. The *Philadelphia Inquirer* portrayed the parade as a welcoming event; one article was titled "Bienvenido" and described a local celebrity whose very presence at the event demonstrated that the parade represents all Latinos.

Maria Porras, Vineland, N.J.–based local morning anchor for Univision TV (Channel 65), is still walking tall over her reception at Sunday's Puerto Rican Day Parade, her first big public appearance. "I was a little bit nervous," Porras said yesterday. "I feel sometimes that I'm not good at speaking in public. But they were so friendly. They received me with a lot of love." She said it was not even an issue that she is not Puerto Rican (she is a native of Venezuela). Porras, 28, who lives in Center City and formerly was an editor for *TV Guide*, says she got a kick out of seeing herself on ABC (WPVI-TV covered the parade) and hearing Mayor [John F.] Street's Anglo pronunciation of "Viva Puerto Rico." Street's heart was in the right place, she said. "It's great when the mayors support Latino events."[50]

The story suggested that Center City cosmopolitans should feel comfortable at the parade, for the Latino community was open, welcoming, and friendly. Even Mayor Street's "Anglo pronunciation" was greeted with amusement rather than consternation. What mattered was that a person's "heart was in the right place" when attending the parade or other Latino events. Parade attendees need not be cultural experts or members of a particular ethnic group.

Such positive reports were still mixed with negative ones. In 2003, an anonymous news brief in the *Philadelphia Daily News* was titled, "15 Arrested after Puerto Rican Day Parade."[51] With trouble came the identification of the parade and its ethnic character as Puerto Rican, despite the various ethnicities represented at the parade and in the week's festivities. According to the newspaper, a crowd gathered at Fifth and Indiana streets after the parade and threw bottles at police officers posted in the neighborhood to ensure peace: "Cops said about 15 people were arrested and may be charged with offenses such as assault or drunk and disorderly behavior."[52] These troubles do not match those of the mid- to late 1990s, when reports of gunshots, violence, and general chaos dominated the headlines.[53]

In 2004, newspaper coverage again turned positive. "A Banner Day for

Puerto Rico" read the headline of one *Philadelphia Daily News* story, which went on to extol the civic contributions of the Puerto Rican community, the beauty of the culture, and the positive energy of the crowd.[54] Governor (and former mayor) Edward Rendell, Mayor Street, and Pennsylvania Secretary of State Pedro Cortes were among those marching up the parkway. The article suggested that the Puerto Rican community had matured, that it felt less of a need to drape the Puerto Rican flag everywhere. Jose Torres, who moved from Puerto Rico to Philadelphia in 1989, remembered how, when he first started attending the parade many years ago, he always carried a Puerto Rican flag and wore its colors. Things were different now. " 'My flag is in here,' Torres said, smiling and tapping his chest. 'In my heart.' "[55]

In 2004, changes in the Latino population also dominated coverage of the parade. A *Daily News* article titled "Puerto Rican Party on the Parkway: Parade Welcomes All Latinos" began by distinguishing the parade of 2004 from the parade of past generations: "This is NOT your parents' Puerto Rican Day parade."[56] The reporter sustained the theme by emphasizing how the city's Latino population had diversified and how that diversity had been incorporated in the parade's repertoire: "Besides watching performers play traditional salsa music, paradegoers will hear guitar rhythms of *bachata* from the Dominican Republic and *banda*, modern Mexican music currently popular in the southwest, say organizers." The changes in the population were notable, as immigrants from Mexico, Guatemala, Peru, Venezuela, Colombia, the Dominican Republic, and other Latin American countries had arrived in Philadelphia in ever larger numbers: "For instance, the Guatemalan population grew 510 percent from 1990 to 2000, according to U.S. Census figures. Dominicans saw a 250 percent spike during the same period." The reporter went on to quote Telemundo personality Maria Del Pilar, the parade's grand marshal, as saying, "Puerto Rico is the heart of Latin America"—reconciling the name of the parade with the diverse populations the parade now represents.[57]

As much as the article emphasized the diversity of the Latino population and its ability to borrow from non-Latino traditions, it also highlighted the boundaries illustrated by the different types of music played during the procession. Hip-hop represented a departure from the traditional music of Latin America, the Caribbean, and Spain; moreover, hip-hop had come to symbolize urban African Americans living in violent circumstances. The organizers' observation that hip-hop would not dominate the music of the parade may be viewed as an attempt to distance themselves from African Americans, who were largely seen as occupying segregated neighborhoods and as not being fully incorporated into American society.

THE CODE OF THE NEIGHBORHOOD

The newspaper reports code Latinos as troublemaking, destructive, conflictual, or chaotic as well as problem solving, contributing to society, and possessing a civic spirit.[58] The binary codes correlate with a general notion that Philadelphia's Latino community is either successfully or unsuccessfully incorporating itself into American society. In *Immigrant America*, sociologists Alejandro Portes and Rubén Rumbaut observe that immigrant groups incorporate into American society in three ways: they assimilate upward, making achievements in education and employment that rival those of native-born (white) Americans; they become selectively acculturated, keeping some parts of their culture that help them navigate American society and thereby make achievements in education and employment that are similar to their white American counterparts; or they assimilate downward, sometimes joining an oppositional subculture, as they reject mainstream norms and fail to make the same achievements in education and employment that native-born Americans do. Underlying these modes of incorporation into society is a set of interlinked codes. While Puerto Ricans are not immigrants per se, they inhabit a neighborhood with other Hispanic American citizens who have migrated to the barrio along with other Latinos who have immigrated from the Dominican Republic, Cuba, Mexico, and other parts of the Caribbean and Central and South America. To say that a group has assimilated upward or that it has successfully engaged in selective acculturation is to say that it has a civic spirit, that it is focused on problem solving rather than on whining, that it contributes to society, and that it is peaceful and law-abiding. A downward-assimilating group is full of antisocial troublemakers who destroy private and public property, break the law, and generate chaos; they are the "street" elements in the neighborhood pitted against those who are "decent"[59] (see table 7).

The Puerto Rican Day Parade is a useful model for illustrating the background representations that permeate mainstream understandings of an ethnic group. The central format of the parade does not vary over time, and the participant roles (marshals, chairperson, invited dignitaries, and congregants) remain stable, even though the individuals occupying those roles differ from one year to the next. For the parade to function as a yearly ritual, it has to be regarded as such by socially sanctioned bodies such as mainstream newspapers. Viewers and participants who uphold the parade represent the sacred (that is, civil society), and those who threaten it represent the profane. Newspaper coverage of the Puerto Rican Day Parade legitimizes myths about members of the ethnic group—how civic-minded

TABLE 7. Latino Neighborhood Codes Embedded in Philadelphia Newspaper Reports about the Puerto Rican Day Parade

Upward Assimilation (Sacred)	Downward Assimilation (Profane)
Civic spirit	Antisocial
Problem solving	Troublemaking
Contributing	Destroying
Law-abiding	Lawbreaking
Decent	Street
Consensual	Conflictual
Peaceful	Chaotic
Incorporated	Isolated

they are, whether they tend to be problem solvers or troublemakers, and whether they arrive on America's shores ready to struggle with an unrelenting work ethic or instead are bent on welfare dependency, violence, and destruction. These ritual codes emerge in the *Philadelphia Inquirer* and the *Philadelphia Daily News* at different time periods. The codes depicting Puerto Ricans and other Latinos as contributing to society can be found in the 1980s and then again starting in 2001 but are notably absent in the mid- to late 1990s. Likewise, the codes depicting Puerto Ricans and other Latinos as destructive and as troublemakers gain traction in the 1990s.[60]

CULTURAL CONSTRAINTS REVISITED

As suggested above, public rituals such as the Puerto Rican Day Parade underscore societal understandings of who the Latinos are and what type of place it is that they inhabit. These perceptions do not result simply from community leaders' attempts to manage newspaper coverage of the event. Certainly there are discussions among Latino leaders and community members about ways to combat stereotypes and make a favorable impression on outsiders, but the Latino leadership does not always agree on a general public relations strategy or on what specific cultural or political activities are appropriate for the parade. Among reporters covering the parade for the *Philadelphia Inquirer* and the *Philadelphia Daily News*, there seems to be no clear set of material or political interests in portraying the parade, the Latino population, or the city's barrio in a positive or negative light.

Because the newspaper outlets describe the parade by highlighting some but not all of its floats, in these descriptions one can find the background beliefs that make the Latino community visible to others while affirming its own collective identity. These background beliefs form the cultural structure that enables some assumptions about the Latino community to be taken for granted but not others.

The newspaper coverage before and after the Puerto Rican Day Parade depicts not only the ceremonial procession but also the neighborhood where many of its participants reside. Since the 1960s, Puerto Ricans and other Latinos have been marching in the parade to send messages to the members of their ethnic group about civic participation, the importance of a strong work ethic, and the consequences of confronting stereotypes in society. At the same time, they send messages to the American public that Latinos make valuable contributions to society and that the neighborhoods inhabited by Latinos are (or can become) "good" places.

7 » Redemption and Revitalization in the Barrio

A Tentative Conclusion

It is difficult to convey the yearning for racial redemption felt by many people of color in the United States, but it needs to be understood if efforts to rebrand ethnic neighborhoods are to succeed. In *The Fire Next Time,* James Baldwin celebrated the centennial of the Emancipation Proclamation and envisioned a day when the dungeon of racism would shake and its chains fall away. To think about redemption in the context of the Philadelphia barrio is to imagine the neighborhood as salvageable, as capable of paying its debts for past sins and as eager to sin no more. Redemption looks inward and backward to a clean core and a better time, a paradise lost with the possibility of being regained. A neighborhood becomes redeemed through ritual cleansing: the gathering of visual symbols, the defense of things sacred, the erection of barriers against things profane. The redeemed declare their land worthy of praise and reject the notion that their home is polluted or polluting.

In their appeals for redemption, Puerto Ricans and other Latinos in Philadelphia have sung various versions of Willie Perdomo's poem "Nigger-Reecan Blues." The barrio residents experience how a highly segregated neighborhood inflicts upon them both "the young Black man's fight" as well as "the old white man's burden." People from outside of the barrio ask, "What are they?" But *the barrio residents* are not expected to speak for themselves in their own terms. They have to fit the definitions of the situation that place them at a disadvantage in the commercial and political marketplace. What the "black ghetto" has meant in the urban ethnographies of researchers and the popular press provides the terms for debate. If you protest these terms, you probably won't be heard; and if you are heard, most of your concerns will be occluded in the public's memory.

In the language of revitalization, the material conditions of the neighborhood form the basis for how it is perceived and how it will progress. Community development corporations typically focus on infrastructure, sidewalks, trash removal, storefront improvements, streetlights, police presence, and safety, all in the belief that fixing material problems will counter the stigma that hampers investment in the barrio. According to this view, the stigma itself results from the objective problems of drugs, violent crime, and the visible deterioration of the housing stock, and the work that impression managers engage in is simply one of trying to change widespread negative assessments about the neighborhood by focusing on actual positive activities. These positive and negative evaluations are objective qualities seen by any reasonable people willing to look without bias.

For the revitalizers, our focus on the sacred and the profane may seem misplaced. What use would religious terms have in a study of the arts, branding, and neighborhood transformation? And why would the characteristics of a population (high poverty, highly ethnic concentration, high crime) be conflated with the characteristics of a place (dirty, unattractive, unsafe)? We sometimes forget that poverty in the United States has more than material qualities. As we saw in chapter 6, newspapers portray the barrio's troubles as intractable and as somehow inherent in the character of the people and the place they inhabit. The violence and drug abuse afflicting the barrio are not simply negative characteristics but indications of how polluted the neighborhood is and how polluting the neighborhood might be for other areas in the city. Newspaper reports of a "crime epidemic" in Philadelphia portrayed it as an infection from the Badlands spreading across the city. A fatal overdose of the prescription painkiller OxyContin that happened outside the barrio was greeted with surprise, as something more likely to have occurred in the Badlands. The barrio provides the negative reference point against which good places are judged. The challenge is to take the community's ethnic identity and to transform it into a positive symbolic resource enabling redemption and revitalization.

PAYING FOR ETHNIC AUTHENTICITY

Ethnicity sells. Ask anyone in Little Italy, New York, during the Feast of San Gennaro, or in Chinatown, Philadelphia, during the Chinese New Year, or in Thai Town, Los Angeles, during Songkran (the Thai New Year). Holidays and festivals from the "home country" signal periods of gift giving, ritual purchases, and performances among a core ethnic group. People from outside of the core group use the visible presence of core group members as evidence of the event's authenticity. It is, after all, how one certifies a "good" Chinese restaurant—lots of "Chinese-looking" families eating there, some ordering their food in Chinese. Similarly, festivals and parades organized and attended by large swaths of a core ethnic population indicate that these events are not staged for tourists but are done for and by the ethnic community. These signals help to sell these events as authentic—worth the time and money it takes to mount them. As tourists and others from outside of an ethnic community shop in the neighborhood's stores, eat in its restaurants, view its art exhibits, and watch its local performers, they are buying into the cultural specificity of the event.

What sells must also cost. The "ethnic look" requires costumes, instruments, performance fees, and transportation for performers; food for receptions; rental of stage equipment; and posters, banners, and radio and newspaper announcements. Moreover, the ethnic look cannot be accomplished through the commercial interchange alone. It must be performed, and for it to be performed well, it is usually rehearsed. Rehearsals happen formally and informally, and in both cases the performers must pay attention to how they wear their costumes along with the attitudes they project. Informal rehearsals abound as young people learn about their culture by participating in local festivals and in impromptu dances on the sidewalk or spontaneous bursts of song at an art exhibition. These behaviors are then recognized as out of the ordinary and attributed to culture—what it means to be Latino, Puerto Rican, Cuban, Dominican, Mexican, or otherwise ethnic.

Beneath the costs in coin and time there is the price of performance. The performance of ethnicity at once bolsters and contests what W. E. B. DuBois refers to as the "wages of whiteness."[1] By this he means the unearned "income" of race or ethnicity found in the deference given by virtue of a person's race or ethnicity, the comfort of knowing that no matter how bad one's situation might get, it would not surpass the low regard held for African Americans (due to slavery) or other minorities (due to colonial exploitation), and that real material privileges accrue by virtue of one's whiteness and that these privileges take the form of having access to education and having one's group dominate societal institutions such as the courts and the police force. The "worst" city neighborhoods are usually Black or Latino, and even white sections of the city experiencing high drug use and high crime rates are not labeled as the lowest of the low. While this "ethnic deficit" robs ethnic individuals of privilege in the general economy, it generates income for them in niche markets. In the niche, consumers want a taste of the ethnic, even (or especially) when it is spiked with danger.[2]

Ethnic authenticity (indeed, authenticity of any kind) places its object on a pedestal while tethering it to the post. Anthropologist Michael Herzfeld uses the metaphors of pedestal and post in The Body Impolitic to emphasize the multiple outcomes stemming from authenticity claims. By being placed on a pedestal, an authentic art form falls under the protection of official institutions and local people informally serving as enforcers of tradition. In "Rethinking Globalization," sociologist George Ritzer describes how these institutions and individuals sometimes reject attempts to modify art for the sake of commercial profit. Hence, art and culture organizations could refuse to accept funds with strings attached that would require them to dilute their cultural programs, and business owners as well as other artists and individuals within the community are willing to contribute money and other resources to support local production of art exhibits, community-wide cultural festivals, and dance performances. Ritzer warns, however, that these guardians of authenticity would be vulnerable to the threat of financial ruin or the political manipulation of wealthy real estate developers because power imbalances still matter for the arts as for other realms of social life. Good intentions do not always prevail in a capitalist economy.

At times, the protectors of authenticity can prevail too much, tethering the art to the post and denying people within ethnic (or indigenous) communities the right to forge their own destinies. It is sometimes forgotten that innovation can occur from within a community for its own sake and not just out of concern for capitalist consumers. When "indigenous" people modify their ritual practices or alter their art forms, their actions are not necessarily intended to satisfy non-indigenous consumers. Rituals and art forms can become obsolete or simply fail to gain appeal; therefore, the producers of these rituals and art forms have to choose between change (becoming "inauthentic") or death (becoming nonexistent). In *Capitalism, Socialism, and Democracy*, economist Joseph Schumpeter refers to this market force as the gale of creative destruction, requiring the destruction of the obsolete but the creation of something better in its place. The new practices, rituals, and objects, however, may be unrecognizable to the people who ought to believe in them most.

The social performance of authenticity depends on the actors' belief in the parts they are playing. This presents a quandary for policy makers and community development practitioners trying to turn the ethnic identity of their neighborhood into a marketable resource. To the extent that people believe in the parts that they are playing, they may consider themselves not as actors enacting a script but as idiosyncratic individuals who happen to love "Latino" food, music, and arts. They are not engaged in a "con game," duping cultural tourists or anyone else into believing their authenticity. Their lives, it may be said, are filled with "contradictions"—disagreements over what the most important priorities of the community are and how the community's collective cultural identity ought to be represented.

The more engaged people within the community are in deciding how they will be represented, the more their image suffers as a people prone to conflict. As they try to sell their identity both to themselves and to others, they pay what DuBois describes as the psychological price of being forced to see themselves through the eyes of mainstream white society because their own particular visions of authenticity are considered too close to the object of interest to obtain objective focus.

BEING FOR SALE WITHOUT SELLING OUT

It would be a mistake to equate the marketing of authenticity with the unadulterated commodification of culture. Not only have we seen debates waged over what is and is not an appropriate presentation of culture and what the limits of commercialization should be (chapters 2 and 3); we have also encountered transgressive artists such as Dan One, the graffiti writer. In his conversation with me, he lamented the mercenary tendencies of some graffiti writers, who were willing to "sell out" to the highest bidder in order "to make paper" (to earn money). When approached by another graffiti writer to participate in painting an image on a car for a dealership, Dan One initially hesitated. "I feel like yo, my name—not just my name—my efforts are not just to promote this company," he explained. "So I told him, 'Okay, we're gonna do this gig, right; we're gonna paint this car, but we're going to paint an oil field with a whole bunch of dead people and skulls on the bottom. How's that?'" Dan One takes satisfaction in demonstrating to those trying to pimp artists that they too are being pimped. Artistic license becomes a weapon for the economically weak.

He especially likes engaging in subversive work. For example, rather than deny his services to a local slumlord who requested that one of his store facades be painted, Dan One consented with impish enthusiasm.

Dan One: Some slumlord wants me to paint his store, so I say, "Okay. I'm gonna paint your store. Let's try to do something that I know is gonna [have] an impact." And the owner goes out and he's like, "It's beautiful. It's beautiful. You know, you got that woman there in the fields collecting." And I'm like, "Yeah, yeah, okay."

Author: And what kind of message would the woman in the field be for you?

Dan One: Well, I'm trying to play the stereotype that women are always put in the field and the men are supposed to be the so-called commanders. But then I flip it around; you know what I mean? I'll do women in the field, but they'll have jeans and a male appeal [appearance]. And my lesbian following will be like,

"That shit was hot 'cause I know what you was doing with that." And I'm like, "Yeah!" See I slip little things in there, you know what I mean?

For the common people, they say, that's nice; that's pretty. But artistically—and remember the art is really telling some story—I'm very strategic when I do my art. [But outsiders don't get it. They look at my work and say things like,] "Oh, it's pretty—a whole bunch of colors." It's just graffiti for them. But they don't know the symbolism behind it, what the colors mean, and I think that's why these art critics say, "It's dangerous." It's because they know the power to be unregulated, free, uncontainable. You can't stop it.

For Dan One and other artists, art and commerce need not occupy separate, hostile worlds, although sometimes they do. And artists need not "sell out," even when necessity requires that they make money so that they can pay their bills. The performers are playful and pragmatic, value rational and aesthetically passionate.

IMPLICATIONS FOR PUBLIC POLICY

The price of authenticity runs to an extreme when it sows the seeds of a neighborhood's destruction. The story told by Sharon Zukin is a familiar one:[3] as a neighborhood near the center of the city becomes more attractive to people with higher incomes, they begin to frequent the neighborhood's businesses and purchase properties. As the demand for real estate within the community increases, so too does the price of the existing stock of real estate and the property taxes. The increase in property taxes and in the cost of materials to maintain those properties forces poorer residents to leave the community for cheaper, less desirable homes in neighborhoods farther away from the city's center. The only policy response that community development corporations have developed is to buy properties while they are still cheap and to sell or lease these properties at below-market prices to people who have long lived in the community. This piecemeal strategy cannot effect widespread protection, but it may be the only recourse for neighborhoods experiencing gentrification.

Public policies promoting cultural tourism and cultural industries in particular neighborhoods must contend with the challenges of deciding what representations of an ethnic neighborhood qualify as authentic and of controlling what representations are in the public domain. Consumers from outside the neighborhood may easily conflate "authentic" with stereotypical attributes. If content and control over its representation are both locally held, authenticity is high. If content is local but control is not, authenticity can wane, unless there is a strong commitment to the maintenance of local content even when this commitment does not prove financially profitable. "Real" culture for the masses comes from within the individual. Too much orchestration indicates too much artifice; therefore, the greater the autonomy of the performers, the more authentic the performance.[4] In the case of highbrow cultural representations, the emphasis is on expertise and the protection of fixed, externally recognized cultural assets.[5] This is the traditional museum model of protecting local, unique representations using a curatorial apparatus.

Foundations that apply a museum model to local art institutions obtain mixed results. In an attempt to "upgrade" cultural offerings, image consultants sometimes employ templates meant to apply generally to all urban neighborhoods participating in cultural tourism. The Greater Philadelphia Tourism Marketing Corporation tries to pay attention to context and to use the particular conditions and histories of neighborhoods as their selling points. But some foundations have refused to fund art exhibitions, performances, and programs that are not "innovative enough," applying a standard of innovation developed at headquarters without regard for the various (underserved) constituencies and other audiences the local arts organizations cater to. For community members participating in branding efforts, the context-specific approach outshines the generic one.

In *How Brands Become Icons*, sociologist and marketing specialist Douglas Holt helps us understand why paying attention to local histories and to the symbols that motivate "insiders" affects branding efforts. Insiders are not unthinkingly carrying out the marketers' plans; they are responding to their own needs for solidarity, self-esteem, and affirmation. The need for affirmation changes as individuals within a group experience what Holt calls "cultural disruptions"—periods of time when they are collectively treated as dangerous to the public good because the coherent identity of the nation seems under threat by their increasing presence. Cultural disruptions are especially acute for Latinos because some politicians view them as not interested in assimilating or, if interested, not capable; hence, their very presence in large numbers can be taken as superficial evidence that American civil society is somehow under threat.

Urban Latino communities with concentrated levels of poverty are seen as threatening and undesirable. To the extent that a Latino neighborhood (or any neighborhood, for that matter) suffers from stigma, it cannot be branded in any way a marketer pleases. In *Stigma*, sociologist Erving Goffman observes that the way stigma is managed depends on whether a community has a discredited identity or a discreditable identity. One with a discredited identity is marked with stigma, and those who come into contact with it readily recognize the shame. This community has two courses of action available: it can isolate itself to avoid rejection or it can acknowledge the stigma, placing the stigma into context and downplaying its detrimental effects by emphasizing its universality along with its historical uniqueness.[6] The Philadelphia barrio has a discredited identity and has largely pursued the second course of action.

If a community is merely discreditable, the stigma is ambiguous or not easily detected. With a disciplined message machine, the stigma can be marketed away through the use of a covering strategy to conceal embarrassing things. Such an approach does not work in places like the Philadelphia barrio, though marketing firms elsewhere have tried to pass over the more unpleasant aspects of a neighborhood's history in an effort to comfort tourists on their way to "the ghetto."[7] Marketers and community development practitioners who acknowledge the stigma and who differentiate the discredited versus discreditable status of the community's identity will be better able to manage the stigma. And marketers and community development practitioners who appreciate and work with the cultural structure in which the neighborhood is embedded will be better able to use arts and culture to transform ethnic neighborhoods.

IMPLICATIONS FOR URBAN STUDIES

Urban studies that take culture into account typically investigate the political and material conditions that make cultural production possible. Had this been my approach, I would have devoted much more space to the gatekeepers at the various foundations funding cultural work, the political agendas of elected representatives, and the economic concerns of business and real estate owners as well as community development corporations. But rather than explore the abode of material interests, I delved into the abode of ideal interests. Symbols and social texts matter both to those trying to deploy them for the sake of economic profits and to those deploying them out of convention, habit, and as an emotional expression of their identity.

For some hard-core structuralists, perhaps my approach to studying the arts and culture in the barrio needlessly puts social structure and political power to one side. A close reading of the ethnography, however, reveals how those structures of power appear in context. I try not to assume the privileged voice of the social scientist floating above the scene and above the people I am studying in order to render an "objective" assessment of how they are working against their own interests or how they are participating in a neoliberal project that transforms culture and daily life into resources that can be exploited in a commercial market. That stance has been taken;

those proclamations made. What is less common is a serious engagement with the cultural structure as it appears in urban settings.

In this book I demonstrate how the narratives people tell about a place (the narrative frames) render it worthy (or not) of intervention by local activists and business owners and how such narratives justify what kinds of investment make sense there. Navigating between the cultural and social structure of the neighborhood helps explain how the narrative frames emerge, what relationship the civil society (ritual) codes in the larger cultural structure have to the frames, and how closely the frames are correlated with the economic behaviors of business owners.

As we saw in chapter 4, the narrative frames are indeed closely correlated with what business owners and community leaders do. Those who see the neighborhood as golden and as capable of shining again profess their predictions that an investment in the community is likely to pay off. Those who see the gold as tainted or who see nothing golden at all are careful not to sink their money into a hole. These local frames do not operate in a vacuum but are associated with larger societal frames about the civil and uncivil segments of society.

A neighborhood becomes constructed as good or bad, but the process of construction is subject to constraints not fully known even to the inhabitants. Although the cultural structure is largely invisible to individuals, it becomes inculcated during public ceremonies. Applying Emile Durkheim's analysis from *The Elementary Forms of Religious Life* to public ceremonies, we see that the ceremonies represent "a system of ideas by means of which individuals imagine the society of which they are members and the obscure yet intimate relations they have with it."[8] Collective beliefs enter into and become organized within the minds of individuals during these focused gatherings, and socially inculcated impulses are "amplified each time [they are] echoed, like an avalanche that grows as it goes along."[9] And these impulses enable individuals to distinguish between the sacred and the profane, the good neighborhood and the bad.

Our cultural analysis of market dynamics in the ethnic enclave suggests fruitful lines of inquiry for comparative analyses of ethnic enclaves and ethnic economies in cities making "the cultural turn" to cultural tourism and the promotion of local cultural industries. Do branding strategies differ between ethnic enclaves and ethnic economies? In other words, do the branding roles and the attention to group boundaries and bonds differ in locales with geographically dispersed ethnic enterprises owned by individuals from various groups compared with locales with geographically concentrated enterprises owned largely by members of the same ethnic group? When is there more or less local control in branding events? How does the history of different racial and ethnic groups affect the resonance of different branding events? Intra- and intercity comparisons will offer more general propositions for how ethnic branding differs in different social spaces and for understanding how branding might strengthen or further weaken economic opportunities in postindustrial cities. The interactive theoretical model presented here pushes us beyond polemic to close empirical observation of the processes of representation and how audience responses shape these representations in the urban ethnic marketplace.

SEEING NEW OPPORTUNITIES

James Baldwin wrote essays about the relational aspects of identity, with "black" being circumscribed by "white," and he participated in panels on racial progress and equality where he emphasized that different experiences lead to different ways of seeing and remembering. Sociologist Stephen Steinberg recounts a 1964 symposium titled "Liberalism and the Negro," in which Baldwin along with Nathan Glazer, Sidney Hook, and Gunnar Myrdal were invited to speak.[10] Baldwin argued that how much racial progress one believes that America has made depends on what one's direct experience with racial discrimination has been. When Hook asserted that ethical principles in American society had become more widespread, Baldwin was incredulous. "What strikes me here," he said, "is that you are an American talking about American society, and I am an American talking about American society—both of us very concerned with it—and yet your version of American society is really very difficult for me to recognize. My experience in it has simply not been yours."[11] In his position at the upper rungs of the social ladder, Hook could see progress within close range, whereas Baldwin had a different vantage point by virtue of his position nearer to society's lower rungs.

The people I interviewed about the barrio had different perspectives about how much progress had been made there. By virtue of their position in society, community leaders saw more subtle forms of progress in the neighborhood than those outside of the community, who were wary of its claims to have been transformed. Individuals within the community who are better off because of the more vibrant commercial activities taking place there are more hopeful, of course; their young people are going to college, and their performers are getting high-visibility gigs.

Less optimistic are those who have lost loved ones to gun violence or who have otherwise suffered directly from the drug gangs fighting for turf or from other social maladies like the ones described by journalist Steve Lopez in *Third and Indiana*. Some of these individuals speak with resentment about their lot in life, wanting desperately to leave the Badlands for safer environs. Others wander the streets like zombies, without work, numbed by painkillers illicitly obtained. Such individuals inhabit not only the barrio but also Center City neighborhoods, where their presence does not define the character of the neighborhoods they inhabit.

How outsiders perceive a neighborhood affects how neighborhood residents see themselves. Sociologist Richard Sennett makes this argument in the workplace, observing that an organization's reputation influences the sense of identity its employees have.[12] Analogously, neighborhoods have composite identities that matter to neighborhood residents and spokespersons as they affirm, contest, and alter what it means to be a member of the ethnic enclave. Well-regarded neighborhoods offer a sense of pride; poorly regarded neighborhoods contribute to a sense of shame and a disinclination to invest or to innovate. Indeed, Sennett notes, "You [come] to know about yourself in relation to the frustrations or anger you experience in an *anchored* social reality outside yourself."[13] When one's anchored social reality is a neighborhood with a discredited reputation, one's sense of self either remains on the defensive or acquiesces to what others are likely to say no matter what one does.

The calendar of big events sometimes gives a boost to one's social reality. Latinos, for example, may be the flavor of the month when newspaper articles about Hispanic Heritage Month shine a spotlight on the neighborhood, but they may be forgotten for the rest of the year. They know that they do not have the material resources to sustain a presence in the broader public eye, so there are no page spreads in the newspaper reminding consumers elsewhere of the wonders of the barrio. A tourist visiting Philadelphia would probably venture into Chinatown and Little Italy but not the Centro de Oro. There is still hope that this uneasy blend of social invisibility and antisocial visibility will yield to a burgeoning market demand for authentic ethnic culture, even for those cultures with "discredited," stigmatized populations.

As late as 2006, the *Philadelphia Weekly* featured an article by Steve Volk titled "Third and Indiana: Get Yer Crack Right Here, Same as Back in the Day." Volk described drug dealers "swarming" around cars like flies to shit, as these vehicles stop at Third or Fourth Street and Indiana Avenue. He mourned the demise of Operation Sunrise, in which the police cordoned off the neighborhood as if it were a war zone. He writes, "The Badlands, which include the lower reaches of Indiana Avenue, have long been some of the city's most notorious streets—a place where an addict can pick up crack or heroin with the ease of picking up fresh vegetables in the Italian Market."[14] What happens in the Badlands is the opposite of what happens in

Little Italy or other "credible" (and credited) areas of the city, if such newspaper reports are to be believed.

A GENUINE ACT OR A MINSTREL SHOW?

What is to be believed about the barrio's character or about the attributes of its ethnic identity? The "performance" of an ethnic identity does not begin and end with an art exhibit, concert, or parade but is continuously negotiated and accomplished. Business owners stage "ethnic-looking" storefronts or target their advertisement to a specific ethnic clientele. Newsletters, posters, and restaurant menus are bilingual. Poems on public murals come from Puerto Rican, Caribbean, Mexican, or other South American writers. The smell of cooking food that wafts out the doors of restaurants and from the windows of homes, as well as the music booming from open windows and passing cars, helps mark the neighborhood's ethnic character.

At the same time, the various audiences witnessing the performance of ethnic authenticity participate in its accomplishment. The performance has to be believed by the audience, because the performers feel this belief (or disbelief) and react in turn. Some social scientists are skeptical that the arts could thrive in a place like the barrio. Their doubt stems from memories of what the community was like in the past and from police reports about incidents in the general area that seem to confirm that not much has changed since then. They therefore question whether I have "gone native" and lost my objectivity in reporting what is happening in this community. To this assertion I respond that I have not turned a blind eye to power dynamics, crime, and poverty, but I have not blinded myself to other factors, either.

Concerns about blindness to the varied dimensions of the community are valid. The neighborhood does face a number of challenges, such as violent crime, drug use, and poverty. The fact that this book captures moments in which people are laughing, their hands clapping in applause, their feet stomping on the downbeat and tapping to the upbeat, does not mean that the author has misrepresented the neighborhood residents as minstrels. In "Minstrel Man," Langston Hughes sees the possibility of having recognizable laughter and unrecognized pain in the performance of ethnic identity for outsider audiences:

> Because my mouth
> Is wide with laughter
> And my throat
> Is deep with song,

You do not think
I suffer after
I have held my pain
So long.

If the outlooks of the performers and their acts of resistance (defying what outsider audiences want to see and hear) were not so evident, I would worry that I had become too intent on finding authentic ethnic performances and had ignored the power relations and social conditions constraining my research subjects. But this book does document those who are holding pain—holding pain while painting a mural, stepping to a musical beat, or lifting their voice in song.

All research is partial, aimed at highlighting a small set of factors and processes leading to a narrow range of outcomes. Because prior research and journalistic exposés have already focused on the reasons why "decent" residents of the barrio should be ashamed of what happens in their neighborhood, I have tried to balance this negative discourse with counterattacks made by local residents, business owners, and community leaders. I refer to their cultural performances and revitalization efforts as counterattacks because I recognize that critiques about "what's wrong with the neighborhood" are not isolated, acultural assessments of the positive and negative attributes of a place; rather, these assessments influence what contours the collective identity may take. The material and symbolic attacks and counterattacks shape the rate and course of transformation in Philadelphia's Latino commercial district and the neighborhood it anchors. Only by thinking about stigma and the social performance of neighborhood identities can we begin to understand *what types* of revitalization projects will be evaluated as feasible (or not) and how the different ethnic identities of neighborhoods influence those evaluations. If we recognize these cultural conditions and understand how they are changing, we will begin to see how the dungeon of racism may be made to shake and its chains to fall away.

Telling It Like It Was

Methods and Data

The lines of investigation I pursued to do the research for this book had a great deal to do with the interactions I had in the field.[1] I read letters deposited in the historical archives, unearthed stories in the newspapers, interviewed people in or about the barrio, and observed and participated in events. My ideas developed as I became more involved in the community and its history. My move from Philadelphia to Ann Arbor during the course of my research also affected how I approached the barrio and how people within it responded to me. How my engagements with the community unfolded partly explains the conclusions I reached, yet I am confident that other qualitative researchers studying the same community would not find my conclusions farfetched. With the neighborhood and many of my research subjects identified, my findings can be roughly replicated and my arguments more thoroughly interrogated.

FINDING OUT ABOUT THE PAST

As I attended folklore performances, concerts, and art exhibits in the barrio, sat in on strategy meetings at Raíces, and assisted with grant writing, I became aware of what was significant to the people I was studying. When I asked individuals about how the community had changed over time and what had helped or hindered positive developments, they pointed to events that seemed significant from their perspective. For example, Steve Lopez's book *Third and Indiana* and Ted Koppel's *Nightline* program on the Badlands stood out for many of the people I interviewed as significant because the book and the television program demonstrated the importance of having some control over the narratives told about the place where one lives or works. Could one book or one television program make the community worse off than it already was? Few seemed to be making that claim, exactly. Many of the people I interviewed claimed instead that the book and the television program seemed to matter whenever they talked to outsiders (or even to each other) about *what would be possible* for the barrio. As I visited various historical archives to learn about the barrio's history, I kept in mind this question of what the barrio's leaders envisioned as being possible and how outsiders (government officials, bankers, consultants, and others) responded to these visions of possibility. I also kept my eye open for disagreements over how the community and its commercial district should evolve.

The Historical Society of Pennsylvania houses the Balch Institute for Ethnic Studies (established in 1971), and the Balch Institute contains a rich collection of documents filed under "Latino" and "Puerto Rican." There I found files from several organizations in the barrio, including the Fifth Street Merchants Association, Puerto Rican Week festival organizers, the Spanish Merchants Association, and Concilio.

Though numerous, the organizational files were uneven in quality. Some memoranda had been excluded, and documents from certain months or years were largely missing. The amount of materials deposited also varied by year and by volume. The Fifth Street Merchants Association files covered 1975–1987 and ran only half a foot in length; the Puerto Rican Week Festival files were equally as short and covered 1979–1987. At the other extreme were the Spanish Merchants Association files, which stretched to 120 feet in length and covered 1970–1988.

In the Fifth Street Merchants Association files, I found a number of memoranda about renovations along North Fifth Street as well as problems that needed to be collectively resolved, such as parking and trash collection. I include a few samples here to provide a sense of the variety of materials contained in these archives. (The material is presented verbatim so that the reader has a raw sense of what is in the files.)

5th Street Merchant Association

General Meeting
Tuesday – April 9, 1977
Law Office Building
6:30 p.m.

Minutes

See Attached for those present.

Mr. Dennis Doeti from Architects Workshop displayed the Blue prints for the 2nd phase project.

Phase 2 should begin within 3 months, that is around the end of July or August.

Sidewalk finish would cover a radius of 9 feet around each corner and/or until the end of the business store.

Complain[t]s were given by the merchants on the construction done on phase 1 which not completed as specify on contract.

a) Paint work is peeling off.
b) Cracks on sidewalk.
c) Basement doors not installed properly.

Investigation on the above matter will be looked upon to see what could be done.

There will be a sidewalk sale in the month of June or July. Further detailed information will be available on the next general merchants meeting.

Meeting was adjourn[ed] at 7:30 p.m.[2]

In connection with the memoranda about the merchants' complaints, the archives also contained the reports drafted by the Philadelphia Architects Workshop and sketches of the new themed streetscapes.

A number of letters to and from the city indicate the Latino community's dissatisfaction with the parking facilities in the barrio. The problem of parking shows up in both the 1970s and the 1980s (the time periods covered by the archives). See, for example, the memorandum from the Philadelphia Citywide Development Corporation and the letter that Mayor Frank L. Rizzo's office issued eight days later, both addressed to Candida Gonzalez, president of the Fifth Street Merchant Association, in 1978. First the memo:

PHILADELPHIA CITYWIDE DEVELOPMENT CORPORATION
SUITE 2032 LAND TITLE BUILDING * 100 SOUTH BROAD STREET *
PHILADELPHIA, PA 19110 * (215) 561-6600

MEMO

To: Candida Gonzalez, Fifth Street Merch. Assoc.
       Francisco Morales, Fifth Street Merch. Assoc.
       Jose Danisevich, Fifth Street Merch. Assoc.
       Bill Salas, Spanish Merch. Assoc.
       Ted Thorne, Office of Housing & Community Development

From: Dane Wells, Manager, NCR [Neighborhood Commercial Revitalization]
           Div., Phila., Citywide Development Corp *DW*

Date: May 18, 1978

Subject: <u>Fifth Street Parking Study</u>

This is to confirm our meeting on Thursday, May 25, at 6:30 PM, at Candy's house, 2732 North Fifth Street, to review the parking situation.

At this meeting, we should attempt to accomplish the following:

(1) Review progress to date (by Candy and Bill).
(2) Review the needs for parking, for example:
    a. How many merchants must now park on the street—tying up "customer spots?"
    b. Where are the peak customer traffic areas?
    c. What are the estimates of customer traffic in those areas now—and projected for the future?
    d. What percentage of the customer traffic drives to Fifth Street?
(3) Review possible sites for parking.
(4) Review possible methods for establishing additional parking.

By the end of this meeting, we should know what additional information we need . . . and we should be able to establish a coordinated and well planned working strategy.

Based on last Tuesday's meeting, I would suggest that this group be able to develop a very specific proposal to submit to Councilman Janotti. Due to Bill and Candy's efforts, he is very aware of the need. Many other neighborhoods, however, are also competing for a limited number of parking funds, and it is our assumption that the better the organization and commitment of the Fifth Street proposal, the better your chances for success.

The meeting on the 25th will review the situation and lay the ground work for future action. I suggest that we try to give ourselves a deadline for the completion of the proposal at that meeting.[3]

Now let's take a look at the mayor's letter, which acknowledges the problem of parking in the city generally but does not assume responsibility for solving the particular problem of parking faced by the barrio residents.

CITY OF PHILADELPHIA
Frank L. Rizzo
Mayor

May 26, 1978

Mrs. Candida R. Gonzalez
President
Fifth Street Merchant Association
Post Office Box 18671
Philadelphia, Pennsylvania 19132

Dear Mrs. Gonzalez:
Many thanks for your letter and your kind comments. You may be sure that this Administration will continue to cooperate with you for the betterment of your neighborhood.

I share your concern for the parking facilities of the City of Philadelphia and I have forwarded a copy of your correspondence to Mr. John Andrew Gallery, Director of Housing and Community Development.

You will be hearing from Mr. Gallery directly.
Sincerely,

FRANK L. RIZZO[4]

Other memoranda in the archives cover the issue of parking along with the details of other revitalization projects. These memoranda indicate that the Latino community saw itself as an emerging ethnic corridor in the city and that city officials wanted to treat the Latino commercial corridor like other commercial corridors in the city.

MINUTES OF THE 5TH STREET MERCHANTS ASS'N
July 15, 1981

In Attendance: John Gerasi, Mike Gonzalez, Emilio Nunez, Gualberto Medina, Marta Diaz, Mike Munoz, Nick Hernandez

Clean-Up Campaign: will commence Wednesday, July 22, 1981. Equipment will be sent to 2825 N. 5th Street and the workers will congregate here to coordinate the campaign.

Off-Street Parking: Mr. John Gerasi reported that the only contiguous parcels that the city has immediately available are 2717, 2718, 2721, 2723, and 2725 North Fifth Street. The city will complete this phase of the off-street parking efforts and then develop several other phases in the very near future.

It was agreed by all persons present that it would be best to start generating parking immediately although it may happen on a piecemeal basis. The merchants agreed to assume responsibility for the parking lot and the President of the 5th Street Merchants Association tendered a letter to Mr. Gerasi to this effect.

Small business, Economic and Housing Development conference: John Gerasi will attempt to develop an agenda of speakers for the conference. We will attempt to hold this conference at the library at 6th and Lehigh. Mr. Gerasi will determine whether the library will be available for one evening during the week of September 21, 1981.

Dorado Village: Gualberto Medina announced that the Pennsylvania Housing Finance Agency (PHFA) has a made a commitment to fund this housing project. It will cost approximately $4.5 million to construct the project.[5]

Another memorandum discusses the parking problem as well as the potential designation of the North Fifth Street as a historic district. The basis for and the advantages to being designated a historic district were not apparent to the Latino leadership at the time the memorandum was written. Should the trolley be removed from North Fifth Street to suit the business owners even if its removal might impair the community's ability to be designated a historic area later? (A number of merchants wanted the trolley line removed because the trolley backed up traffic and made the delivery of supplies more problematic because it sometimes got stuck.)

MINUTES OF THE 5TH STREET BUSINESS ASSOCIATION MEETING OF
JUNE 2, 1987

The meeting was held at the HACE Mall, 2921–27 North 5th Street, Suite 109 at 9:00 a.m.
Those in attendance were:
Aura Villalta
Jim Harris
Marta Diaz
Carlos Acosta
Andres Gautier
David Cosme

Also present was:
Tom Almarini

. . .

Marta Diaz expressed having some difficulty understanding why our area would be considered a historic site to which Jim made it a point of clarifying by simply stating that the Trolley car is meant to be preserved (plus, it does not contribute to air pollution).

4. Mrs. Diaz complained about the number of abandoned cars along 5th Street to which Jim promised to write a letter to remove the abandoned cars.
5. Clean-up of Orkney Street is scheduled for this coming weekend, June 6th. Jim suggested that we consider converting the lot which runs from 2945 to 2949 Orkney Street to a Tot-Lot. However, Carlos feels that it should be used for urgently needed parking. Questions and doubts were raised as to people wanting to park there to which Aura and Marta said they would be most willing. Mrs. Villalta suggested that we conduct a survey to get an idea of how area businesspersons, customers and residents feel about parking on Orkney Street.

MINUTES
June, 1987
Page Three

It was also mentioned that 5th & Indiana is a suitable site for public parking— accommodating 28 cars—and that the City should make it possible for us to acquire this lot....

The meeting was adjourned at 10:10 a.m.[6]

In my interview with Max Izaguirre, the dry cleaner, he told me that when he arrived in the barrio, the stone-paved streets grew slick whenever it rained, creating hazardous conditions for pedestrians and delivery people, and trucks often got stuck behind the trolley as it made its way through the narrow passage. City boosters wanted to keep the old streets and the trolley to preserve the character of the neighborhood, but local entrepreneurs wanted to pave over the stones and remove the trolley. As Max told me this story, I recalled the memoranda in the Balch Institute's collection, and I mentioned the discussion I had come across in the Fifth Street Merchants Association files. Max was pleased by this affirmation, and at the end of the interview he showed me some drafts of the gateway to the Fifth Street corridor drawn up by a group of architects. It may be that he had intended to show me the drafts all along or that my awareness of the various plans executed and discussed in the community motivated him to share these with me. In any case, I wanted to express my respect for his time by demonstrating that I had done my homework before coming to the interview.

In addition to the memoranda and letters at the Balch Institute, I took advantage of Taller Puertorriqueño's archives, known as the Eugenio María de Hostos Archives Center at the Free Library of Philadelphia at Sixth and Lehigh. The archives run for about thirty feet and contain an extensive collection of documents, including letters sent by representatives of Taller to local newspapers about how those newspapers were representing Puerto Ricans and other Latinos; other documents include additional newspaper clippings, organizational files, pamphlets, and a set of oral histories titled "Batiendo La Olla" (Stirring the Pot), the latter a bilingual account of the experiences of Puerto Ricans in Philadelphia in the 1970s.

When I talked with Johnny Irizarry, the former executive director of Taller, about the content of this book, Johnny suggested that I include testimony from the Human Relations Commission about how Puerto Ricans and other Latinos were violently ejected from some Philadelphia neighborhoods. Johnny thought that these reports and others contained in the city's archives would give me a firm grounding in the environment of reception for Latinos in Philadelphia. The Urban Archives at Temple University provided further newspaper clippings, including stories about Latino's homes being firebombed in order to persuade them to leave the neighborhood and public debates about Puerto Ricans in particular and Latinos who were perceived to be unaccustomed to "American" standards of cleanliness.

SNOOPING AND HELPING OUT

Interviews with nineteen business owners and another eighteen individuals who were active in the community illustrated some of the different perspectives people have about how the neighborhood is being rebranded.[7] Of course, it is one thing to be told what people think and quite another to see whether their words match their deeds. An invitation to volunteer at Raíces enabled me to observe this and to interact further with the community. As the following sections demonstrate, the interviews I conducted and my work as a volunteer and board member at Raíces took place at all hours of the day and night, and my "research time" could not be easily segregated from my personal time.

The Interviews

It was after 11 on a Monday night when my mobile phone rang. I was preparing my nightly ablutions while staying with dear friends (an artist and a curator) in Old City for a few days. I had returned to Philadelphia to look for a graffiti artist to interview for the book. How could I talk about the graffiti wall in my chapter on the Philadelphia Neighborhood Tour but not include an interview with the creator of the wall? (I thank Mitch Duneier for pointing this out.) Graffiti artists are not listed in the phone book, nor are they to be found in the same place at a regular time each day. How would I find one, especially this one? I sent out some queries to some of the people I interviewed and asked them to pass my information along to a graffiti artist who might be willing to be interviewed for the project. Fortunately, Gil González replied, saying that he had been in touch with Dan One about me and had told Dan One that I am "a brother" with good politics, so it was cool to talk to me. Gil couldn't guarantee anything, but Dan seemed interested. (Michigan's Institutional Review Board for the Protection of Human Subjects did not permit ethnographers to contact people directly through chain referrals. Instead, we were expected to have our information passed along to potential respondents who have to contact us first. These requirements made it even less likely that a hard-to-reach person might actually be reached, so I was worried that he might not call.)

Then the phone rang. "Is now a cool time to talk?" Dan One asked. Of course, the answer was yes. I stumbled around my friend's living room and dug into my computer bag to find my tape recorder. Ever mindful of the Institutional Review Board restrictions, I interrupted Dan to tell him that I would like to record our brief conversation and to give an abbreviated description of the consent form for participation in the study. "I know. I know. I know," Dan One replied, somewhat impatiently. "Can you meet tomorrow afternoon?" he asked. I told him that I was flying out in the afternoon but could return in a few weeks.

I worried that I might miss Dan One completely and thought briefly about changing my return flight (at great expense), but I realized that I would soon be back on the East Coast. In a few weeks I had a meeting at the National Science Foundation down in Washington, D.C., and had deliberately left some extra days free at the end of the meeting before scheduling my return to Ann Arbor. (As an ethnographer living away from my field site, I had to remain vigilant about creating unstructured periods of time when research subjects might be available to meet with me.) While at the NSF meeting, I confirmed with Dan One the day and time he was available and boarded an early morning Amtrak train so that I could arrive at his girlfriend's house in South Philly by noon. We talked for about three hours before he escorted me to the city bus that would get me back (via the metro) to the Amtrak station. He was hard to reach because of the uncertain legality of graffiti art; other people I interviewed were hard to reach for different reasons.

I wanted to interview the business owners at their businesses so that I could see what types of people were coming in to make purchases and how the business owners interacted with their customers. Many of the business owners I interviewed, especially those participating in the neighborhood's revitalization efforts, found themselves stretched thin, so when they needed to reschedule appointments, it was usually their meeting with me that got moved. I understood and encouraged this behavior because I could not guarantee that my writing a book about their struggles would benefit them materially, and I stressed this at the outset. I usually met them for the first time in their place of business, told them about the research project, and asked for a time when I might return to conduct an interview. In some instances, business owners would say that they had time right then, so long as I did not mind being interrupted. I immediately took them up on the offer, not wanting to lose an opportunity that might be hard to come by later, particularly after I moved to Ann Arbor. I stood while conducting an interview if the business owner was standing behind a counter or reshelving items while talking with me. On some occasions I brought coffee and pastries to an interview as a sign of appreciation, particularly when I knew that I would be spending some time with members of the staff as well.

While in Michigan, I managed to obtain a cash fund to pay people forty dollars for participating in the study. I did this as a way to express my thanks for their time. Often people felt uncomfortable taking the money from me, given that I was writing a book about their community, and sometimes they only took the money after I assured them that the money was not coming out of my pocket but was coming from the university. At other times, they allowed me to simply leave the money with the organization where they worked to help with an upcoming children's program. When the cash fund ran out, I sometimes used my savings to offer cash payments to interviewees, but the limited funds available prevented me from retrospectively paying all the people I had interviewed over the two years I lived in Philadelphia.

Some of the interviews I conducted could be completed on the appointed day, though not always at the appointed hour. Small-business owners have to fill the gaps when workers do not show up or customers have urgent needs. Pete Varona, the beer distributor, told me that the demands of running his business sometimes caused him to miss doctor's appointments and other important meetings. Even as Pete apologized for not being able to meet with me until two hours later than scheduled, he also impressed upon me how this was not a situation of his own choosing. On days when I was planning to meet with a business owner, I did not schedule more than one conversation in a four-hour period because I recognized the need to be flexible. I also prepared for numerous interruptions depending on the time of day and the day of the week, and I knew that when I started an interview or an informal conversation with one individual, I might be easily pulled into a conversation with several other people with lots to tell me. Were I to keep my eye on my watch, I might interrupt the flow of our conversations and, worse, offend those who were being generous with their time.

There were certain periods in which interviewing anyone was nearly impossible, such as the Feria del Barrio, the events of Hispanic Heritage Month (including the Puerto Rican Day Parade), and religious holidays. There were also moments when big deals were being negotiated. For example, after Rey Pastrana was freed from prison, I went back to Philadelphia to meet him. He was eager to tell his story, but he warned me that he was busy working with Congreso de Latinos Unidos on a deal for a school and had some other issues that had arisen with some of his businesses. He could give me some general time periods that looked open, but he would not know for sure until an hour or so beforehand. With Rey, the third time was the charm: he had hoped that he would have time on a Thursday, but called me that morning to say that it would be impossible, so we could try for Friday; on Friday I went to his restaurant, Isla Verde, at the Plaza Americana, hoping that he might have an opening after 3 p.m., but he was waylaid in a meeting with contractors. Finally, Saturday arrived, and although he had to postpone our conversation until later that day, by the time we met at his restaurant it was early evening, and he ordered a bottle of red wine for our table and insisted that I order the best dishes on the menu. I had demonstrated with humility my eagerness to meet with him and to be flexible with his schedule, and he reciprocated with openness and a sumptuous meal. I could have misread his rescheduling as a lack of interest or I could have decided that the interview wasn't worth the wait, but I am glad that I did not misinterpret the fact that the man was busy and was juggling a number of different projects and responsibilities at once.

I knew too much about the history of the community not to include Rey in the book in one form or another. I had tried to interview him back in 2005 while I was living in Philadelphia. I saw him win the award for his contributions to the Latino community at the Feria and had called his office to say that I was writing a book on ethnic entrepreneurship and would like to interview him for it. He seemed exuberant, but warned me that there was a lot happening right then and I should call back in a few weeks when things calmed down. Things didn't calm down. Rey was in some legal trouble, and it looked as if the best I could do was interview the people who knew Rey and cite the newspaper reports quoting him; however, he was released from prison in time for me to include a conversation with him in the book, and one of the book's reviewers insisted that I find him since his story seemed essential to understanding the ways in which the Latino commercial district and the surrounding neighborhood were changing.

I interviewed Rey, along with most of the people in this book, in English. To ensure that language barriers did not prevent some business managers or owners from participating in the study, I translated the consent form into Spanish and offered to conduct the interview in Spanish. I had a few interviewees who looked me up and down and said, "And you can do this in Spanish, too?" To test me they then asked that I explain the study in Spanish to them. This usually resulted in the interviewee smiling broadly and then cutting me off. "Okay. Okay. Pretty good," one guy noted at the end of my spiel. Then he switched the conversation over to English, where it remained for the rest of the interview. In only one case did the respondent choose to speak in Spanish for the entire interview. Maria Acevedo was eighty-eight years old and spoke in a soft voice. I strained to hear her and had my tape recorder on so that I could listen to her responses several times. Fortunately, her grandson was also in the store at the time and stepped in to translate simultaneously without being asked.

Language differences went beyond the mother tongue. Some of the people I interviewed distinguished me from other blacks by virtue of how I spoke. In my early days in the barrio, one of my interviewees said, "You're not from Philly, are you?" After I said that I was from South Carolina, she said, "That makes sense. You're from the South. You don't carry yourself like blacks here in Philly, and you don't talk like them, either." In that same conversation, she asked me where I learned Spanish. After I explained that I'd lived in Costa Rica while working on my first book, she remarked, "That's makes sense, too. You don't talk like Puerto Ricans or Mexicans or Dominicans. I *can* understand you. It's very formal. Very polite." These comments about my language, accent, and demeanor made me cautious about assuming that I could just blend in with the people of the barrio. After I had been in the barrio for a few years, some people assumed that I was Puerto Rican or Dominican and said so—otherwise, why would I be spending so much time there? I also noticed that conversations would switch from English to Spanish to English, sometimes within the same sentence. It was always assumed that I could follow along, and whenever my face grimaced or I scrunched my forehead, someone usually asked if I understood what was just said. If I said that I caught only half of it, the inquiring individual would offer a quick translated summary of the conversation.

Just as the tongue speaks a language, so too do the hips, the wrist, and the neck. The language of the body marks an individual's sexuality, and such markings, no doubt, influenced how I interacted with some of my interviewees. The effect of my body language seemed to matter when I was interviewing a Latino gentleman who told me about a conversation in which some of his colleagues had spoken negatively about some gay guys who had come by their booth. He told his colleagues that money is money, and that they should treat gays like any other consumer. He wanted me to know that he "is cool" with gays and does not hold any prejudices toward anyone. It is not a topic I raised, so I assume that my mannerisms led him to raise it.

Once I remember walking to the Raíces office at Fifth and Somerset. I had parked a block and a half north of it and was walking along the sidewalk in the afternoon, clad in khaki slacks and a blue-and-white checkered shirt with brown leather loafers. I noticed a muscular, dark brown guy who stood about five foot eight with his shirt unbuttoned halfway down his torso. He nodded to me as I walked by and then began walking behind me. His steps kept an even pace with mine and I looked back over my shoulder to see if anyone else was walking with him. He flashed a smile and tilted his head back as if beckoning me. I turned the corner at Somerset. He did too. Then I stopped briefly to survey the traffic before crossing the street so that I could dart into Raíces. He stopped in his tracks just before I made my escape and said, "Umf. Look at that ass." It was a pickup line, for sure. I nodded robotically to acknowledge the comment, then walked with a stiff back and a focused gaze straight to the office door. What I had done to indicate either my gayness or my willingness to be pursued, I cannot say. On another occasion, while I stood at a bus stop in the barrio, two guys slowed their convertible, rolled down their right window, and asked me for directions to a Latino gay bar nearby. Such pickups did not happen often, but they did make me wonder how my demeanor might influence whether people were willing to be interviewed by me. In my experience growing up in South Carolina, I recalled being told that I was not supposed to walk the same way as my twin sister or I would give people "the wrong idea" about who I am. Perhaps I was walking, again, as if I had "sugar in my pants."

Do I always give "the wrong idea," I wondered? I once found myself being accosted by a woman on the steps of the Free Library where Taller's archives are housed. I was standing still, waiting for the library to open, when she approached me and began talking about one of her favorite erotic authors. I responded to her questions with monosyllabic answers in the hope that she would stop asking me if I liked reading erotica and what types of things I liked to do sexually. I did not feel threatened but annoyed. Had I given the impression that I was looking for company or that I would be interested in the type of literature she preferred? Perhaps she wanted to unnerve me, a bespectacled thirty-some guy, wearing blue slacks and a white collared shirt with a black leather satchel over his shoulder. Perhaps she toyed with me for sport. This experience did make me wonder what kind of vibe I gave to people I encountered. Before going into the community, I had hoped that my academic purpose would trump my sexuality and my race, because I feared that these attributes might distract or discourage potential interviewees. After entering the field, I discovered that just being myself, not pretending to be someone I am not, ultimately made me more palatable to the people I interviewed.

I did have a moment when I was not being myself in front of a research subject. I was at Woody's, a Center City gay bar, when I encountered a guy I had interviewed in the barrio. He was with another guy I had seen in the barrio and whom I presumed to be his boyfriend. The research subject seemed to want to make a deeper connection with me as a friend, but I feared that I would annoy his companion and I also feared that he would realize that I had had a few gin and tonics too many. It seemed fine to me to observe him and others "in their natural habitat" even when "they" did unflattering things, but it seemed not so fine to have a person I was studying gaze upon me. That night he told me that sometimes he needed to get away from everything going on in the barrio. I think that he wanted to say more, but with the usual dynamic of the observer and the observed fully overturned, I found myself unable to seize the opportunity to probe for more. I excused myself from the bar, but in retrospect I wish I had been honest with him about my embarrassment and initiated a conversation (however uncomfortable) about his life as a business owner in the barrio who happens to be gay.

Participant-Observation

When I am being observed, probed, or judged, I try to comport myself with dignity and cover what I perceive to be my flaws. I noticed that this was true of many of the people I met in the barrio. It is easy to take a great deal of care in presenting oneself to others for brief episodes and sporadic encounters, but it becomes more difficult to do so when important issues must be faced immediately. I happened to be on the board of Raíces when the organization was looking for a new executive director and when funders were watching closely to see if the organization would survive the leadership transition. I saw how people within and outside of the organization responded to a budget crisis that left the new executive director without salary and health insurance for a number of months.

There was a silver lining with the budget crisis. With so much at stake, my fellow board members were speaking their minds about who they perceived to be their allies and their enemies. I excluded this information from the book because it would have amounted to gossip, but it did help me navigate the social terrain. My vocation as professor gave me some cover and helped me insist on my neutrality, but even with my diplomacy, I am sure that there was an assumption that I was not neutral and therefore needed to be handled carefully for a while, especially by people in competing arts organizations. We were all seeking funds from the same sources, and we all recognized the need to avoid openly competing with one another.

As people in organizations sought funding, they assumed that I might have some good connections to offer through my work at the university or that I would otherwise have valuable knowledge or experience that they might put into practice. I was often asked for advice, and I knew that withholding advice on matters where I had some expertise would be considered needlessly rude. My strategy was to be the last one to speak and to spend my time trying to summarize the positions I heard my interlocutor and others take. I usually ended with my assessment of what the risks were of taking the positions that people had already staked out. This allowed me to demonstrate that I was listening intently and to serve as a sounding board for them. It also kept me from advocating a course of action without regard for the consequences. Had one of my "great ideas" gone wrong, my salary and my ability to pay my bills would remain unaffected. I did not live in the community, and within two years of working in the community I had moved out of state. If those within the community happened to make a mistake, they could at least know that they took the time to figure out what the possible risks were, especially because they still lived in the neighborhood and would see the consequences of their decisions on a daily basis for years to come.

Some of these discussions would have provided the book with a rich context for the decisions that Raíces was making, but I had to withhold any information that I obtained as a board member not meant for public consumption. If I saw something in the meeting minutes that I wanted to include in the book, I waited until I was outside the context of a meeting to ask the executive director to elaborate on it for the book. For example, in the minutes for one meeting, the board discussed how the organization's landlord would have to respond promptly to damage done to the mural on the exterior of the building because Raíces was part of an image makeover for the commercial district. When I had lunch with the executive director a few weeks later, I told her that I thought that particular discussion would be interesting to include in the book. We then talked about it, and I included in chapter 3 what I had learned in our discussion. This strategy enabled me to respect the privacy of the organization and to be transparent in how I was using my position as a board member to advance my book project.

When I attended art or performance events, I saw writers from the Latino newspapers *Impacto* and *Al Día* among the audience. In these events there was no expectation of privacy. Similarly, when I first started attending dress rehearsals, some parents would ask whether I was with the press. Some were disappointed to learn that I wasn't, because they were hoping to have their child featured in a story. My presence at dress rehearsals and at final performances helped me get to know some of the performers casually and to see how some of them would arrive to rehearsals late because they worked far away and traveled by public transportation. They would change clothes, removing their work uniforms to put on costumes. At other times, I would see Yolanda arriving with a van full of young people who had to be collected in different areas of the barrio stretching much farther north than the commercial district. I also saw parents talking to their children, offering moral instruction and making comments to the entire group of parents and onlookers about the importance of arts programs for their children. I saw how people behaved and was able to get them to tell me about events I had observed firsthand: "Remember yesterday, when so-and-so did such-and-such?" or "What's going on right now? I'm a little confused."

GOING BACK AND MAKING IT BETTER

When I attended rehearsals, marched in the parades, and interviewed people individually, I told them that I would come back with a draft of the book for them to comment on before its publication.[8] I had hoped that my return would be mostly celebratory: I would read excerpts; they would comment on them; I would thank them; they would thank me; and I would incorporate their comments into the manuscript. That is not exactly how my revisit went.

After our interview in the summer of 2008, Carmen Febo, the executive director of Taller, offered to host a discussion about my book at Taller the following summer. By the time June 2009 rolled around, I was knee-deep in work with Raíces as the board was undertaking a new strategic plan and as Veronica Castillo-Pérez, the executive director, was focusing on the organization's fiscal health. At the same time, Taller was reeling from budget and reduced staff time, yet Carmen still managed to produce a handsome poster.

Taller had also reduced its hours of operations and would now be closed on Saturdays, except for special events. (My talk was scheduled for a Saturday.) Veronica changed the time of our strategic planning meeting (scheduled the same day!) so that the board could come to my talk. I sensed that I was becoming more trouble than I was worth.

When I arrived at Taller, I immediately looked for Daniel de Jesus but didn't see him. Carmen told me that some people couldn't make it back on this particular Saturday. Then I realized that some of her staff members

Postcard announcing author's presentation at Taller.

would be picking up part-time work to supplement their reduced working hours at Taller.

About twenty people were in attendance, and I was nervous. I opened the talk with an overview of the book and was about to read a passage aloud when I was interrupted.

Carmen Febo: First of all, I'd love to hear some excerpts about the flavor and the language that you're using.

Author: In that case, I'm going to actually read… Yes, and there's a hand back there as well. Yes, sir.

Jesse Bermudez: I want to know if there is some kind of section that addresses the work that has been put together by organizations in respect to the development of the cultural and business district in this area. And I know that [although] you've mentioned quite a bit so far in your conversation, I never heard the name of AMLA surface anywhere in your book. Our organization was the one who set out to create and push this whole issue of how culture builds community, starting way back from when the William Penn Foundation [was] in this area looking at cultural clusters around the entire city. So I think that maybe, you know, things like that need to be included. Also my good friend Wilfredo Gonzalez who has been in this community for a long time, has been a hub for musicians and artists.… So I would really like for you to do a little bit of investigating on that and get some information on that in your book.

(Rumblings of conversation take place, but I cannot make out what people are saying.)

Author: Yes, I'm glad that you brought that up.… One of the difficulties is that I go out and try to find people, and then we play phone tag or sometimes people don't quite get back to me, and AMLA was one of the groups that I really tried hard to get for the book. I didn't get an actual interview but I did pull [from] other sources. . . . In chapter 2 of the book, [about] the [Philadelphia] Neighborhood Tours, Patricia Washington talks about AMLA being her main contact, working with Jesse Bermudez, and that's certainly in the book, and that's how the [Philadelphia] Neighborhood Tours came into [this neighborhood].

Jesse Bermudez: Right. (*He nods his head approvingly.*)

Author: I did try to find someone from AMLA, and it didn't quite happen—

Jesse Bermudez: You found 'em. I'm here. (*Claps his hands on "here."*)

Author: Good. . . . Thank you. I want to put [in] more on AMLA.

Jesse Bermudez: I'll give you a contact number to reach me.

Author: Okay. Then we can do a phone interview so that I can incorporate that into the final book. This is great for me.

Jesse Bermudez: Right.

Author: And I think the Centro [Musical] too.

Jesse Bermudez: You should do more research. Because [there's] a lot going on. . . . You should get more involved in the community, and you would learn a lot more about what we do, to help out the community. I think in the future, you're good, but I think it will make the result much better.

Author: Thank you. Is there anything in particular that you think should definitely be included that you don't think is in here right now? I'm also happy to share some chapters with you. . . .

Wilfredo Gonzalez: Like Jesse Bermudez says, let's get together. . . . We got a lot of organizations, from Concilio all the way down. . . . We have a big number of organizations, but you have to knock on doors.

Author: Yes.

Wilfredo Gonzalez: And once you do that, let's get together. And let's go from there. Taller need[s] help. The whole Latino community need[s] help. And we need people like you to represent us, to make sure you get the right word out there. I think you can do it.

Author: Okay, thank you. Okay, maybe I should give you, let me give you an excerpt from—

Wilfredo Gonzalez: You need homework. . . . OK, you're doing other communities around Philadelphia?

Author: No, I'm just doing this community, the Centro de Oro, but the talk is—

Wilfredo Gonzalez: We're gonna give you plenty of headaches—

(*Lots of laughter in the room*)

Audience member: Oh, no!

Wilfredo Gonzalez: —once you get to know us.

Author: ... One of the difficulties of doing this kind of work as an academic is that there are two very distinct audiences. There's an audience that is less interested in what's going on and much more interested in how this study speaks to other studies.... One of the earlier versions of the draft of this book had a lot of extra things about organizations and things that had to be cut because it wasn't focused enough.... So one of the difficulties is to try to pull together something that is both focused and yet does not do a disservice to groups and voices that are in the community, which is why I'm here many months before the draft of the book is done. And it is also very hard to tell people what is in the book before you've actually written a version of it. Let me read a couple of pages from chapter 2, "Latin Soul, Latin Flavor: Performing the Authenticity of Place":

This chapter explores how people within the community perform the Latin neighborhood's authenticity for tourists. As we see in the case of Philadelphia, although it may be in the interest of local city boosters to portray ethnic neighborhoods as an authentic site ripe for exploration, the city's boosters often find that they are not able to do this in any way that they please. The actors acknowledge their community's past difficulties and some of its current challenges. This community is not a sanitized Disneyland, functioning solely for the pleasure of its paying customers. Instead, we encounter a contingent of actors whose sense of dignity and self-respect is tied into how their community is represented. They want to get into the authenticity game, but they want to do it in a way that respects the community's cultural heritage. This is not to say that money is not a motivating factor. According to Patricia Washington, the initiator of the Philadelphia City Neighborhood Tours and vice president of the Greater Philadelphia Tourism Marketing Corporation, "Tourism was a strategy to replace the manufacturing industry, which in a lot of northeastern cities was disappearing. So our governor, our mayor, our legislature, our city council are all behind this idea of tourism being a replacement industry for the lost manufacturing jobs. So of course, the neighborhoods wanted to get into this. They wanted to benefit also or learn how they could benefit from this multibillion-dollar industry." Discussing how city governments and those in the entertainment industry exploit the blues in Chicago, for example, to stimulate local economic growth, David Grazian critiques the rhetoric of diversity and mul-

ticulturalism that enables the commodification of local cultural traditions....
I'm going to skip through a little bit of this discussion of Grazian.

The initiation of the Neighborhood Tour to the Latino community came
from within the community and happened in part because the initiator, Jesse
Bermudez, the president of AMLA... already had a social relationship with Patricia Washington from her years working with nonprofits. As she tells it, they
wanted to learn from what Chicago had done, but they felt no obligation....
"We realized that there are a lot of similarities between Philadelphia and Chicago... and the lived experiences of the residents could not be ignored for the
sake of the visitors comfort," etc.

Then I describe what happens on a particular [tour] that was led by Joseph Gonzalez, with Bill Salas in attendance. Bill is thoroughly quoted in the first chapter because he talks about community development being a holistic enterprise
in which both the arts and the physical development of the community have
to be taken into account.... When I had trouble finding contacts with AMLA,
I'd find someone who had worked with AMLA to make sure I got AMLA in, and
then I would take a few things from the web that would mention AMLA in other
chapters, etc. So that was the compromise position. One of the things that's difficult is often I end up with not the perfect scenario, but if I have lemons, I will
make lemonade.

Audience: Aha.

Audience member: Right. That's it.

Author: And then hope that someone shows up like today.

(*Audience members applaud and talk among themselves.*)

Wilfredo Gonzalez: Applaudo.

. . .

Author: I'm here until Tuesday morning. I'll be back later in the summer, and if
we have to, we can do it over the phone, even, but I want to make sure that we
get [Jesse's] actual voice....

Carmen Febo: Wilfredo has this music store and this music connection, but his
vision is about that connection and the opportunities here.

Veronica Castillo-Pérez: I think you actually mention Wilfredo and Centro Musical when you speak about my arrival here and how [Centro Musical] was one of
the first businesses that actually donated a guitar to Raíces to do our fund-raiser
when I first got here.

Author: Yes.

Veronica Castillo-Pérez: But in the bigger picture, as Carmen says, it is important.

Jesse Bermudez: To say how long of a period [Wilfredo has] been around and how much he's done. And the fact that his store is a hub. We transmit live radio programs on Saturday, in and out of there. It's a big artists' hub.

Author: And one of the things that I have also with Wilfredo and Centro Musical is in chapter 4 on the businesses, because we had a brief, forty-minute interview, but we talked more about Centro Musical, your experience coming into the neighborhood, so you're certainly there in that particular chapter. You're also talked about in chapter 3, in terms of how business owners are actually making contributions to arts organizations.

Jesse Bermudez: That's real important.

Author (looking from Jesse to Wilfredo): And then you [Wilfredo] show up again because there were some protests. There was a young man who was shot in the back by police, I think. And there was a protest. And your name was in the papers for leading this protest and threatening to bring the parade to a halt.

(Wilfredo looks puzzled.)

Author: Am I remembering well, back in the nineties? I think your name was mentioned there.

Carmen Febo: It may be a different Wilfredo. *(Everyone chimes in at once.)* There's Wilfredo Rojas. Wilfredo Rojas is the activist. It's another Wilfredo.

(At this point in the presentation, I'm horrified: one of the documents I consulted in the Balch Institute's collection named the owner of Centro Musical as Wilfredo Rojas rather than Wilfredo Gonzalez. I am relieved, at the same time, that this mistake was caught before the book's publication.)

Author: Yep, you're right.

Wilfredo Gonzalez: I'm on the business side.

Jesse Bermudez: Wilfredo was a Young Lord, back in the day. That gives you an idea.

Carmen Febo: Not this Wilfredo.

Author: The other Wilfredo.[9]

The session ended much better than it began. I admitted my mistakes and recorded the error that I had made with Wilfredo's last name. I also readily admitted that I should have worked harder to find Jesse Bermudez, but Jesse soon learned that I made efforts to contact him and that I had spoken with a number of other people to get information about him. When we later spoke by phone for an interview, Jesse thanked me for interviewing him and for taking the time to try to get the story right.

I wanted to write a book that people in the community could read about a place that they recognized as home. I also wanted to describe my research methods with honesty because the identity of the researcher (whether it's racial/ethnic, sexual, or class identity or a combination of them all) affects how ethnographic research is undertaken. I am sure that my book remains one-sided—that I captured a small piece of a much larger reality. By telling it like it was, specifying my own ignorance, and making plain how I saw and heard what I did, I hope to enable other researchers to improve upon what I have done.

Notes

CHAPTER ONE

1. Dávila, "Empowered Culture?"; Dávila, *Barrio Dreams*.

2. Harvey, *Spaces of Capital*.

3. See Molotch, "The City as a Growth Machine"; Logan and Molotch, *Urban Fortunes*.

4. Zelizer, *The Purchase of Intimacy*.

5. Logan and Molotch, *Urban Fortunes*.

6. Sociologist Jeffrey Alexander argues that social performances do not rely solely on how adept individuals are at playing their parts; rather, they resonate to the extent that they draw on existing symbols and shared understandings within society. See Alexander, "Cultural Pragmatics."

7. For a discussion of iconic brands, see Holt, *How Brands Become Icons*.

8. See, for example, Rojas, "The Enacted Environment in East Los Angeles."

9. On the power of language, see Bourdieu, *Language and Symbolic Power*.

10. Grazian, "The Production of Popular Music as a Confidence Game."

11. For a discussion of art worlds, see Becker, *Art Worlds*.

12. Similarly, in his study of a Puerto Rican housing project in Boston, Mario Small recognizes that the way an individual sees the neighborhood influences the types of activities she engages in to improve it. See Small, *Villa Victoria*.

13. I do not want to imply that "staging" happens purely in the service of economic and political goals. Personal attachment to a sense of place and to cultural symbols means that the same narratives that branders are manipulating structure the motivations of the branders and the other people in the neighborhood performing the identity of place. As a cultural sociologist, I essentially invert the front- and backstage of the performance. See Goffman, *The Presentation of Self in Everyday Life*; Goffman, *Encounters*. I treat what happens behind the scenes (backstage) as the *foreground* and people's core beliefs about the neighborhood as well as its underlying economic and political structures as the *background*. Background representations (culture) can have autonomy in motivating action.

14. Sociologists Alejandro Portes and Rubén Rumbaut use the concept of the environment of reception to show how it affects the ease with which different immigrant groups adapt to the United States. Portes and Rumbaut, *Immigrant America*. As explained in the text, my use of the concept is different.

15. I draw on Jeffrey Alexander and Philip Smith's work to argue that these news stories reflect a deeper structure of shared understandings in American society. See Alexander and Smith, "The Discourse of American Civil Society."

16. Urban sociologist Elijah Anderson examines how individuals within the black ghetto make the distinction between "decent" and "street" behaviors. See Anderson, *Code of the Street.*

17. Perceptions of neighborhood disorder depend on the percentage of minorities there and the poverty rate, independent of how much trash there is, according to Sampson and Raudenbush, "Seeing Disorder."

18. Whalen, *From Puerto Rico to Philadelphia*, p. 6. For more history of the Puerto Rican migration to Philadelphia, see Vázquez-Hernández, "From Pan-Latino Enclaves to a Community."

19. Whalen, *From Puerto Rico to Philadelphia*, p. 51.

20. Ibid., p. 50.

21. Koss, *Puerto Ricans in Philadelphia*, pp. 66–67.

22. Ibid., p. 64.

23. Taller Puertorriqueño, "Batiendo la Olla," p. 43.

24. Ibid., p. 41.

25. These percentages far exceed the threshold set by sociologists Richard Alba, John Logan, and Kyle Crowder for defining an ethnic neighborhood—namely, "a set of contiguous [census] tracts, which must contain at least one tract where a group is represented as 40% or more of the residents and whose other tracts each have a level of ethnic concentration among residents of at least 35%." Alba, Logan, and Crowder, "White Neighborhoods and Assimilation," p. 893.

26. The Census uses the term "Hispanic" rather than "Latino." Most people I interviewed used "Latino," and some took offense at "Hispanic." One informant liked to joke, "Hispanic? I'm not his panic, and I'm not her panic, either." In *Latinos, Inc.* Arlene Dávila explains that "Hispanic" is the term used by the U.S. Bureau of the Census and is thereby state sanctioned. It is the literal translation of the term *Hispano*, designating that one descends somehow from Spain, a characterization that has taken on a racial tone in the United States. Dávila writes: "By the 1960s and 1970s, the terms 'Hispano' and 'Hispanic' were seen to be contrary to the cultural nationalism that accompanied larger struggles for civil empowerment by both Chicanos and Puerto Ricans and thus as a denial of their identity and a rejection of their indigenous and colonized roots. Ironically, it was shortly after these cultural struggles that the US government coined the official designation of 'Hispanic' [for] anyone of Spanish background in the United States" (p. 15). The younger generation of marketers interviewed by Dávila tended to use the term "Latino" while the older generation more often used "Hispanic."

27. Dribben, "Visitors See a Street Scene of Revitalization."

28. Some readers might be curious about where these cross streets and this city ward are in relation to the famous seventh ward studied by W. E. B. DuBois in *The Philadelphia Negro*. The old seventh ward where DuBois conducted his study is now the fifth ward. (The fifth borders the eighteenth, which borders the thirty-first and the twenty-fifth.) The interviews for this book come from the eighteenth, twenty-fifth, and thirty-first wards.

29. Dribben, "Visitors See a Street Scene of Revitalization."

30. Interview, February 14, 2007.

31. Interview, June 20, 2008.

32. Interview, June 25, 2008.

33. In his presidential address before the Society for the Study of Social Problems, Howard Becker exhorts social scientists in general and ethnographers in particular to reject the false dichotomy between being scientifically rigorous and being emotionally attached to the subject. See Becker, "Whose Side Are We On?"

34. Mitchell Duneier uses Ovie Carter's photographs to offer a visual voice to the experiences of the people he studied. Duneier, *Slim's Table*; Duneier, *Sidewalk*.

CHAPTER TWO

1. Interview, February 1, 2007.

2. E-mail communication, August 16, 2010.

3. Grazian, *Blue Chicago*, p. 206.

4. The reported percentages exclude the numbers following the decimal point. As a result, these percentages total 98 percent rather than 100.

5. GPTMC, "Neighborhood Tourism Network: A Five Year Overview" (memo to Meryl & EC from Patricia & Libby, January 24, 2007), p. 8.

6. The invitation itself was part of the performance, for it referenced a set of narratives and rhetorical configurations that resonated with the intended audience. Social performances are not merely a matter of strategically manipulating the impressions that others have about a particular situation, à la Goffman. Instead, social performances are *guided* by these cultural configurations and background texts. See Alexander, "Cultural Pragmatics," p. 550.

7. GPTMC, "Neighborhood Tourism Network," p. 9.

8. http://www.gophila.com (accessed September 20, 2006). This site has since been replaced by a new visitor site titled Philadelphia and the Countryside, http://www.visit philly.com.

9. The online description exploited a phenomenon recognized by John Urry in his studies of the tourist city: "People encounter the city [and its neighborhoods] through their senses" (p.71). See Urry, "Sensing the City."

10. Media studies scholar Michael Schudson observes that calendars function as "important knowledge-fixing (and knowledge-activating) mechanisms... [and as] culturally sanctioned forms of public memory." Schudson, "How Culture Works," p. 163.

11. Zerubavel, *The Fine Line*.

12. This question of local control reminds me that the mingling of market-based tours and ethnic neighborhood life need not be a zero-sum game, though sometimes it is. In her analyses of money, markets, and social life, Viviana Zelizer warns against facile accounts of markets as desecrating the sacred and deflowering the innocent (Zelizer, "Beyond the Polemics of the Market"; Zelizer, *The Purchase of Intimacy*). Instead she argues that people act creatively in commercial marketplaces; in addition to family, religion, and neighborhood, marketplaces provide an arena in which relationships are built and group solidarities affirmed. Even scholars such as George Ritzer, who writes about how globalization has led to the proliferation of standardized products gutted of local meanings, acknowledges that such dire outcomes need not come to pass. See Ritzer, "Rethinking Globalization."

13. Anderson, *Code of the Street*, pp. 15–34.

14. See Tajfel and Turner, "An Integrative Theory of Intergroup Conflict."

15. Fernández-Kelly and Konczal, "Murdering the Alphabet," p. 1165.

16. Interview, June 18, 2009.

17. The image is now Taller's logo, replacing the Puerto Rican flag and castle guard in the original logo. This change was made after the organization consulted with marketing specialists and considered how the Latino population in Philadelphia was developing and diversifying. While some people in the community opposed the change, others applauded it, recognizing the heart as a unique artifact that would be easily remembered by anyone who had visited Taller's facilities in the barrio.

18. Jacobs, *The Death and Life of Great American Cities*.

19. http://www.tallerpr.org/visit_pages/visit.htm (accessed September 20, 2006). The website has changed; I include its original link and texts here to indicate what I saw when I took the tour. The most recent URL (as of August 26, 2010) is http://www.tallerpr.org/B/Education-Programs/Visitenos--A-Cultural-Encounter.aspx.

20. Historical Society of Pennsylvania, Balch Collection, MSS 119, Box 1, Folder 8.

21. Ibid.

22. Zelizer, *The Purchase of Intimacy*.

23. Gottdiener, *The Theming of America*; Harvey, *Spaces of Capital*; Zukin, *The Cultures of Cities*.

24. Dávila, "Empowered Culture?"

25. Seymour, "Puerto Rican Celebration a 'Party Day.'"

26. See Lamont, *The Dignity of Working Men*; Lamont and Molnár, "How Blacks Use Consumption to Shape Their Collective Identity."

CHAPTER THREE

1. I use the term "art worlds" the way Howard Becker does, to refer to "the network of people whose cooperative activity, organized via their joint knowledge of conventional means of doing things, produces the kind of art works that the art world is noted for." Becker, *Art Worlds*, p. x.

2. For more on how cultural events and field trips generate different forms of social capital, see Small, *Unanticipated Gains*. My discussion of social capital in this context acknowledges that different types of people come to know the barrio's organizations through attending art events. By getting to know the community in this way, these people act as a resource, sharing information, money, or other investments. This constitutes social capital, since these resources are being made available to people in the barrio by virtue of the social relationships forged in these art events.

3. Ethnic art worlds exist within what Elijah Anderson calls the "cosmopolitan canopy": "neutral social settings, which no one group expressly owns but all are encouraged to share, situated under [a] kind of protective umbrella." See Anderson, "The Cosmopolitan Canopy," p. 21. The cosmopolitan canopy functions as a space in which people share a common interest, leaving behind their particular groups to mix with other cultures. Because the art world often transcends traditional notions of gender (and gendered places) and racial as well as ethnic barriers, the art world is not perceived as being exclusive or owned by any one group. Cosmopolitan canopies enable those moving within them to cross racial and ethnic boundaries and thus to further intercultural understanding. The cosmopolitan canopies in the Philadelphia barrio distinguish themselves by emphasiz-

ing the particular (the *ethnos*) rather than the universal (the *cosmos*), but the interactions within them succeed nonetheless in fostering dialogue among those who cross racial, ethnic, and class boundaries.

4. Blumer, "Race Prejudice as a Sense of Group Position."

5. Charles, "The Dynamics of Racial Residential Segregation"; Massey and Denton, *American Apartheid*; Wilson, *When Work Disappears*.

6. Interview, September 7, 2005.

7. Interview, January 30, 2007.

8. Interview, December 8, 2008.

9. All quotations in this section come from field notes, October 14, 2005.

10. It seemed to me that the workers could have been Mexican in origin, but the tone of this remark suggested that "Mexican" was meant pejoratively. The commentators certainly intended to indicate that these city workers were not Puerto Ricans who lived in the neighborhood.

11. Interview, June 19, 2007. See also the discussion in the appendix.

12. All quotations in this section come from field notes, June 10, 2005.

13. All quotations in this section come from Field notes, February 10, 2006.

14. The song is believed to have originated during the American Civil War and to have been a popular rhyme among African-American children.

15. Interview, February 14, 2007.

16. Bourdieu, *Distinction*.

17. Interview, September 7, 2005.

18. Caroulis, "Carmen Febo."

19. Interview, February 14, 2007.

20. Interview, June 12, 2008. El Concilio de Organizaciones Hispanas de Filadelfia (the Council of Spanish Speaking Organizations of Philadelphia), founded in 1962, is a social services organization in Philadelphia. The Young Lords, founded in 1959 as a Puerto Rican gang in the Lincoln Park neighborhood of Chicago, was transformed into a political rights movement after Mayor Richard J. Daley evicted Puerto Ricans from that neighborhood and other areas in 1966. The Young Lords eventually established branches in metropolitan areas throughout the country, including Philadelphia. APM (the Association of Puerto Ricans on the Move), founded in 1970, is a social services organization in Philadelphia.

21. Interview, October 28, 2008.

22. Ibid.

23. Eugenio María de Hostos Archives Center, Taller Puertorriqueño, Subseries: Administrative Papers V, Box 5.

24. Interview, June 12, 2008.

25. Interview, October 27, 2005.

26. Ibid.

27. Interview, January 30, 2007.

28. Ibid.

29. Interview, October 29, 2005.

30. Ibid.

31. Ibid.

32. Interview, October 27, 2005.

33. E-mail communication with Mike Esposito, June 21, 2009: "I actually had the initial idea in 1991 and approached Yolanda early on to join me in this venture. I was going solo for about a year, with Yolanda attending some meetings and providing resources until she helped me as stage manager at Fiesta en la Plaza 1992 (Fiesta 1992 for short) at Upper Darby High School (June 7, 1992). From that moment on we worked as a duo. In the end we decided to call each other cofounders in recognition of all the hard work and dedication that Yolanda brought to the organization."

34. Interview with Mike Esposito, October 27, 2005.

35. Ibid.

36. Ibid.

37. Field notes, September 22, 2006.

38. Ibid.

39. Ibid.

40. Field notes, June 13, 2008.

41. Interview, November 5, 2009.

42. Ibid.

43. Ibid.

44. Ibid.

45. Ibid.

CHAPTER FOUR

1. LaBan, "Isla Verde."

2. Interview, June 6, 2009.

3. Ibid.

4. Ibid.

5. Ibid.

6. Ibid.

7. In *City on the Edge*, sociologists Alejandro Portes and Alex Stepick describe a similar trajectory followed by a prominent ethnic entrepreneur in Miami's Little Havana. Miguel Recarey, owner of the largest Cuban firm in the United States in the mid-1980s, ran afoul of the law by using his political connections to skirt the rules and build an enviable commercial empire. Recarey's Internal Medical Centers (IMC) benefited from political connections that allowed him to evade the rules for obtaining lucrative government subsidies. Even President George H. W. Bush's brother, Jeb, and other politicians in Florida treated Recarey as a man to be admired and respected. By 1987 the government had indicted Recarey for bribery. Soon thereafter, he disappeared, preferring obscurity to prison.

8. The narratives of entrepreneurs show us how culture influences the way similarly situated people respond to the same objective conditions. In addition, understanding social structure and the political economy of cities helps us grasp how the visions of what is possible are constrained. Mario Small argues that "different cohorts will respond to the same structural conditions if they conceive of the neighborhood through different cultural 'frames.'" Small, "Culture, Cohorts, and Social Organization Theory," p. 20.

9. *Santerismo* is a religious practice that merges Puerto Rican *Espiritismo* (Spiritism) and *Santería* (Way of the Saints), the latter a blend of Roman Catholicism, Native American traditions, and the Yoruba religion of West Africa.

10. Interview, June 16, 2008.

11. Ibid.

12. Ibid.

13. Interview, February 14, 2007.

14. Ibid.

15. Ibid.

16. Ibid.

17. Interview, April 25, 2006.

18. Ibid.

19. Interview, March 19, 2006.

20. Ibid.

21. Ibid.

22. The city's neighborhoods get coded as being on either side of a civic binary: good/bad, sacred/profane, civil/uncivil society. For more on civil society codes, see Smith, "Codes and Conflict"; Alexander and Smith, "The Discourse of American Civil Society."

23. Interview, June 16, 2008.

24. Ibid.

25. Ibid.

26. Ibid.

27. Ibid.

28. Portes and Shafer, "Revisiting the Enclave Hypothesis"; Portes and Stepick, *City on the Edge*.

29. When I saw him several days after our interview, I was entertaining the crowd during a street demonstration of the *bomba* and the *plena*. He and other business owners use these performances as a welcome break and a reminder that they live in an interesting, culturally rich place, but their time constraints are real.

30. Interview, June 16, 2008.

31. Interview, June 12, 2008.

32. Ibid.

33. Ibid.

34. Ibid.

35. Interview, December 15, 2005.

36. Ibid.

37. Interview, June 18, 2007.

38. Interview, March 3, 2006.

39. Ibid.

CHAPTER FIVE

1. See Steve Lopez's 1995 columns in the *Philadelphia Inquirer*; for example, "Bleeding Hearts in the Badlands" and "A Memory Recovered from amid the Weeds." Also see David Zucchino's articles in the *Philadelphia Inquirer*, appearing in the early nineties, that popularized the Badlands image: "In the Badlands of the City, Drugs Still Riding High," "A Huge Heroin Bust," "How an Illicit World Flourishes Just Three Miles from City Hall," and "The Badlands: In the Grip of Drugs."

2. Greenberg, *Branding New York*, pp. 19–20.

3. The three areas were bounded respectively by the following streets:

1. On the east by Sixth Street, on the south by Green Street, on the west by Tenth Street, and on the north by Susquehanna Avenue.
2. On the east by Tenth Street, on the west by Broad Street, on the south by Vine Street, and on the north by Thompson Street.
3. On the east by Broad Street, on the south by Spring Garden Street, on the west by Twenty-third Street. The northern border of this area is irregular. Between Twenty-third and Seventeenth Street, Fairmount Avenue is the northern edge. At Seventeenth Street, the northern boundary runs down Seventeenth Street to Poplar Street and then down Poplar Street back to Broad Street. (Commission on Human Relations, *Puerto Ricans in Philadelphia*, p. iv)

4. Ibid., p. i.

5. The list of characteristics in this sentence is ordered by the ranking made among non–Puerto Rican respondents. Most respondents ranked language highest as an indication of how Puerto Ricans differed from non–Puerto Ricans, while the smallest percentage ranked cleanliness as a distinguishing factor. Commission on Human Relations, *Philadelphia's Puerto Rican Population*, p. 52.

6. Ibid., p. 58.

7. Commission on Human Relations, *Clinical Inquiry into Incidents of Intimidation and Mob Pressure Forcing Minority Families to Vacate Their Homes*, pp. 26–27.

8. Ibid.

9. Ibid., pp. 35–36.

10. Schermer, "Memorandum to Community, Civic and Religious Leaders," pp. 2–3.

11. Commission on Human Relations, *Philadelphia's Puerto Rican Population*, pp. 22–23.

12. Historical Society of Pennsylvania, Balch Collection, MSS 114, Box 110, Folder 1.

13. Ibid. This document reported demographic statistics about the Puerto Rican population, including health and housing conditions as well as the population growth rate.

14. Historical Society of Pennsylvania, Balch Collection, MSS 118, Box 1, Folder 7. This document is a memorandum from the Economic Development Administration addressed to leaders of the city's commercial corridors.

15. Davidson, "Property Values Up, Old Shopping Strip on 5th St. Bounces Back with New Life."

16. Ibid., p. 25.

17. Ibid.

18. Ibid.

19. Ibid.

20. Ibid.

21. Historical Society of Pennsylvania, Balch Collection, MSS 114, Box 110, Folder 21.

22. Historical Society of Pennsylvania, Balch Collection, MSS 118, Box 1, Folders 1, 5, 7.

23. Philadelphia Architects Workshop, "Storefront Design Criteria," pp. 4–5, Historical Society of Pennsylvania, Balch Collection, MSS, 118, Box 1, Folder 7.

24. Ibid., pp. 6–7.

25. Historical Society of Pennsylvania, Balch Collection, MSS 118, Box 1, Folder 6.

26. Historical Society of Pennsylvania, Balch Collection, MSS 118, Box 1, Folder 7.

27. Boyle, "Puerto Rican Business Thrives."

28. Waldinger and Lichter, *How the Other Half Works*.

29. Tienda, "Puerto Ricans and the Underclass Debate," p. 106.

30. Ibid.

31. Whalen, *From Puerto Rico to Philadelphia*, p. 199. Social scientists tended to blame the culture of poverty for the ills facing Puerto Ricans, other Latinos, and African Americans. See Mills, Senior, and Goldsen, *The Puerto Rican Journey*; Fitzpatrick, *Puerto Rican Americans*; and Lewis, *La Vida*.

32. Quoted in Whalen, *From Puerto Rico to Philadelphia*, p. 199.

33. Ibid., p. 205.

34. Historical Society of Pennsylvania, Balch Collection, MSS 114, Box 158, Folder 35 (emphasis in original).

35. Williams, *Crackhouse*.

36. Golub and Johnson, "Crack's Decline," pp. 6–8.

37. Adamson, "Cops Crack Down on Badlands Crime"; Adamson, "Sweeping the Creeps off Streets"; Goodman, "Police Operation Restored Hope to Kensington after Sunrise"; Goodman, Lowe, and Gibbons, "Operation Sunrise Rolls In"; Tkacik, Moore, and Adamson, "Party's Over Day 1."

38. Goldman, "NY Attack on Crime a Success"; Moore, "ACLU: We Back Police Clean-Up."

39. Goldwyn, "Churches Help to Combat Crime"; Tkacik, "Flock Is Hard to Reach."

40. See chapter 6 for a discussion of plans to picket Mayor Edward Rendell at the Puerto Rican Day Parade over the shooting of Radames Bonilla. The shooting and planned protests are discussed in Latty, "Puerto Rican Activists to Picket Rendell at Parade."

41. E.g., Interview, October 28, 2008.

42. Seifert and Stern, "'Natural' Cultural Districts."

CHAPTER SIX

1. For sociological studies of parades or commemorations or both, see Armstrong and Crage, "Movements and Memory"; Etzioni, "Toward a Theory of Public Ritual"; Olick, "Genre Memories and Memory Genres"; Saito, "Reiterated Commemoration"; Schwartz, "The Social Context of Commemoration"; Spillman, "When Do Collective Memories Last?"; and Wagner-Pacifici and Schwartz, "The Vietnam Veterans Memorial."

2. Interview, June 12, 2008.

3. The FBI maintained that agents entered the house intending only to serve an arrest warrant on Ojeda Ríos, who had been a fugitive and was wanted in connection with the robbery of an armored truck in 1983. The FBI also stated that they had merely returned fire and had acted in self-defense. But some political activists remained unconvinced, noting that the FBI shot Ojeda Ríos in the neck and left him in his home fatally wounded. "It was an execution squad, because the FBI never intended to arrest Ojeda Ríos but to kill him," Antonio Camacho told reporters for the online socialist newspaper *The Militant* (Richards, "FBI Agents Kill Puerto Rican Militant"). The killing ironically took place on Grito de Lares (Cry of Lares), the pro-independence movement's annual commemoration of the 1868 rebellion against Spanish colonization.

4. For the contrasting character of neighborhoods, see Hunter and Suttles, "The Expanding Community of Limited Liability."

5. See Tiebout, "A Pure Theory of Local Expenditures."

6. Alexander and Smith, "The Discourse of American Civil Society."

7. Cooke, "For Area Hispanics, Celebration amid the Struggles" (emphasis added).

8. Ibid. (emphasis added).

9. Ibid.

10. Sama, "For Puerto Ricans, a Day of Pride."

11. Seymour, "Puerto Rican Fest Floats Out in Style."

12. Ibid.

13. Ibid. See also Adamson, "Violence Mars Puerto Rico Day"; Couloumbis, "Puerto Ricans Honor Heritage"; Lowe, "Police, Latino Leaders Want a Trouble-Free Festival."

14. Cooke, "For Area Hispanics, Celebration amid the Struggles."

15. Colimore, "It's a Parade-Filled Weekend: Hispanic, German Festivities Planned."

16. Seymour, "Puerto Rican Fest Floats Out in Style."

17. Campbell, "A Day for Puerto Rico."

18. Holmes, "Bittersweet Celebration: Hugo Shadows Puerto Rican Parade."

19. Copeland, "A Celebration of Latino Heritage."

20. Cooke, "For Area Hispanics, Celebration amid the Struggles."

21. Seymour, "Puerto Rican Celebration a 'Party Day.'"

22. Ibid.

23. Copeland, "A Celebration of Latino Heritage."

24. Campbell, "A Day for Puerto Rico."

25. Historical Society of Pennsylvania, Balch Collection, MSS 119, Box 1, Folder 18.

26. Gonzalez, "Puerto Rican Parade on the Parkway."

27. Ibid.

28. Cooke, "For Area Hispanics, Celebration amid the Struggles."

29. Santiago, "Puerto Rican Pride Braves the Rain."

30. Latty, "Puerto Rican Activists to Picket Rendell at Parade."

31. Ibid.

32. Adamson, "Violence Mars Puerto Rico Day."

33. Ibid.

34. Ibid.

35. Ibid.

36. Latty, "Post-Parade Festivities Set."

37. Lowe, "Police, Latino Leaders Want a Trouble-Free Festival."

38. Meltzer, "Officials' Goal."

39. Ibid.

40. Couloumbis, "Puerto Ricans Honor Heritage."

41. Pradhan, "Tight Security Again for Puerto Rican Day."

42. Colimore, "It's a Parade-Filled Weekend."

43. Latty, "Post-Parade Festivities Set."

44. Panaritis, "Georges Doesn't Rain on Parade."

45. Ibid.

46. Lowe, "Police, Latino Leaders Want a Trouble-Free Festival."

47. Schogol, "At Hispanic Heritage Month Events the Mood Is Somber."

48. Ibid.

49. Ibid.

50. Klein, "Bienvenido."

51. *Philadelphia Daily News*, "15 Arrested after Puerto Rican Day Parade."

52. Ibid.

53. Ibid.

54. Medina, "A Banner Day for Puerto Rico."

55. Ibid.

56. Medina, "Puerto Rican Party on the Parkway."

57. Ibid.

58. For more on binary codes and the cultural structure, see Alexander and Smith, "The Discourse of American Civil Society"; Smith, "Codes and Conflict."

59. Anderson, *Streetwise*; Anderson, *Code of the Street*.

60. Of course, it would be a mistake to reify these codes and force them onto these different time periods in a mechanical way. The codes indicating that the Latino community is civil get mixed in with codes indicating otherwise. Unanticipated acts of violence and displays of chaos push the profane set of codes into the foreground of the public discourse. Actors from the community also work to minimize the profane and to maximize the sacred, as they confront stereotypes and emphasize Latinos' contributions to society generally. Changes in the economic fortunes of the city and the neighborhood as well as large-scale demographic shifts and political events (such as the September 11 attacks) also influence which ritual codes resonate in the newspaper reports.

CHAPTER SEVEN

1. DuBois, *Black Reconstruction in America, 1860–1880*.

2. Smith, "New City, New Frontier"; Grazian, *Blue Chicago*.

3. Zukin, *Loft Living*; Also see Harvey, *Spaces of Capital*.

4. I consider the correlation of autonomy and authenticity further in Wherry, "The Social Sources of Authenticity in Global Handicraft Markets"; also see Fine, "Crafting Authenticity."

5. I am using the term "highbrow" similarly to Lawrence Levine in *Highbrow/Lowbrow*, referring to the esoteric performances that appeal to the upper classes.

6. Rivera, "Managing 'Spoiled' National Identity."

7. Grazian, *Blue Chicago*.

8. Durkheim, *The Elementary Forms of Religous Life*, p. 227.

9. Ibid., p. 212.

10. Steinberg, "The Liberal Retreat from Race during the Post–Civil Rights Era."

11. Quoted in ibid., p. 18.

12. Sennett, *The Culture of the New Capitalism*.

13. Ibid., p. 74 (emphasis in original).

14. Volk, "Third and Indiana."

APPENDIX

1. See Whyte, *Street Corner Society*.

2. Historical Society of Pennsylvania, Balch Collection, MSS 118, Box 1, Folder 3.

3. Historical Society of Pennsylvania, Balch Collection, MSS 118, Box 1, Folder 6.

4. Historical Society of Pennsylvania, Balch Collection, MSS 118, Box 1, Folder 5.

5. Historical Society of Pennsylvania, Balch Collection, MSS 118, Box 1, Folder 3.

6. Historical Society of Pennsylvania, Balch Collection, MSS 118, Box 1, Folder 4.

7. See Charmaz, *Constructing Grounded Theory*; Strauss and Corbin, *Basics of Qualitative Research*.

8. I have modeled my discussion of going back to the field on Duneier's appendix in *Sidewalk*.

9. The discussion took place June 6, 2009.

Works Cited

Adamson, April. "Cops Crack Down on Badlands Crime: Operation Sunrise Targets Drug Traffic in Kensington." *Philadelphia Daily News*, June 15, 1998, p. 4.
———. "Sweeping the Creeps off Streets: Dealers, Hookers on Hiatus." *Philadelphia Daily News*, June 18, 1998, p. 5.
———. "Violence Mars Puerto Rico Day." *Philadelphia Daily News*, September 22, 1997, p. 7 (Local).
Alba, Richard D., John R. Logan, and Kyle Crowder. "White Neighborhoods and Assimilation: The Greater New York Region, 1980–1990." *Social Forces* 75 (1997): 883–909.
Alexander, Jeffrey C. "Cultural Pragmatics: Social Performance between Ritual and Strategy." *Sociological Theory* 22, no. 4 (2004): 527–73.
———. *The Meanings of Social Life: A Cultural Sociology.* New York: Oxford University Press, 2003.
Alexander, Jeffrey, and Philip Smith. "The Discourse of American Civil Society: A New Proposal for Cultural Studies." *Theory and Society* 22, no. 1 (1993): 151–207.
Armstrong, Elizabeth A., and Suzanna M. Crage. "Movements and Memory: The Making of the Stonewall Myth." *American Sociological Review* 71, no. 5 (2006): 724–51.
Anderson, Elijah. *Code of the Street: Decency, Violence, and the Moral Life of the Inner City.* New York: W.W. Norton, 1999.
———. "The Cosmopolitan Canopy." *Annals of the American Academy of Political and Social Science* 595 (2004): 14–31.
———. *Streetwise: Race, Class, and Change in an Urban Community.* Chicago: University of Chicago Press, 1990.
Baldwin, James. *The Fire Next Time.* New York: Dial Press, 1963.
Becker, Howard S. *Art Worlds.* Berkeley: University of California Press, 1982.
———. "Whose Side Are We On?" *Social Problems* 14, no. 3 (1967): 239–47.
Blumer, Herbert. "Race Prejudice as a Sense of Group Position." *Pacific Sociological Review* 1, no. 1 (1958): 3–7.
Bonilla-Silva, Eduardo. *Racism without Racists: Color-Blind Racism and the Persistence of Racial Inequality in the United States.* 3rd ed. Lanham, MD: Rowman & Littlefield, 2010.

Bourdieu, Pierre. *Distinction: A Social Critique of the Judgement of Taste*. Translated by Richard Nice. Cambridge: Harvard University Press, 1984.

———. *Language and Symbolic Power*. Edited by John B. Thompson. Translated by Gino Raymond and Matthew Adamson. Cambridge: Harvard University Press, 1991.

Boyle, Bruce. "Puerto Rican Business Thrives." *Bulletin*, September 19, 1976.

Campbell, Roy H. "A Day for Puerto Rico." *Philadelphia Inquirer*, September 28, 1987, p. B5.

Caroulis, Jon. "Carmen Febo: The Doctor Believes in the Healing Power of Art." *Philadelphia Inquirer Magazine*, February 10, 2001.

Charles, Camille Zubrinsky. "The Dynamics of Racial Residential Segregation." *Annual Review of Sociology* 29 (2003): 167–207.

Charmaz, Kathy. *Constructing Grounded Theory: A Practical Guide through Qualitative Analysis*. Thousand Oaks, CA: Sage, 2006.

Colimore, Edward. "It's a Parade-Filled Weekend: Hispanic, German Festivities Planned." *Philadelphia Inquirer*, September 27, 1986, p. B4.

Commission on Human Relations. *Clinical Inquiry into Incidents of Intimidation and Mob Pressure Forcing Minority Families to Vacate Their Homes*. Philadelphia: City of Philadelphia, 1960.

Commission on Human Relations. *Philadelphia's Puerto Rican Population: A Descriptive Summary Including 1960 Census Data*. Philadelphia: City of Philadelphia, 1964.

———. *Puerto Ricans in Philadelphia*. Philadelphia: City of Philadelphia, 1954.

Cooke, Russell. "For Area Hispanics, Celebration amid the Struggles." *Philadelphia Inquirer*, September 19, 1983, p. A1.

Copeland, Larry. "A Celebration of Latino Heritage: 5,000 Turn out for Puerto Rican Week Parade." *Philadelphia Inquirer*, October 1, 1990, p. B6.

Couloumbis, Angel. "Puerto Ricans Honor Heritage: About 10,000 People Gathered on the Parkway to Commorate Puerto Rican Day with a Parade and Cultural Festival." *Philadelphia Inquirer*, September 27, 1999, p. B1.

Davidson, Joe. "Property Values Up, Old Shopping Strip on 5th St. Bounces Back with New Life." *Bulletin*, December 21, 1975, pp. 23, 25.

Dávila, Arlene. *Barrio Dreams: Puerto Ricans, Latinos and the Neoliberal City*. Berkeley: University of California Press, 2004.

———. "Empowered Culture? New York City's Empowerment Zone and the Selling of El Barrio." *The Annals of the American Academy of Political and Social Science* 594, no. 1 (2004): 49–64.

———. *Latinos, Inc.: The Marketing and Making of a People*. Berkeley: University of California Press, 2001.

Dribben, Melissa. "Visitors See a Street Scene of Revitalization: Different Places, Same Problems." *Philadelphia Inquirer*, April 4, 2008, p. B1.

DuBois, W. E. B. *Black Reconstruction in America, 1860–1880*. New York: Free Press, [1935] 1995.

———. *The Philadelphia Negro: A Social Study*. Philadelphia: University of Pennsylvania Press, [1899] 1996.

Duneier, Mitchell. *Sidewalk*. New York: Farrar, Straus and Giroux, 2000.

———. *Slim's Table: Race, Respectability, and Masculinity*. Chicago: University of Chicago Press, 1992.

Durkheim, Emile. *The Elementary Forms of Religous Life*. Translated by Karen E. Fields. New York: Free Press, [1912] 1995.

Etzioni, Amitai. "Toward a Theory of Public Ritual." *Sociological Theory* 18, no. 1 (2000): 44–59.

Fernández-Kelly, Patricia, and Lisa Konczal. "Murdering the Alphabet: Identity and Entrepreneurship among Second Generation Cubans, West Indians, and Central Americans." *Ethnic and Racial Studies* 28, no. 6 (2005): 1153–81.

Fine, Gary Alan. "Crafting Authenticity: The Validation of Identity in Self-Taught Art." *Theory and Society* 32, no. 2 (2003): 153–80.

Fitzpatrick, Joseph P. *Puerto Rican Americans: The Meaning of Migration to the Mainland*. Englewood Cliffs, NJ: Prentice-Hall, 1971.

Goffman, Erving. *Encounters: Two Studies in the Sociology of Interaction*. Indianapolis: Bobbs-Merrill, 1961.

———. *The Presentation of Self in Everyday Life*. Garden City, NY: Doubleday, 1959.

———. *Stigma: Notes on the Management of Spoiled Identity*. Englewood Cliffs, NJ: Prentice-Hall, 1963.

Goldman, Henry. "NY Attack on Crime a Success: The Aggressive, Unrelenting Police Effort is Similar to What Philadelphia Seeks to Achieve with Operation Sunrise." *Philadelphia Inquirer*, June 21, 1998, p. E3.

Goldwyn, Ron. "Churches Help to Combat Crime: Cooperating with Police Crackdowns." *Philadelphia Daily News*, June 22, 1998, p. 22.

Golub, Andrew L., and Bruce D. Johnson. "Crack's Decline: Some Surprises across U.S. Cities." *Research in Brief*. Washington, DC: National Institute of Justice, 1997.

González, Gilberto. *Three Rings*. Bloomington, IN: Xlibris, 2009.

Gonzalez, Juan. "Puerto Rican Parade on the Parkway." *Philadelphia Daily News*, September 24, 1982, p. 63.

Goodman, Howard. "Police Operation Restored Hope to Kensington after Sunrise; The Residents Must Maintain Their Gains." *Philadelphia Inquirer*, August 16, 1998, p. B1.

Goodman, Howard, Herbert Lowe, and Thomas J. Gibbons Jr. "Operation Sunrise Rolls In: The Cleanup Starts in Kensington; Drug Arrests and Anti-Graffiti Work Were Only Part of the Effort to Help a Troubled Area of the City." *Philadelphia Inquirer*, June 16, 1998, p. A1.

Gottdiener, Mark. *The Theming of America: American Dreams, Media Fantasies, and Themed Environments*. 2nd ed. Boulder: Westview Press, 2001.

Grazian, David. *Blue Chicago: The Search for Authenticity in Urban Blues Clubs*. Chicago: University of Chicago Press, 2003.

———. "The Production of Popular Music as a Confidence Game: The Case of the Chicago Blues." *Qualitative Sociology* 27, no. 2 (2004): 137–58.

Greater Philadelphia Tourism Marketing Corporation (GPTMC). "Neighborhood Tourism Network: A Five Year Overview," January 24, 2007, memorandum to Meryl & EC from Patricia & Libby.

Greenberg, Miriam. *Branding New York: How a City in Crisis Was Sold to the World*. New York: Routledge, 2008.

Harvey, David. *Spaces of Capital: Toward a Critical Geography*. London: Routledge, 2001.

Herzfeld, Michael. *The Body Impolitic: Artisans and Artifice in the Global Hierarchy of Value*. Chicago: University of Chicago Press, 2004.

Holmes, Kristin E. "Bittersweet Celebration Hugo Shadows Puerto Rican Parade." *Philadelphia Inquirer*, September 25, 1989, p. B3.

Holt, Douglas B. *How Brands Become Icons: The Principles of Cultural Branding*. Boston: Harvard Business School Press, 2004.

Hughes, Langston. "Minstrel Man." In *The New Negro: Voices of the Harlem Renaissance*, edited by Alain Locke, p. 144. New York: Touchstone, [1925] 1997.

Hunter, Albert J., and Gerald D. Suttles. "The Expanding Community of Limited Liability." In *The Social Construction of Communities*, edited by Gerald D. Suttles, pp. 44–80. Chicago: University of Chicago Press, 1972.

Jacobs, Jane. *The Death and Life of Great American Cities*. New York: Random House, 1961.

Klein, Michael. "Bienvenido." *Philadelphia Inquirer*, October 3, 2002, p. D2.

Koss, Joan Dee. "Puerto Ricans in Philadelphia: Migration and Accommodation." PhD diss., University of Pennsylvania, 1965.

LaBan, Craig. "Isla Verde." *Philadelphia Inquirer*, May 15, 2005, p. M6.

Lamont, Michèle. *The Dignity of Working Men: Morality and the Boundaries of Race, Class, and Immigration*. Cambridge: Harvard University Press, 2000.

Lamont, Michèle, and Virág Molnár. "How Blacks Use Consumption to Shape Their Collective Identity: Evidence from Marketing Specialists." *Journal of Consumer Culture* 1, no. 1 (2001): 31–45.

Latty, Yvonne. "Post-Parade Festivities Set." *Philadelphia Daily News*, September 25, 1998, p. 25 (Local).

———. "Puerto Rican Activists to Picket Rendell at Parade: They Want Action on Police Review Board." *Philadelphia Daily News*, September 23, 1993, p. 20 (Local).

Levine, Lawrence W. *Highbrow/Lowbrow: The Emergence of Cultural Hierarchy in America*. Cambridge: Harvard University Press, 1988.

Lewis, Oscar. *La Vida: A Puerto Rican Family in the Culture of Poverty—San Juan and New York*. New York: Random House, 1965.

Logan, John R., and Harvey L. Molotch. *Urban Fortunes: The Political Economy of Place*. Berkeley: University of California Press, [1987] 2007.

Lopez, Steve. "Bleeding Hearts in the Badlands." *Philadelphia Inquirer*, January 18, 1995, p. B1.

———. "A Memory Recovered from amid the Weeds." *Philadelphia Inquirer*, September 5, 1995, p. A1.

———. *Third and Indiana*. New York: Penguin, 1995.

Lowe, Herbert. "Police, Latino Leaders Want a Trouble-Free Festival: They Announced a Plan to Help Keep Things Calm in Festivities after the Puerto Rican Day Parade." *Philadelphia Inquirer*, September 9, 1998, p. B2.

Massey, Douglas, and Nancy Denton. *American Apartheid: Segregation and the Making of the Underclass*. Cambridge: Harvard University Press, 1993.

Medina, Regina. "A Banner Day for Puerto Rico." *Philadelphia Daily News*, September 27, 2004, p. 5 (Local).

———. "Puerto Rican Party on the Parkway: Parade Welcomes All Latinos." *Philadelphia Daily News*, September 24, 2004, p. 45 (Features).

Meltzer, Marc. "Officials' Goal: Peace at Puerto Rican Bash." *Philadelphia Daily News*, September 22, 1999, p. 15 (Local).

Mills, C. Wright, Clarence Senior, and Rose Kohn Goldsen. *The Puerto Rican Journey: New York's Newest Migrants*. New York: Russell and Russell, [1950] 1967.

Molotch, Harvey L. "The City as a Growth Machine: Toward a Political Economy of Place." *American Journal of Sociology* 82, no. 2 (1976): 309–32.

Moore, Jeremy. "ACLU: We Back Police Clean-Up." *Philadelphia Daily News*, June 17, 1998, p. 27.

Olick, Jeffrey K. "Genre Memories and Memory Genres: A Dialogical Analysis of May 8, 1945 Commemorations in the Federal Republic of Germany." *American Sociological Review* 64, no. 3 (1999): 381–402.

Panaritis, Maria. "Georges Doesn't Rain on Parade: Despite Worries about Family, Puerto Rican Fest Was Upbeat." *Philadelphia Inquirer*, September 28, 1998, p. B1.

Perdomo, Willie. "Nigger-Reecan Blues." In *Where a Nickel Costs a Dime*, pp. 19–21. New York: W.W. Norton, 1996.

Philadelphia Daily News. "15 Arrested after Puerto Rican Day Parade." September 29, 2003, p. 20 (Local).

Portes, Alejandro, and Rubén G. Rumbaut. *Immigrant America: A Portrait*. 3rd ed. Berkeley: University of California Press, 2006.

Portes, Alejandro, and Steven Shafer. "Revisiting the Enclave Hypothesis: Miami Twenty-Five Years Later." In *The Sociology of Entrepreneurship*, edited by Martin Reuf and Michael Lounsbury, pp. 157–90. San Diego: JAI Press, 2007.

Portes, Alejandro, and Alex Stepick. *City on the Edge: The Transformation of Miami*. Berkeley: University of California Press, 1994.

Pradhan, Suman. "Tight Security Again for Puerto Rican Day: Police and Organizers Hope to Repeat Last Year's Success with Relatively Peaceful Parade and Festivities." *Philadelphia Inquirer*, September 21, 1999, B2.

Richards, Ron, "FBI Agents Kill Puerto Rican Militant," *The Militant* 69, no. 39 (October 10, 2005), http://www.themilitant.com/2005/6939/index.shtml (accessed September 1, 2010).

Ritzer, George. "Rethinking Globalization: Glocalization/Grobalization and Something/Nothing." *Sociological Theory* 21, no. 3 (2003): 193–209.

Rivera, Lauren. "Managing 'Spoiled' National Identity: War, Tourism and Memory in Croatia." *American Sociological Review* 73 (2008): 613–34.

Rojas, James T. "The Enacted Environment in East Los Angeles." *Places* 8, no. 1 (1993): 42–53.

Saito, Hiro. "Reiterated Commemoration: Hiroshima as National Trauma." *Sociological Theory* 24, no. 4 (2006): 353–76.

Sama, Dominic. "For Puerto Ricans, a Day of Pride." *Philadelphia Inquirer*, October 1, 1984, p. B2.

Sampson, Robert J., and Stephen W. Raudenbush. "Seeing Disorder: Neighborhood Stigma and the Social Construction of 'Broken Windows.'" *Social Psychology Quarterly* 67, no. 4 (2004): 319–42.

Santiago, Denise-Marie. "Puerto Rican Pride Braves the Rain." *Philadelphia Inquirer*, September 26, 1988, p. B2.

Schermer, George. "Memorandum to Community, Civic and Religious Leaders; Subject matter, Purposes and General Plan for a Clinical Inquiry into Incidents of Intimidation and Mob Pressure Forcing Minority Families to Vacate Their Homes." December 8, 1960. Philadelphia City Archives.

Schogol, Marc. "At Hispanic Heritage Month Events the Mood Is Somber: Some Celebrations Set for Sept. 15 to Oct. 14, Have Been Canceled, Others Will Be Muted." *Philadelphia Inquirer*, September 27, 2001, p. B2.

Schudson, Michael. "How Culture Works." *Theory and Society* 18, no. 2 (1989): 153–80.

Schumpeter, Joseph A. *Capitalism, Socialism, and Democracy.* London: Allen and Unwin, 1976.

Schwartz, Barry. "The Social Context of Commemoration: A Study in Collective Memory." *Social Forces* 61, no. 2 (1982): 374–402.

Sennett, Richard. *The Culture of the New Capitalism.* New Haven, CT: Yale University Press, 2006.

Seymour, Gene. "Puerto Rican Celebration a 'Party Day.'" *Philadelphia Daily News*, September 27, 1982, p. 8 (Local).

———. "Puerto Rican Fest Floats Out in Style." *Philadelphia Daily News*, September 29, 1986, p. 17 (Local).

Small, Mario Luis. "Culture, Cohorts, and Social Organization Theory: Understanding Local Participation in a Latino Housing Project." *American Journal of Sociology* 108, no. 1 (2002): 1–54.

———. *Unanticipated Gains: Origins of Network Inequality in Everyday Life.* New York: Oxford University Press, 2009.

———. *Villa Victoria: The Transformation of Social Capital in a Boston Barrio.* Chicago: University of Chicago Press, 2004.

Smith, Neil. "New City, New Frontier: The Lower East Side as Wild, Wild West." In *Variations on a Theme Park: The New American City and the End of Public Space*, edited by Michael Sorkin, pp. 61–93. New York: Hill and Wang, 1992.

Smith, Philip. "Codes and Conflict: Toward a Theory of War as Ritual." *Theory and Society* 20, no. 1 (1991): 103–38.

Spillman, Lyn. "When Do Collective Memories Last? Founding Moments in the United States and Australia." *Social Science History* 22, no. 4 (1998): 445–77.

Steinberg, Stephen. "The Liberal Retreat from Race during the Post–Civil Rights Era." In *The House That Race Built*, edited by Wahneema Lubiano, pp. 13–47. New York: Vintage, 1998.

Seifert, Susan C., and Mark J. Stern. "'Natural' Cultural Districts: Arts Agglomerations in Metropolitan Philadelphia and Implications for Cultural District Planning." Dynamics of Culture Working Paper #2005-2, Social Impact of the Arts Project, University of Pennsylvania, 2005.

Strauss, Anselm C., and Juliet Corbin. *Basics of Qualitative Research: Techniques and Procedures for Developing Grounded Theory.* Thousand Oaks, CA: Sage, 1998.

Strobach, Paula G. "The Attitudes of Philadelphians towards Their Puerto Rican Neighbors." In *Puerto Ricans in Philadelphia*, by Arthur Siegel, Harold Orlans, and Loyal Greer, pp. 50–62. Philadelphia: Institute for Research in Human Relations, 1954.

Tajfel, H., and J. C. Turner. "An Integrative Theory of Intergroup Conflict." In *Differentiation between Social Groups: Studies in the Social Psychology of Intergroup Relations*, edited by Henri Tajfel, pp. 33–47. London: Academic Press, 1978.

Taller Puertorriqueño. "Batiendo la Olla ('Stirring the Pot'): A Cross-Generational Comparison and Self-Study by Second Generation Puerto Ricans in Philadelphia." Oral history project. Washington, D.C.: National Endowment for the Humanities, 1979. Available online at http://www.eric.ed.gov/PDFS/ED337553.pdf.

Tiebout, Charles. "A Pure Theory of Local Expenditures." *Journal of Political Economy* 64, no. 5 (1956): 416–24.

Tienda, Marta. "Puerto Ricans and the Underclass Debate." *The Annals of the American Academy of Political and Social Science* 501, no. 1 (1989): 105–19.

Tkacik, Maureen. "Flock Is Hard to Reach: To Help Addicts and Hustlers, She Goes Where They Live." *Philadelphia Daily News*, July 28, 1998, p. 8.

Tkacik, Maureen, Jeremy Moore, and April Adamson. "Party's Over Day 1: Kensington Lowlifes Crawl Off, Residents Hail All-Out War on Drug Dealers, Addicts, Hookers, But Fear They'll be Back in Business Later." *Philadelphia Daily News*, June 16, 1998, p. 4.

Urry, John. "Sensing the City." In *The Tourist City*, edited by Dennis R. Judd and Susan S. Fainstein, pp. 71–86. New Haven, CT: Yale University Press, 1999.

Vázquez-Hernández, Víctor. "From Pan-Latino Enclaves to a Community: Puerto Ricans in Philadelphia, 1910–2000." In *The Puerto Rican Diaspora: Historical Perspectives*, edited by Carmen Teresa Whalen and Víctor Vázquez-Hernández, pp. 88–105. Philadelphia: Temple University Press, 2005.

Volk, Steve. "Third and Indiana: Get Yer Crack Right Here, Same as Back in the Day." *Philadelphia Weekly*, May 24, 2006, http://www.philadelphiaweekly.com/news-and-opinion/third_and_indiana-38415289.html (accessed September 1, 2010).

Wagner-Pacifici, Robin, and Barry Schwartz. "The Vietnam Veterans Memorial: Commemorating a Difficult Past." *American Journal of Sociology* 97, no. 2 (1991): 376–420.

Waldinger, Roger D., and Michael I. Lichter. *How the Other Half Works: Immigration and the Social Organization of Labor*. Berkeley: University of California Press, 2003.

Whalen, Carmen Teresa. *From Puerto Rico to Philadelphia: Puerto Rican Workers and Postwar Economies*. Philadelphia: Temple University Press, 2001.

Wherry, Frederick F. "The Social Sources of Authenticity in Global Handicraft Markets: Evidence from Northern Thailand." *Journal of Consumer Culture* 6, no. 1 (2006): 5–32.

Whyte, William Foote. *Street Corner Society: The Social Structure of an Italian Slum*. Chicago, University of Chicago Press, [1943] 1993.

Williams, Terry. *Crackhouse: Notes from the End of the Line*. New York: Penguin, 1993.

Wilson, William Julius. *When Work Disappears: The World of the New Urban Poor*. New York: Knopf, 1996.

Zelizer, Viviana A. "Beyond the Polemics of the Market: Establishing a Theoretical and Empirical Agenda." *Sociological Forum* 3, no. 4 (1988): 614–34.

———. *The Purchase of Intimacy*. Princeton: Princeton University Press, 2005.

Zerubavel, Eviatar. *The Fine Line: Making Distinctions in Everyday Life*. Chicago: University of Chicago Press, 1993.

Zucchino, David. "The Badlands: In the Grip of Drugs." *Philadelphia Inquirer*, April 6, 1992, p. A1.

———. "How an Illicit World Flourishes Just Three Miles from City Hall." *Philadelphia Inquirer*, April 5, 1992, p. A1.

———. "A Huge Heroin Bust." *Philadelphia Inquirer*, July 24, 1991, p. A1.

———. "In the Badlands of the City, Drugs Still Riding High." *Philadelphia Inquirer*, April 3, 1991, p. A1.

Zukin, Sharon. *The Cultures of Cities*. Cambridge, MA: Wiley-Blackwell, 1996.

———. *Loft Living: Culture and Capital and Urban Change*. Baltimore: Johns Hopkins University Press, 1982.

Index